D1383020

The Merchant Adventurers
General Editor: Ralph Davis, Ph.D.

Far Eastern Trade 1860-1914

The Merchant Adventurers

Far Eastern Trade
1860-1914

FRANCIS E. HYDE, Ph.D.

Chaddock Professor of Economic History,
University of Liverpool

Adam & Charles Black
London

First published 1973
A. & C. Black Ltd
4, 5 & 6 Soho Square, London W1V 6AD
ISBN 0 7136 1345 9

Printed in Great Britain by
T. & A. Constable Ltd., Edinburgh

Contents

48705

List of Tables

List of Maps

Acknowledgements

THIS book owes much to the help and encouragement of many colleagues: to the inspiration of the late Professor Percy Maude Roxby, who, as Professor of Geography in the University of Liverpool, first aroused the author's interest in the social and economic problems of China; to Professor G. C. Allen for insights into the economic development of Japan; to Professor C. D. Cowan, who organised a series of seminars on south-east Asia and later published the results of the discussions; and to Dr K. C. Liu, whose work on shipping in Chinese waters paved the way to a new understanding of the river and coastal trades. The author is also greatly indebted to the late Mrs Hugh Rathbone and to Mr B. L. Rathbone for permission to use the papers of Rathbone Bros. and Co.; to Sir John Nicholson for an agreement to use the Holt papers, including the books, accounts and reports of the Ocean Steam Ship Co.; and to the directors of John Swire and Sons for their permission to make full use of the business archives of their firm. To his colleague, Dr Sheila Marriner, the author is especially grateful, first through collaboration at the time when she was writing her book on Rathbones of Liverpool and secondly in joint authorship of *The Senior*, an account of the life of John Samuel Swire. To Professor G. H. Peters of the Department of Economics in the University of Liverpool for work on population rates of growth and Mr Philip Cottrell, of the Department of Economic History in the University of Liverpool, the author acknowledges their help and expert advice. Finally, the debt to others must include within the list Mrs Hilda Fleming who typed, revised and corrected the text and the author's wife, who not only read the proofs and undertook the burden of compiling the index but who also, throughout the writing of the book, gave him much needed help and encouragement.

Preface

APART from information obtained from the records of shipping companies, the background material for this volume is drawn chiefly from published sources. Nevertheless, an attempt has been made to collate the results of recent research and present it against a reasonably wide background. In this way, it is hoped that the reader might be given the facts about Far Eastern trade in depth and perspective.

The interesting and informative studies by Allen and Donnithorne, and under the editorship of C. D. Cowan, have emphasised the nature of the impact of Western capital and technology upon the traditional, political and economic structure of the Far East. What is perhaps less readily understood is that the provision of main line steamship services between Europe, China, Japan and the Netherlands East Indies not only created a life-line but also stimulated local commercial development. Coastal and river trades were given added importance; considerable cross-trades were given impetus and a vast *entrepot* trade was centred upon the ports of Singapore, Batavia, Hong Kong, Shanghai and Yokohama. There was also a quickening of commercial tempo through the creation of banks and other financial institutions, and by direct investment. New forces were liberated which, in turn, gave spontaneity and dynamism to economic growth. This, however, differed in scope and form from one country to another; Malaya's economy became increasingly dependent on the production of rubber and tin; that of Siam on rice, while China and Indonesia abandoned old staples in favour of new ones. Japan alone achieved a broader and yet more highly integrated structure including revolutionary changes in agriculture, industry and commerce. For considerable sections of indigenous populations, standards of living improved and numbers increased, the Pacific was bridged and the Far East was drawn into an expanding world economy.

If trade is considered as one generating source of expansion, capital and all its ancillary functions may be regarded as another. For this reason, it has been deemed relevant to include a chapter on the various ways in which capital was applied to the promotion of trade, such uses varying with the objectives pursued and tempered by changes in commercial environment, chronology and the demand for resources. On this subject, the views expressed are illustrative only of Western attitudes but, throughout the narrative, there is ample evidence of the growing power of local capital, from Chinese merchants in Singapore and Bangkok, from Japanese merchants in China and from Chinese shipping companies in all local trades. The inference is fully justified that, whereas Western capital played a dominant role in opening up the Far East to trade, an increasing proportion of promotional activity was, by 1914, passing into local control. This, at least, was one valid conclusion to be drawn from this study of Far Eastern trade. For the rest, the author would ask the indulgence of the reader in his appraisal of the source material. Under the terms of reference, this volume is meant for a fairly wide readership as well as for the academic specialist, and it is hoped that the level of presentation will prove to be of interest to all readers and stimulate further discussion and inquiry.

The University of Liverpool   F. E. H.

CHAPTER I

The Opening of the Far East to Western Enterprise

THE term 'Far East' is a comprehensive designation for a vast area of the world's land and sea surface. Within its boundaries there lives approximately one quarter of the world's population, comprising widely different races, tongues and religions each with distinctive customs, folklore and history. The great land mass of China, with its teeming population, ancient cities and prosperous ports, is central to the whole, bordered to the west by what are now Indo-China, Thailand and the Malayan peninsula. To sea-ward runs the great arc of Pacific islands, starting with the old 'spice' islands which in the seventeenth century came under Dutch influence and later became known as the Netherlands East Indies. Today, they form the greater part of the widely dispersed territory known as Indonesia. Finally, the chain is completed by the island empire of Japan and the conglomerate Philippines. On the periphery stand India and Burma, the former having become subject to an increasing British control since the eighteenth century and the latter also to British influence during the second half of the nineteenth century.

The impact of European culture on these ancient civilisations in the East was much less significant than the influence of Western commercial enterprise. In fact, Chinese (and later, Japanese) artistic ideas did much to alter and shape the pattern of Western cultural development in the eighteenth and nineteenth centuries. Nevertheless, the two-way exchange of ideas and practice ulti-mately led to an acceptance of foreign barbarians in the East and to the emergence of China and Japan as participants in an extend-ing international economy.

Before 1834, Britain's trade with China had been conducted within the compass of the East India Co.'s monopoly. By the beginning of the nineteenth century, such trade had become part of a triangular pattern of settlement between India, China and Britain.[1] The Pacific trade was, up to 1830, financed largely from the Philippines, at that time the distribution channel for the supply of Mexican silver dollars, a currency acceptable in China and accumulated as a result of trade between Manila and Acapulco.[2] With the cessation of the East India Co.'s monopoly, however, the way was cleared for a more diversified system of trade and finance. This was but a precursor to the events which led to the opening of China to the West, though it was an important antecedent to the more dynamic commercial development which ran parallel with the linking of China and Europe by means of the steamship and the telegraph after 1860.

How was this vast and diverse area known as the 'Far East' opened up to the acquisitive grasp of European merchants and shipowners? The explosive forces which burst open the enshrouding bonds of dynasty and ancient legal and customary restriction were generated as much by contact with India as with European merchants. Furthermore, the impact of new ideas stimulated a process of change among the vast populations and, in China itself, a series of revolutionary upheavals which ultimately transformed both the political and economic structure of the country as a whole. The influences from India were fundamentally European in origin, though they were given oriental gloss and thereby made more attractive to Eastern economies. They were directly the result of an extension of British control over the mainland of India; Punjab was added to the East India Co.'s monopoly in 1849, lower Burma with Rangoon in 1852, and Oudh, the last independent Moslem state, in 1856. Side by side with this extension of territory for commercial purposes went reform. During his governor generalship of India, Lord Dalhousie introduced railways, the electric telegraph and uniform postage, three great engines of social improvement which led eventually to the unification and centralisation of government and to the breakdown of aristocratic

---

[1] See M. Greenberg, *British Trade and the Opening of China, 1800-1842* (1951), Chapter I, *et passim*.
[2] W. E. Cheong, 'Trade and Finance in China, 1784-1834', *Business History*, Vol. VII, No. 1, January 1965, pp. 34-47.

privilege and feudal autonomy. The powerful opposition to these reforms was, in fact, responsible for the Indian Mutiny, a bloody episode in history which, when quelled, gave Britain a virtual control over the whole sub-continent. A period of sustained economic expansion followed the suppression of rebellion and a large scale investment of British capital took place after the East India Co. ceased to function in 1857. In commercial terms the traditional trades of India were thrown open to Western enterprise under conditions of free competition. An immediate extension of Western practice took the form of joint stock legislation in 1858, the use of the managing agency and the establishment of the supremacy of the agent over his board of directors. The resumption of railway construction in 1858 and 1859 helped to stimulate agricultural production for export, because all the main railway lines led to the ports, and British administration had extended over all the fertile valleys of the peninsula. In this process, capital was drawn into the production of new staples of trade: jute in Bengal, tea in Assam, rice in Burma, coffee and tea in Ceylon, and cotton in Bombay. Bombay became the telegraphic terminus for the European cable, while Galle on the southernmost tip of Ceylon performed a similar service for east Asia, and Calcutta grew into a vast importing and exporting centre, linking Europe with China *via* Singapore. The final stimulus to this transforming development was caused by the opening of the Suez canal in 1869, an event which turned Bombay into a steamship port and opened up the Far East by the provision of speedier communications with the West.

Meanwhile in China, the stimulation of enterprise in India had parallel repercussions. Following the short Opium War in 1841, the Treaty of Nanking was signed, the chief provisions of which opened up the ports of Shanghai, Amoy, Foochow and Ningpo to foreign trade. British consuls were allowed to reside in these ports; import duties were limited to 5 per cent *ad valorem* and, after 1843, favoured nation treatment was accorded, together with extra-territorial jurisdiction of consuls.[1] This was the first of the 'unequal' treaties which reduced China from its 'position as the central nation to that of an equal in the family of nations'.[2] These privileges

[1] G. C. Allen and Audrey G. Donnithorne, *Western Enterprise in Far Eastern Economic Development: China and Japan* (1954), Appendix D, p. 266.

[2] For an extension of concessions under subsequent treaties, see G. C. Allen and Audrey G. Donnithorne, *op. cit.*, pp. 127 *et seq.*

were extended during the next fifty years under subsequent treaties to a large number of other ports, both on the coast and along the Yangtse River. There also followed the first naval surveys of the China coast in 1842-43, and so began a century of effort to open China to the outside world.

One of the important commercial results of the Treaty of Nanking was the confirmation of Britain's possession of Hong Kong, one of the finest harbours in eastern Asia. That island port became the centre of the opium trade and the source of expansive enterprise once the steamship had conquered the route to the Pacific. In this process the Peninsular and Oriental Co. had acted as pioneer. In 1845, it had secured a share of the bi-monthly mail to Bombay and extended its service from Galle to Singapore and Hong Kong, placing London in contact with the new base within a period of 54 days instead of the customary 89 days.[1] By thus establishing a fast link with China, the P. and O. began to encroach upon the opium and silk trades, as well as upon the other traditional trades of the sailing ship companies. Other results quickly flowed from this extension of maritime activity. By using Galle from 1845 to tranship the mails from Singapore and Hong Kong, the P. and O. used the Straits of Malacca rather than the Straits of Sunda and made Penang into a port of call. Furthermore, by creating Singapore as a half-way port between India and China it facilitated the extension of the overland route to Batavia, and enabled the Dutch government, from 1845, to establish links with Singapore for the carriage of passengers and mail to Java. The successful extension of these shipping routes over half the world was an augury of greater development in the future when steamships, powered by compound-tandem engines, were to open up the trade of the Far East to European domination through the use of such ports as Penang, Singapore, Shanghai and Hong Kong.[2]

The next phase in the struggle to bring China within an international trading economy was set within the boundaries of China itself. The Taiping Rebellion was, in one sense, an active result of the disruptive influence from the West, in that it was a peasant

---

[1] Boyd Cable, *A Hundred Year History of the P. and O.* (1937), p. 102; also D. A. Farnie, *East and West of Suez* (1969), p. 22.

[2] F. E. Hyde, *Blue Funnel: A History of Alfred Holt and Co., 1865-1914* (1956), p. 24; also Sheila Marriner and F. E. Hyde, *The Senior: John Samuel Swire, 1825-1898* (1967), pp. 114-21.

rebellion against the Manchu, the Mandarin and the foreigner. The rebellion began in the hills of Kwansi near Canton, in 1851, and became the herald of a century of revolution in the Middle Kingdom. The revolt spread rapidly and, in 1853, Wuchang, Hanyang and Hankow fell into rebel hands. Advancing down the Yangtse, the insurgents captured Kiukiang and Angking, finally establishing themselves in March of that year in Nanking. Sending expeditions to the north they penetrated as far as the neighbourhood of Tientsin, but were finally driven back to the Yangtse in 1855. Many foreign merchants, under the belief that the rebels had adopted Christianity, gave them qualified support, but when it became clear that their attitude to foreigners was no whit less obstructive than that of the Pekin government, this support dwindled and was replaced by open hostility. For a time the ports on the Yangtse were cut off and Shanghai itself was threatened. A joint Anglo-French expedition was sent to aid the imperial forces in 1860 and the rebellion was finally suppressed in 1864.[1] As a result of this rebellion, there was a flight of refugee capital and enterprise from the interior to the protection of the consular cities and ports, among them Hong Kong and Shanghai.[2] There was a further and, perhaps, more fundamental change in the traditional channels of trade. The revolt of the nine southern provinces diverted not only their taxes from Pekin to Nanking, but also the shipments of northern tea from Canton; green tea and silks were diverted to Shanghai. The destruction of silk weaving looms in Nanking during the course of the rebellion forced raw silk upon the export market through Shanghai in 1852-53, and encouraged its shipment at very high freights *via* the overland route. Black teas were diverted from Canton to Foochow which was the nearest port to the Bohia Hills.

Shanghai's new foreign settlement attracted native and foreign merchants. Much of the hoarded capital in the old city was given room for profitable employment. Within a short time, this city developed a civic pride and consciousness through the establishment of municipal and land regulations; a new municipal council used its authority to administer the imperial maritime customs in 1854. From 1855, Shanghai and Hong Kong were linked together by foreign steamship services, pioneered by the American firm of

[1] *Cambridge Modern History*, Vol. XI (1934 ed.), pp. 820-1.
[2] G. C. Allen and Audrey G. Donnithorne, *op. cit.*, p. 19.

B

Russell and Co.[1] Finally, the involvement in the Taiping Rebellion led to a stimulation of trade, first under the Treaty of Tientsin in 1858 which opened the great rivers of China to foreign trade, and permitted merchants and missionaries to penetrate the interior of China, and secondly, through the Treaty of Pekin in 1860 which ended a period of twenty-five years of struggle, and re-organised the basis of relations between Europe and China. This latter treaty ceded Kowloon to Hong Kong and legalised Chinese emigration in English interests. Henceforth supplies of cheap Chinese labour could be transported in British ships to work the rice-fields in Siam and the tin fields of Malaya. The opening of ports on the Yangtse and the elimination of Chinese junks from the river below Nanking created new opportunities for local steamship enterprise, and led to the foundation in 1862 of the Shanghai Steam Navigation Co., with the American firm of Russell and Co. as its managing agents.[2] The great inland tea market of Hankow was first reached by ocean steamship in 1861, by the river steamers of the Shanghai Steam Navigation Co. in 1862, and by sailing vessels in 1863, thus giving Chinese merchants freedom of choice between the two markets of Hankow and Shanghai.

These events stimulated the expansion of Shanghai into a shipping centre of international importance. The diversion of traffic from central China, already begun in 1854, away from the overland routes to Canton into the river and coastal routes to Shanghai, greatly helped in effecting this change of status. After 1863, Shanghai became a terminal port for the European coasting trade in Chinese produce, and was linked to Hong Kong by the Shanghai Steam Navigation Co. Ten years later, it had become the focus of intense rivalry between the shipping interests on the river, in the shape of the American firm of Russell and Co. and the British firms of Jardine Matheson and Co. and John Swire's China Navigation Co. We shall trace the course of this rivalry in a subsequent chapter. Meanwhile, during the 1860's, Shanghai's population, trade and revenue expanded faster than those of Hong Kong, it had become the main centre of European trade in China, benefiting by the opening of Japan to the east, of the Yangtse to

---

[1] Kwang-Ching Liu, *Anglo-American Steamship Rivalry in China, 1862-1874* (1962), pp. 19 *et seq.*

[2] *Ibid.*, pp. 32 *et seq.*

the west, and by the inducement which its deep water harbour at Woosung offered to the new steamship owners from Europe. In short, this port, because of fortuitous political circumstances, realised to the full the potentialities of its geographical position at a time when the insistent pressure of Western enterprise required such a base on the China coast. It controlled the trade of the whole Yangtse basin, a mighty commercial highway stretching for some 3,200 miles from the eastern sea to Tibet, and navigable for more than half its length. Shanghai had access to the 100 million inhabitants of the most fertile, productive and populous region of the Chinese empire. It could collect teas and silks for export, and channel opium and Western products inland. Finally, as the most northern ice-free port on the coast, it could serve as the centre for transhipment between coastal navigation to the north and the south, as well as between coastal and river navigation.

*

No less important than this opening of China to trade were the movements of a similar character to establish commercial contacts with Japan, Burma and Siam. As we have seen, the impact of Western ideas in China produced the Taiping Rebellion. In Japan, the revolution of 1868 overthrew the Tokugawa Shogunate, a revolution instigated by anti-foreign sentiment which had been growing in intensity since the appearance of Perry's black ships in 1853. The emperor, Matsuhito, who took over the government in 1868 and died in 1912, profited from the centralisation of administration which followed, as well as from the unconditional obedience to authority, in ordering a new competence for the emergent Meiji state as a moral entity. Japan pursued independence very largely because of its poverty. To Western eyes, Japanese commercial potentialities and scope for future development were limited, and accordingly the country was neglected as an outpost of Western development. The upward surge of Japan's new national spirit was, therefore, the sponsor of rapid industrial and commercial renaissance.

Whereas Japan had previously possessed only the agrarian techniques of China and other east Asian countries, it now began to import the industrial know-how of Western civilisation. The importation of capital goods began so as to build up industrial resources. Foreign competition, however, forced concentration on the production of those commodities for which there were natural advantages. Thus, for a time, Japanese exports consisted principally of teas for the American market and silk for the weavers of Lyons. This latter commodity, however, was subject to historical and political pressures. Resenting the support which the French government had given to the Tokugawa Shogunate, Japan insisted on exporting all the raw silk to Lyons *via* London and Liverpool and would accept in exchange only Birmingham and Manchester goods.[1] The links between Britain and Japan were strengthened in the following decades. The first Japanese foreign commercial loan was floated in London in 1870, for the construction of a railway. This linked the old and the new capitals and, with its completion in 1872, was the first railway to be opened in east Asia. By integrating all the alien imports from the West into a culture which continued to be specifically oriental, Japan at one and the same time increased in economic strength while retaining a national outlook and characteristics.

In the three larger riverine countries to the north of Malaya, namely Burma, Siam and Indo-China, the pattern of development and of economic expansion was different from that in either China or Japan. Burma was brought successively under British rule following the wars of 1824-26, 1852 and 1885. Before British influence became predominant, however, the focus of the Burmese kingdom had been the interior dry zone and, though Arakan and Tenasserim had been annexed in 1826, it was not until the seizure of the Irrawaddy delta in 1852 that there was any significant change in the pattern of Burma's agrarian economy. At this time, the delta was sparsely populated by comparison with the dry zone, largely because the Burmese had never succeeded in controlling the severe floods of the Irrawaddy River. British administrators quickly realised the economic potential of these hot, humid lowlands and, wishing to encourage the Burmese to grow a cash crop in order to possess resources to buy British manufactures, set about bringing the delta into productive use. British engineers, using Indian labour, built a series of protective embankments interspersed with irrigation channels. The Burmese population was encouraged to settle in the area and bring the land into cultivation. The policy inducing settlement was based upon the offering

---

[1] See below, Chapter VII.

of 15-acre plots to those who participated in the process of re-
clamation.[1] The scheme was successful and, by the mid-1860's, a
massive shift of population had begun to take place from the
surrounding hills and from the dry zone. With the establishment
of rice-fields and small scale productive units for the preparation
of the crop for market, Indian middlemen and seasonal labourers
began to move in. Within three decades the Irrawaddy delta had
become the greatest rice exporting area in the world. From this
stage onwards, notwithstanding the annexation of Burma (including the dry zone) in 1885 and the systematic development of
oil-fields after the turn of the century, as well as the production
of teak from a few isolated areas, the delta became the mainstay
of the country's economy. Rice provided well over 60 per cent of
Burma's export trade before 1914 as compared with 10 per cent
for oil and smaller percentages for teak and non-ferrous metals.[2]
Apart from these products, however, the majority of the country's
production outside the delta continued to be derived from sub-
sistence-type agriculture. Whatever may be said of Britain's
exploitation of Burma's primary resources, efforts were made to
increase the population's capacity to import the manufactured
products of the West. To this extent, therefore, there was some
improvement in standards of living which could be directly
attributed to foreign enterprise.

The pattern set by the British in Burma was followed by the
French government in Indo-China. French rule was extended over
Cochin China and Cambodia between 1862 and 1867, over Annam
and Tonkin from 1882, and over Laos between 1893 and 1904.
Here again, the first areas which were taken over were those which
were sparsely populated. In an attempt to make the Mekong delta
a profitable area for commercial agriculture, French engineers
began, in 1870, to construct a series of drainage channels similar
to those cut by British engineers on the Irrawaddy. This enabled
rice production to increase with a labour force drawn mainly from
the lowlands of Cochin China.[3] Furthermore, although there was a
considerable influx of Chinese middlemen and labourers into the

[1] Charles A. Fisher, 'Some Comments on Population Growth in South-
East Asia, with special reference to the period since 1830', C. D. Cowan
(ed.), *The Economic Development of South-East Asia* (1964), p. 60.

[2] *Ibid.* Before 1939 the percentages were rice 40 per cent and oil 20
per cent.

[3] *Ibid.*, p. 62.

Mekong rice-fields, there was no mass migration of population comparable in scale with that in Burma.

In the densely populated area of Tonkin, the plan for economic development had to follow a different pattern from that of the export economy of the south. The resources in coal and non-ferrous metals were exploited and the abundant supplies of cheap labour were directed into industrial occupations with the establishment of textile factories and construction plants.[1] The direction of French investment in Tonkin had more in common with their (and other European) investment in China than with that in the rest of south-east Asia. Thus, French Indo-China had two distinct economic and demographic centres in the northern and southern deltas respectively. Even so, these areas formed but a small part of the region as a whole and, while Western capital did much to improve the economic potentialities of the river lands, vast tracts of countryside still remained subject to peasant subsistence forms of agriculture.

The third river area to be brought under rice cultivation was that of the Menam delta in Siam. In its development as a rice exporting region, its progress followed that of the British pattern in the Irrawaddy delta. Although Siam did not come under colonial rule, except in so far as several outlying portions of the kingdom were added either to the French sphere of influence in Indo-China or to the British sphere in Malaya, the Bowring Treaty with Britain in 1855 opened the country to Western trade. Siam was fortunate in possessing a forward-looking monarchy and at least two kings were men of outstanding ability: Mongkut and Chulalongkorn. Under the direction of these two men Siam succeeded in pursuing a policy of 'divide and rule in reverse'.[2] By utilising British and Chinese resources in commercial affairs, by adopting the French legal system and by bringing in Danish administrators to reorganise the police force, these two monarchs maintained independence in the direction of Siam's economic policy. This policy was governed by geographical considerations in that the lower Menam valley offered the best prospect for the cultivation of rice, a commodity upon which both a flourishing export trade and a relatively high standard of living could be based. By con-

---

[1] *The Economic Development of South-East Asia* (1964), p. 62.

[2] *Ibid.*, p. 63, see also James C. Ingram, *Economic Change in Thailand since 1850* (1955), Chapters 1-3.

trast with Burma, however, the delta had been for many centuries the core of the Siamese state; but even so, the density of population there was low and there was land to spare for cultivation. For the most part, therefore, the expansion of the rice acreage in the lower Menam valley was undertaken spontaneously by the local peasantry.

As elsewhere in south-east Asia, the prospects flowing from the institution of a commercial agricultural system led to an influx of immigrants, in this case particularly of Chinese. In order to protect Siam's newly-found prosperity against external pressure, therefore, the government built a series of railways to link the outlying regions with Bangkok and, following the completion of the first of these to Korat in 1900, the north-eastern province began to participate, in a secondary capacity, in the rice export trade. Elsewhere in Siam, however, the subsistence character of the economy remained relatively unchanged until the outbreak of the Second World War. The emerging production of teak, rubber and tin after 1900 represented only minor geographical extensions of the more highly capitalised production of such commodities in Burma and Malaya respectively.

Thus, in the period immediately preceding the coming of the steamship to the Far East, vast and extensive changes had taken place in political and economic terms, to make the area as a whole more acceptable to the acquisitive instincts of Western capitalists. In China this took the form of a less autonomous system of central authority and the opening up of the coast and ultimately of the interior to trade. In Japan, the traditional régime was swept away and, in its place, a new authority determined, while maintaining independence, to profit from the contact and relationship with Europe. The extension of British control over India and Burma, the historical hegemony of the Dutch in the East Indian islands and the newly acquired interests of the French in Indo-China provided powerful and dynamic stimuli to change. In the process, the population of the area was given incentive to seek new sources of livelihood and migration was accompanied by a new dynamism. For centuries economic growth had been circumscribed by politics and geography. Now, within the space of a single generation, a new technology was to bring prospects of increasing returns and, in its impact, geographical barriers were to be overcome and political environments changed. Only the inscrutable mind of the

East itself could formulate a judgment as to whether these interventions from the West would eventually be regarded as significant in the long history of ancient civilisations, or whether they were but irritating episodes in an otherwise inherently evolutionary form of social and economic structure.

*

So far, we have touched upon the impact of Western ideas in the political and economic reorientation of specific areas in the Far East. Equally important were the effects of change upon migration and the growth of population in the area as a whole. For the first time, the indigenous mass of humanity, existing at little more than bare subsistence level, found new prospects in the pursuance of livelihood under capitalistic and competitive conditions which not only offered inducements for the acceptance and use of more intensive methods of production, but also created attractive opportunities for employment overseas. The result was two-fold in character. With increasing resources, population growth was stimulated in the traditional agricultural areas; and, with the abolition of restrictive legislation against movement, migration began to be an accepted fact, supplies of labour flowing from the depressed lands to those whose primary production was in process of transformation through the application of foreign capital.

As Charles Fisher has pointed out, the relatively low average density of population in south-east Asian countries compared with that in India, China and Japan 'has long been recognised as one of the cardinal facts in the social geography of this region'.[1] It is, perhaps, of some relevance in explaining both the movement and the growth of population in those areas more specifically influenced by the spirit of Western enterprise. In 1958, south-east Asia had a total population of 197 million, representing a density of 126 to the square mile. This, in Fisher's calculation, was approximately one-third the density in India and China within the Wall 'and about one-fifth that of Japan'.[2] At first sight, this is a somewhat surprising contrast between neighbouring and superficially similar areas; though in retrospect, the variability in the rates of economic growth in specific parts of the region should afford more than an adequate explanation of such differentiation. There is, however,

[1] Charles Fisher, op. cit., p. 48.
[2] Ibid.

reason to believe that these differences were greater in the nineteenth century than they are today. In order to give credence to any argument concerned with population and its growth, the source material must be given critical examination and, as far as possible, comparability. Charles Fisher has, in fact, made an exhaustive inquiry into the reliability of population statistics and we have accepted his findings as the basis for this survey. Nevertheless, despite qualifications, there seems to be broad agreement that the average rate of growth in south-east Asia was higher than that in India, China and Japan.[1] This was certainly true of Java where, as Carr-Saunders showed, there was an annual average rate of growth of 2·2 per cent between 1850 and 1900, though this rate fell to 1·3 per cent between 1900 and 1930.[2] The point of interest here is that such a high rate should have been maintained over such a lengthy period.

The total population of the Dutch East Indies rose from 11·0 million in 1830 to an estimated 70·5 million in 1940, giving a 6·4-fold increase with an annual average rate of growth of 1·7 per cent. By comparison, Siam's population increased from 2·7 million in 1830 to 8·27 million in 1911. This amounted to a three-fold increase and a 1·4 per cent annual average rate of growth. In 1830, Indo-China's population was approximately 5·2 million, that for Malaya 0·4 million and for Burma 4·0 million. An independent estimate for Indo-China for 1911 and the censuses for Malaya and Burma for the same year give totals of 17·0 million, 2·64 million and 10·1 million respectively, thus providing annual average rates of growth of 1·5 per cent, 2·3 per cent and 1·2 per cent. As with figures of population growth for other Eastern countries in the nineteenth century, the ranges quoted above are liable to qualification within specific time spans, but the measures used provide us with a sufficiently accurate order of magnitude to illustrate our argument. Perhaps the major conclusion to be drawn from these figures is that, with the coming of Western authority, there was a lowering of the death-rate from a previous level of 35 to 40 per thousand, while the birth-rate remained at a figure somewhat above the original death-rate. This ensured a more than favourable comparison with rates of growth in other Far Eastern territories.

Such a conclusion can be supported, as Fisher has demonstrated,

[1] W. G. East and A. E. Moodie (eds.), *The Changing Map of Asia* (1950), pp. 182 *et seq.*
[2] A. M. Carr-Saunders, *World Population* (1936), pp. 280-2.

by a number of supplementary factors. In the first place, the institution of law and order in the delta lands, the peninsulas and the islands (backed, if necessary, by military authority) reduced the incidence of civil strife and inter-dominion warfare. In the second place, the general increase in economic welfare and opportunity together with related controls for the avoidance of famine in poor seasons, led to more stable conditions. Consequently, there was a more propitious environment in which population growth could take place. These factors were, in turn, given further stimulus by an increase in knowledge, particularly that concerned with hygiene and the spread of sanitary practice. These views can certainly be supported by evidence from all the areas and localities which come within the scope and the application of Western ideas. In some cases, such as in the tin areas of Malaya, in the ports and on plantations, the diffusion of such knowledge was extensive far beyond the original limits of inception. The wealth produced from these points of contact was sufficient to pay for new systems of communication (for example, the road and railway network in western Malaya) and thereby to bring about an extension of influence. It was the existence of excellent transport facilities which, in large measure, determined the planting area of the newly-imported product of rubber, a product which added immeasurably to the prosperity of both Malaya and Indonesia, to the growth and sustenance of an increasing population and to the improvement of living standards.[1] This was true in Malaya, despite the fact that much of the labour employed on the rubber estates consisted of Indian immigrants. The Malays themselves preferred to grow rubber as a cash crop on their own land, outside the discipline of an estate system.

An alternative thesis, concerning the impact of Western capital and ideas upon demographic movements in south-east Asia, stems from the premise that the areas significantly influenced by Western capital and commerce were relatively small in relation to the rest of the area as a whole. In this context, the abnormally high rate of growth in the population of Malaya (and to a lesser extent in Siam) is explained in terms of immigration. As we shall see later, the Holt ships carried an increasing flow of Chinese labour into areas of increasing production. In such circumstances, therefore, new economic opportunities were much less a prime cause of

[1] See below, Chapter VI.

growth in population through a lowering of malnutrition and hence of death-rates; it was, rather, the attraction of new groups into an existing society, under the inducement of potentially large rewards. Thus, in eastern Malaya, where there was no tin mining and rubber planting, rates of population growth were much lower than in western Malaya and approximated rates of growth for south-east Asia as a whole.[1] One cannot obviously make a deduction from this single fact, but it is one piece of evidence which could probably be supported by other instances leading to a tentative conclusion that the creation of new economic opportunities was not necessarily a pre-condition of a high growth rate in the period between 1815 and 1914.

Nevertheless, there is some force in the contention that the extension of foreign authority over certain areas in the Far East by imposing law and order, made possible a freer use of native resources and, consequently, provided favourable conditions for population growth. The introduction of French rule and adminis-tration over Indo-China in 1884, for example, was followed by a rapid increase in agricultural productivity. As a result, population grew so rapidly that it eventually outstripped local resources and foodstuffs had to be imported. Similarly, after the British annex-ation of Burma in 1885, the institution of a new land-holding policy led to a massive influx of population from the surrounding hills and the dry zone into the Irrawaddy delta. This was quickly followed by a rapidly growing immigration of Indian merchants and seasonal labourers so that, within twenty years, this region had a high density population and the highest rate of growth for rice production in the world. Before the extension of British authority in Malaya, foreign influence had been confined almost entirely to the ports of Singapore and Penang. The ceaseless strife between warring sultanates not only impoverished the land but inhibited the use and exploitation of natural resources. It was only after 1874, when British protection was extended to the tin mining areas of the west coast, that production began to increase. Between 1890 and 1910, the output of tin ore increased ten-fold, population at an estimated three-fold and the revenue of Perak alone rose from 226,000 Straits dollars in 1875 to 4,034,000 by 1893. The increase of security in the pursuit of livelihood, therefore, must be considered as an important element contributing to growth in population.

[1] Charles Fisher, *op. cit.*, p. 67.

If this was true in Malaya, Burma and Indo-China, it was no less the case in China after the Taiping Rebellion and in Japan after the civil war of 1877, where population increased by about 10 million with each succeeding decade.

*

If, in demographic terms, the benefits accruing from Western enterprise were unequally distributed, the same cannot be said of commercial enterprise. In this case, the concentration of skill and capital was resident in the colonial ports which stretched in a ring on the periphery of ancient empires. They were created as new centres of commerce and of administration and were distinct from the traditional centres of culture in those countries which they served. These ports were foreign to Asia in origin, nature and function. They were usually won and maintained by military power; once established, they were sustained by sea power. In China, as we have seen, they emerged as the consular cities (1847) and later became Treaty ports (1881) endowed with full authority. More often than not they were built on neglected sites, usually island sites, with a protective barrier of water surrounding them. Suakin, Massawa, Zanzibar, Bombay, Penang, Singapore and Hong Kong are examples of this; they enjoyed maximum access to cheap water routes for the bulk transport of produce by both land and sea.

The commercial creed which motivated and inspired settlers in these ports gained in strength in proportion to its world-wide diffusion. That creed was centred upon belief in the market, the price mechanism, a money economy and free trade. While these axioms of a commercial policy were relevant in the West, they were not valid in the East. Their dogmatic application in unsuitable conditions was, therefore, a measure of sublime ignorance of eastern economic structures. In Western eyes, however, trade was the great leveller; it diverted energy from wasteful war-time pursuits and made the market rather than the battlefield the focus of activity. In this respect, commerce appeared less a source of profit than an instrument of civilisation.

We have already referred to the growing strength of Shanghai and Hong Kong as outposts of this new civilisation; but, of all the colonial ports which were to have influence on the course of commercial development, Singapore must be regarded as of prime

importance. With the opening of the Suez Canal and the establishment of competing steamship services to China and to East
Indian ports, Singapore assumed a strategic and dominating
position in the trade between Europe and the Pacific. Thence-
forward the Straits of Malacca rather than the Straits of Sunda
became the shortest route for the new steamship trades in eastern
waters, benefiting Penang and Singapore at the expense of
Batavia.[1] For a time, Penang, having become a port of call for
steamships, increased its shipping even faster than Singapore.
Singapore, however, eventually developed the potentialities of its
central position as an *entrepot*. It extended its lines of communication with Burma and Siam to the north and with the East Indies
and Australia to the east and the south. Western steamship owners
made it a base for their agency houses; and the new harbour west
of the original settlement on the Singapore river (used by the P.
and O. since 1850) developed at the expense of the old harbour.
The increase in shipping by one-third between 1869 and 1871
compelled the expansion of dock facilities. The growing port
became a centre for Indian and Chinese immigrants; its first
Chinese commissioner was appointed in 1870 and, in the same year,
the Hong Kong and Shanghai Bank opened an agency.[2] The vast
expansion of the *entrepot* trade shifted the lines of communication
away from Batavia to the more strategically situated point on the
new routes between Suez and Shanghai.

In this fact lay the key to future expansion in the trade between
Europe and the Far East. The steamship was the quickener of the
new spirit of enterprise. The first ship to reach Singapore *via* the
Suez Canal was *Thabor* from Marseille in 61 days, the *Sin Zanzing*
from Glasgow and *Sakana* from London in 58 days; *Shantung*
made the voyage from Glasgow in 42 days and, finally, *Pei-Ho*
broke all previous time in June 1870 by arriving from Marseille in
29 days.[3] The conquest of time and space had been accomplished
by Western engineering skill and technology and had brought the
wealth of the East to the warehouses and markets of the West with

---

[1] F. E. Hyde, *Blue Funnel, op. cit.*, pp. 49-52; see also W. Makepeace,
G. E. Brooke, R. St. J. Bradell, *One Hundred Years of Singapore* (1921),
and G. Boggars, 'The Effect of Re-opening of the Suez Canal on the
Trade and Development of Singapore', *Journal of the Malayan Branch
Royal Asiatic Society*, Mar. 1955.
[2] *Ibid.*
[3] D. A. Farnie, *op. cit.*, p. 174, quoting *China Mail*, 17 March 1870.

speed and efficiency. In the process, Singapore had become the pivot of the chain between the age of steam and steel and the ox-cart and rickshaw; between capital-intensive economies and peasant cultivation.

In maritime terms, the opening of the Suez Canal sharpened the differences between the first steamship lines and the later ones. In this respect, the monopoly of the P. and O. in the carriage of mail, passengers and cargo was threatened by the new and vigorous Ocean Steam Ship Co. founded by the brothers Alfred and Philip Holt, in 1865.[1] Their first iron ship, powered by compound-tandem engines, reached Shanghai in July 1866. Thereafter, as we shall see, this company established its hold not only on the trade with Chinese ports but also on that with the Straits Settlements; by pursuing an active policy designed to tap the lucrative trades of the East Indies, Burma and Siam, the Holts also participated with increasing success in the *entrepot* trades of Singapore.

Apart from the P. and O., however, the antecedents of Holts' Blue Funnel Line ships to Far Eastern waters were sporadic in service and uncertain in performance—that is to say, as far as steamship enterprise was concerned. Nevertheless, the effects of the Taiping Rebellion, the boom in Hong Kong and the emergence of Shanghai as a free city induced British and European shipping companies to send out ships. The well documented voyage of the Harrison Brothers' *Admiral Grenfell* (which earned a net profit of £20,000 on a single voyage to Shanghai in 1857) is an excellent example of this.[2] As the steamship began to acquire superiority over the sailing ship, shipping companies sought the establishment of more regular contacts. Thus the Ben Line started a service some time before 1860, Brocklebanks in 1860 and the Shire Line in 1861. These, together with the exploratory voyages of the ships of the French company, Messagéries Impériales, and the active promotion of American interests in the Yangtse trade by Russell and Co., set a pattern for future shipping development.[3]

One additional company promotion, concerned with Far Eastern

[1] F. E. Hyde, *Blue Funnel, op. cit.*, pp. 41-2.
[2] F. E. Hyde, *Shipping Enterprise and Management* (1967), p. 10.
[3] G. Blake, *The Ben Line* (1956), pp. 36 *et seq.*; J. F. Gibson, *Brocklebanks, 1770-1950* (1953), Vol. I, pp. 272 *et seq.*; K. C. Liu, *op. cit.*, pp. 112 *et seq.*

shipping, needs to be mentioned. The Calcutta and Burmah Steam Navigation Co. established in 1856, after the second Burma War, by William MacKinnon, founder of the Bengal merchant house of MacKinnon, McKenzie and Co., was renamed in 1863 the British India Steam Navigation Co. It had extended its operations to the Persian Gulf in 1862 in association with the Euphrates and Tigris Steam Navigation Co. Ltd., which had been started in 1861 by T. Lynch of Bagdad. Through its affiliated Netherlands India Steam Navigation Co. Ltd., it secured the carriage of mail between Singapore and Batavia in 1862. By its registration in the Netherlands in 1865, the company obtained access to Dutch colonial ports in the Far East on equal terms with national shipping and thus provided a linking service between those companies trading direct with Chinese ports with its own peripheral services to Burma and the Dutch islands of the East Indian archipelago.[1]

In these various ways, therefore, the scene was set for the opening up of China, Japan, Malaya and the riverine kingdoms of Burma, Siam and Indo-China to the Western merchant and shipowner. The centres of operation were those of the new steamship ports equipped with the capital stock of a technological civilisation. The vast areas of cultivation in such traditional products as tea and silk were brought within the scope of scientific promotion; the Western merchant houses and banks provided the means of exchange to carry the produce to Western markets. Indigenous populations were given additional sources of livelihood and the relaxation of restrictive legislation on the free movement of the individual saw the beginnings of a new pattern of migration. Supplies of labour were thus made available for the production of tin, rice, tobacco, sugar, rubber and vegetable oils. Inevitably, the East was drawn into the pattern of consumption of Western countries, and tied thereto by the lines of communication created by the railway, the telegraph and the steamship. The explosive force of Western capitalism and commercial acumen was about to disrupt the centuries-old and traditionally based economies of approximately one-quarter of the world's inhabitants.

[1] See Boyd Cable, *op. cit.*, pp. 202-4.

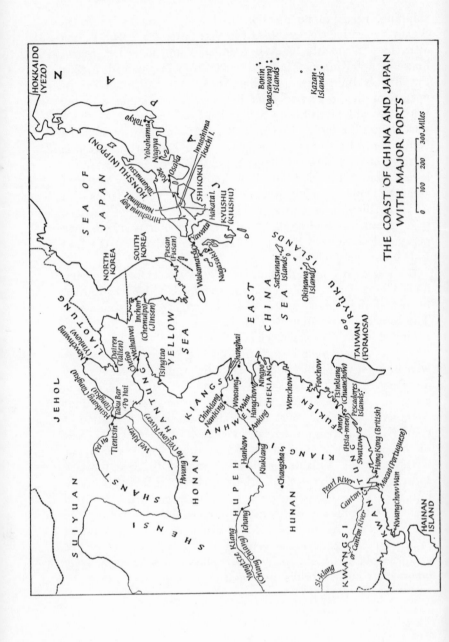

THE COAST OF CHINA AND JAPAN
WITH MAJOR PORTS

0   100   200   300 Miles

CHAPTER II

The New System of Communication: 1865-1890

THE most obvious result of the opening of the Suez Canal in 1869 was that, by shortening the distance and the voyage time, the trade of the Far East was brought within the acquisitive grasp of the steamship owner and his agents. In this context the Canal was an important and a culminating factor in a long series of events, mainly technological in character, which made it possible for the steamship to engage profitably in long hauls. As a consequence, the Far East, already freed from the trade monopoly of the East India Co., was brought into closer contact with the spirit of Western enterprise. Under the spur of the new steamship agents, the tempo of commercial activity increased and the flow of goods and services was stimulated. These broad generalisations merely serve to set the framework for a complete picture in which commercial rivalry, cut-throat competition, political aspirations and financial exploitation played their parts. In this process, the wealth to be derived from a lucrative trade was the lure, and the steamship was the key to its attainment.

Much has been written about the technological development of the steamship.[1] All that need be said here is that the brothers

---

[1] See for example, *Minutes of Proceedings of the Institute of Civil Engineers*, LI, Part 1 (1878), Session 1877-8, No. 1, 511; 'A review of the Progress of Steam Shipping during the last quarter of a Century' by Alfred Holt; R. J. Cornewall-Jones, *The British Merchant Service* (1898); J. Napier, *Life of Robert Napier* (1904); J. Kennedy, *The History of Steam Navigation* (1903); J. A. Ewing, *The Steam Engine and other Heat Engines* (1894). For a more technical account see J. Price, 'On Iron and Steel as Constructive Material for Ships' in *Transactions of the Institute*

Alfred and Philip Holt, having launched the Ocean Steam Ship Co. in 1865 (the Blue Funnel Line), firmly believed that the mechanical problem of sending a ship to China had been solved. The ships for the company were built of iron with the latest design of hull, having a length of about eight and a half times the beam. Powered by compound-tandem engines they had a low coal consumption per indicated h.p. per hour and were, therefore, economical to run. Furthermore, by placing the orders for his ships in periods of depression, Alfred Holt was able to secure the advantages of low costs of construction. In these ways, the Holt ships were given the requisites for returning a profit on each individual voyage. Compared with the famous clipper ships, sailing home from the China coast with approximately 1,000 tons of cargo in a time of 120 to 130 days, the Holt ships with a capacity of 3,000 tons were scheduled to take 77 days on the homeward voyage.[1] As a result, though steamship freight rates continued to be higher than sailing ship rates for a few years, the bulk of the tea cargoes passed to steamships. By 1869, Alfred Holt could claim with a degree of satisfaction that the performance of his steamships in bringing back new tea had been excellent.[2] The ships had not only beaten all competitors but had delivered a volume of tea just short of 9,000,000 lb. to the London market nearly a week before their nearest rivals. As a result, the Holt teas sold at 2d per lb. more than those carried in other ships.[3] This achievement put an end to the forebodings of merchants and the prophecies of sailing ship owners about the use of steamships in Chinese waters. It was, for the Holts, a climax of effort and a presage of future development.

Among Holts' earliest competitors were the Peninsular and Oriental and the French Company, Messagéries Maritimes, both subsidised for the carriage of mails. During the 1870's, however,

---

of *Mechanical Engineers* (1881), and discussion of the paper; also F. C. Marshall on 'The Progress and Development of the Marine Engine', *ibid.*, pp. 449 *et seq.*; F. C. Smith, *A Short History of Naval and Marine Engineering* (1937); H. J. Dyos and D. H. Aldcroft, *British Transport* (1969), pp. 238-42.

[1] F. E. Hyde, *Blue Funnel*, *op. cit.*, p. 24; R. H. Thornton, *British Shipping* (1939), p. 66.
[2] Holt MSS., Alfred Holt's Diary, 13 Oct. 1869.
[3] *Ibid.*

these were joined by a number of British lines, the Glen owned by MacGregor Gow and Co. of Glasgow, the Castle owned by Thomas Skinner and Co., the Shire founded by Captain D. J. Jenkins, as well as other companies operating ships in Chinese waters, such as the British India Steam Navigation Co. and Jardine Matheson and Co. The main cargoes carried outwards were woollens, cotton piece-goods and small manufactures, while those homewards consisted of tea, tobacco, silk, rice, and later sugar tin, rubber and copra.

Once the technical difficulties of sending a steamship to the Far East had been overcome, the second major problem, that of making voyages on newly-established routes pay their way, had to be tackled. This involved the British companies in the protection of their interests, particularly in periods of fluctuating and adverse trading conditions. Such action took the form of agreements and the equalisation of freight rates, the allocation of cargoes, and the amalgamation or absorption of companies. The design was primarily aimed at the elimination of destructive competition between rival British shipping lines, but at a later date it was instrumental in strengthening the competitive position of those firms in the bitter struggles which developed with the Dutch and German companies in the cross-service trades, and in the direct trade with Java and other island ports of south-east Asia.

As already stated, the Holt ships were undoubtedly superior to those of other companies during the 1860's and early 1870's; but within ten years they were being outpaced and outclassed by the newer ships of the Glen, Shire and Castle Lines. The combined fleets of these competitors numbered 22 ships, most of which were capable of steaming home from China in less than 45 days, whereas the fastest Holt ship took 50. The *Stirling Castle*, crack vessel of the Castle Line, made the voyage from London to Hankow in 1882 in just under 29 days, a phenomenal speed at that time. The P. and O., having survived the critical years following the opening of the Suez Canal, was now under the forceful managerial hand of Thomas Sutherland. Under his direction the P. and O. achieved efficiency and again became a serious rival to other lines engaged in the China trade.

Competition on the basis of the steamship's performance was not, however, an all-important factor in the difficult economic and commercial situation which influenced shipping policy after 1875;

though according to John Swire it remained a matter of importance to the successful operation of Holts' Ocean Steam Ship Co.[1]
This was so because Holts stubbornly refused to alter the design
and motive power of their ships. Furthermore, they refused to
admit that the problem of low coal consumption, a problem which
they had overcome in the years before the opening of the Suez
Canal, was no longer such an important factor in giving them a
competitive advantage once that Canal had become a route to the
Far East.[2] Apart from such considerations, however, there were
other pressing problems which had to be faced by all steamship
companies, not least among which were changes in the balance
between outward and homeward cargoes, falling levels of freight
rates, the establishment of contacts in the main ports and the
division of trade between British and foreign shipping lines. By
tackling these problems in a new and revolutionary way, the
organisation of steamship trades to the Far East was not only given
a greater degree of efficiency, but became a model for other routes
throughout the world.

*

As far as the China freight market operated in the 1870's, it was
complex and highly diverse in structure. In the first place, there
was a broad division between sailing ship and steamship rates at
every port. In general, steamship rates, despite fast voyage times,
continued to be higher than those for clippers. This was partly
a reflection of a lingering prejudice against steamships on the part
of merchants and partly of the need to cover risks against higher
capital loss by steamship owners. In the second place, freights
were fixed for different commodities as between one steamship
and another or between competing sailing ships in accordance
with projected voyage times. Thirdly, the level of rates was also
governed by the supply of shipping on berth at a port at a given
time. Finally, the overall pattern of rate determination for regular
cargo-liner companies could be adversely affected by the intervention of casual or tramp steamers, though their competition was
less effective in the carriage of higher quality cargo (such as new
season's tea) which required special conditions of transport. With
the rapid increase in the volume of steamship tonnage on the China

[1] Holt MSS., Swire correspondence, Swire to Philip Holt, 11 April
1879, and Swire to A. Crompton, 5 Dec. 1879.
[2] *Ibid.*, Swire to A. Holt, 7 Dec. 1880.

route, the effect was seriously to decrease the level of rates and, consequently, the earning capacity of individual shipping companies. By 1879, the whole position had changed once again; the years from 1865 to 1870, considered as a period of pioneering in the use of steam power, were followed by a flow of resources into the trade, and a multiplication of the companies engaged. This, in turn, led to an intensification of competition, a fall in rates and a decrease in net voyage profits.

In some respects the operation of steamships added to, rather than diminished, the complexities in the structure of the freight market. Sailing ships in direct competition had always been subject to wide degrees of fluctuation in rates and very often incurred high costs for towage and berthing.[1] Insurance rates also varied widely from port to port. In 1886, the year of the great tea race, when the clippers *Ariel*, *Taeping* and *Serica* left Foochow bar on the same tide and docked in London 99 days later on the same tide, freights which had started at between £4 to £5 per ton, owing to shortage of tonnage at Shanghai, fell to £1 10s. od by September. In general, freights outwards were about £2 10s od per ton, a figure which was considered to be high; but the steamship was soon to alter the whole situation. Holts' ship *Agamemnon* made the passage from China in 66 days in 1868. She had loaded part of her cargo at £8 8s od per ton. It happened, however, that teas were superior at Foochow this particular year, and freights opened there at £5 10s od and did not fall below £2 10s od. In the following year freight rates began at £4 os od in nearly every port and remained relatively high except at Shanghai.[2] On the whole, the steamships loaded at about £2 per ton above the rates for clippers.

It is not necessary to give a detailed account of fluctuations in the freight market for the carriage of every product. A general index, based on average rates at the main ports for both steamships and sailing ships, would show that the figures fell during the 1860's from £8 to £4 per ton. After 1870, the effect of the opening of the Suez Canal was shown in the steamships' virtual monopoly of the carriage of tea from Foochow, the sailing ships having to accept late charters for Australia: whereas steamships could command a

[1] Voyage accounts 1860-75, for specified ships from Rathbone MSS. and Killick Marton MSS.

[2] David R. MacGregor, *The China Bird* (1961), p. 95. Freight lists based on information in Jardine Matheson MSS.

rate of £4 10s 0d with an addition of 10s for the first ships home, the clippers were forced to accept a rate of £2 10s 0d; by August these rates had dipped to £1 10s 0d. There was a slight improvement in 1872 and, in the following year, the level of rates was higher than in any since 1869. This improvement, however, was short-lived. By 1878 freight rates had fallen to such low levels that sailing ships were unable to cover costs and steamships were barely able to maintain services and return a profit. For the period from 1870 to 1878, average rates declined from just over £4 a ton to about £1 15s 0d a ton. In such conditions, the principal steamship companies, increasingly aware of the damaging effects of augmented competition, sought to safeguard their capital resources by embarking upon a policy of co-operation and agreement. This led to the establishment of the first China Conference, a *modus vivendi* which formed the pattern for future relationships between shipping companies and merchants engaged in the Far Eastern trade.

*

As we shall see later, Alfred Holt broke away from the traditional form of commercial relationship undertaken by established agents and correspondents on the China coast. He employed two new firms, Butterfield and Swire at Shanghai and Walter Mansfield and Co. at Singapore. Butterfield and Swire were mainly responsible for the provision of cargoes from the interior and along the China coast, while Mansfield tapped the lucrative trades of Malaya and the East Indian islands. It was, however, to the forceful genius of John Samuel Swire that Holts and other British shipping companies turned in their efforts to combat competition, and it was Swire who persuaded the steamship owners to accept agreement with a view to minimising the hazards of the trade.

At this point, it is pertinent to inquire how Swire gained such a keen insight into the competitive structure of the China trade and how, as a result of this, he was able to persuade other British shipowners to enter into mutually protective agreements for the ordering of their trade. It is certain that his ideas, which eventually led to the formation and organisation of the first China Conference, sprang from his struggle to break into the China coast and Yangtse River trades. In 1872, Swire had founded the China Navigation Co., the fleet consisting of river boats and coastal steamers (these latter coming under a separate organisation known as the Coast Boats Ownery), to trade and carry cargoes to the wharves at Shanghai. Even before the establishment of this company, uniform rate agreements were in force between rival shipping lines. Thus, when Swire's ships entered the Yangtse trade they were subjected to an immediate opposition from the American firm of Russell and Co. This conflict, however, was quickly resolved by an agreement to pool earnings, each company being allowed an equal number of sailings.[1] This agreement was followed by a second in 1874 between Jardine Matheson's China Coast Steam Navigation Co. and Russells, with the object of maintaining uniform rates in the trade between Shanghai and Tientsin.[2] This agreement worked well and, when the native China Merchants Co. bought Russells' Shanghai Steam Navigation Co., John Swire concluded that the Yangtse River trade would continue to be governed by a divided monopoly for some years to come.[3]

Swire's forecast, however, was not fulfilled. The native Chinese company refused to accept an equal division of the river trade and demanded a two-thirds' share. This obstruction culminated in a rate-cutting war to the injury of the two companies engaged in the struggle. Eventually a compromise was reached in 1877 under what was known as a joint purse arrangement. Under this agreement the China Merchants were to receive 55 per cent and the China Navigation Co. 45 per cent of the pooled earnings.[4] From this experience it became clear to Swire that pooling agreements worked more equitably than uniform rate agreements, a conclusion which was greatly to influence his future course of action.

Viewing the situation on the China coast as a whole, Swire was convinced by 1878 that, in order to bring organisation into the steamship trades, some more comprehensive agreement of the joint purse type would have to be negotiated. His influence and energy were, therefore, directed towards this end. By September 1879, a joint purse agreement was reached for the Canton River

[1] Sheila Marriner and F. E. Hyde, *The Senior, op. cit.,* p. 62.
[2] *Ibid.,* p. 136; also K. C. Liu, *British-Chinese Steam Ship Rivalry in China 1873-1885*; C. D. Cowan (ed.), *The Economic Development of China and Japan* (1964), p. 52.
[3] Swire MSS., Swire to W. Lang and J. H. Scott, 5 Jan. 1877; Sheila Marriner and F. E. Hyde, *op. cit.,* p. 137.
[4] *Ibid.*

and there was a hopeful prospect of settlement on the Yangtse and Tientsin routes. In short, Swire had worked out and had put into operation the elements of pooling agreements (and, in fact, had adopted the principle of deferred rebates). Some time before these events his attention had been drawn to the problem of increasing competition between rival shipping companies serving the main line route between Britain, Europe and the Far East. He now understood more clearly the relative effectiveness of the various devices whereby competition could be reduced and freight rates raised. He was witness to the benefits conferred upon both weak and strong companies under the terms of a Conference or quasi-Conference agreement, the stronger having to make payment to the weaker, while all participants profited from the regulation of competition and through the rise in the general level of rates. Consequently, when the first China Conference between the main shipping companies was formed in 1879 with Swire as chairman, its pattern and organisation was the end product of much experience gained in Chinese shipping operations. To Swire, the essentials for such a Conference were to overcome certain general problems affecting the operation of steamship companies running services to the Far East and, in particular, to protect Holts both from these difficulties and from the adverse results of their own unprogressive attitudes.

As we have already seen, the chief difficulties arose from the excess of shipping capacity on particular routes, from seasonal fluctuations in demand for produce and imbalance between outward and homeward cargoes. The problem of excess capacity was a direct result of overbuilding by the main cargo-liner companies during the 1870's but this, in turn, was aggravated by the inroads of tramp steamers. An overall Conference agreement equalising freight rates would, it was thought, help to solve this problem, though pooling arrangements might be more efficacious in dealing with seasonal fluctuations and the imbalance between the import and export trades. Against the background of this crystallising opinion, the first China Conference came into being in September 1879. Its main provisions incorporated a classified list of freight charges and deferred rebates designed to secure the loyalty of merchants to Conference vessels.

A Shipping Conference as such was, and still is, a flexible instrument. By virtue of an agreed rate-fixing device, undercutting on the carriage of specific cargoes can be avoided and a harmonious relationship between participants maintained. Within this framework, however, there is considerable scope for individual negotiation both as to rates and as to cargoes carried, provided always that the rest of the Conference members agree to the specific terms. In this sense, a Conference is not a monopoly, but rather an oligopoly in which members, by maintaining degrees of competitive strength, may also sustain the profitability of their enterprise. In short, the company with the most efficient ships and the most highly skilled organisation could, within the limits imposed by Conference decisions, usually make the biggest profit. As an adjunct to this however, the Conference, through its acceptance and use of various types of pooling agreements, sought to equalise earning capacity in the interests of the less efficient firm. In this respect the Conference system is open to criticism on the grounds that the underwriting of weak firms inevitably keeps the cost of a shipping service at an artificially high level. Nevertheless, a Conference was usually maintained by a series of relatively short-term agreements, under which terms relating to ships and cargoes were in constant process of negotiation. Coverage and membership were liable to expand and contract; terms and agreements were changed and modified to meet the wishes of members, to meet the demands of shippers, to conform to new patterns of trade and to govern additional shipping routes. From the start it was recognised that, if such agreements were to remain effective, they must include both British and foreign shipping companies. The first China Conference circular was signed by the P. and O., Messageries Maritimes, the Ocean Steam Ship Co., the Glen, Shire and Castle Lines, Gellatly, Hankey and Sewell, Norris and Joyner, and Shaw, Williams and Co.[1] By 1884, the Ben Line was a full member and by 1885 the list also included the China Mutual. Thereafter admissions were reasonably all-embracing, North German Lloyd and Kinsin Lines in 1893, 'Shells' and Rickmers in 1894, specified ships of Austrian Lloyd and Rubattinos in 1896, and by the end of the 1890's Nippon Yusen Kaisha had been included. This catholic quality of membership gave the Conference vitality and strength of organisation. Had it lacked this quality, it could never have satisfied the demand of, and catered for the needs of, shipowners and traders.

[1] Swire MSS., Swire to A. Hankey, 15 Aug. 1879.

The first agreement, which began on 1 September 1879, was very largely experimental. It covered both the outward and the homeward trades and was timed for a short period of operation, the outward agreement being due to expire in four months and the homeward in six. In the event, both were terminated in four months. The Outward Conference was renewed immediately and, apart from one major revision in 1885, lasted until the autumn of 1887.[1] On the whole, the outward agreements worked well apart from one or two minor difficulties, such as the allocation of cargoes between ships sailing from London and from Liverpool. This, however, was a difficulty not peculiar to Far Eastern Conferences; it applied generally to all other Conferences.

Holts' Ocean Steam Ship Co. was somewhat differently placed from the other signatories to the outward agreement. The company was a chief carrier for Lancashire cottons and Yorkshire woollens, comprising some two-thirds of all such cargoes to China and two-fifths of those exported to Japan in Conference vessels. John Swire knew that Holts' trade was vulnerable and it was far from inevitable that Lancashire and Yorkshire products should continue to be exported through Liverpool. In the first place, it took longer and cost more to sail ships from Liverpool; in the second place, freight rates from London contained an allowance for rail charges, and it needed only a slight discrimination in rail charges to divert cargoes from Liverpool to London. Finally, exporters of piece-goods had constantly to wage a bitter struggle with the monopoly position of the railway companies serving Liverpool on the one hand and the Mersey Docks and Harbour Board on the other. At first, Swire had maintained that, in fairness, equal rates should be paid from London and Liverpool, so that shipping rates and railway charges should amount to the same aggregate for specific classes of goods.[2] It was not difficult for the P. and O. to tap Liverpool berths. On the other hand, it was in the general interest of all companies within the Conference to keep Holts' ships sailing from Liverpool in order to prevent outsiders sailing from that port at rates undercutting those on London ships. Holts could always threaten to invade the London berth; in fact, they had sailed some ships from London using Gellatly, Hankey and Sewell as their agents. By 1881, Swire recorded that one-third of

---

[1] Sheila Marriner and F. E. Hyde, *op. cit.*, p. 161.
[2] *Ibid.*, p. 162.

Holt departures were from London. In order to give a fair return on all voyages, therefore, the relative levels of freight rates from Liverpool and London were varied from time to time and for different commodities. Sometimes equivalent rates were fixed, but it became standard practice for Liverpool rates to be lower than those from London. Rates in favour of Liverpool had some effect upon the shipment of cargoes, though it was evident that a very slight movement in rates could swing the balance from one port to another. For this reason, Swire became more than ever convinced that a common purse arrangement was essential in the best interests of all shipping companies in the Conference. Such an agreement was in force between Holts and the Glens in the early 1880's and with the China Mutual in 1885. Apart from arrangements of this kind, Outward Conference agreements were satisfactorily in operation at least until 1887.

The various Homeward Conferences, however, were fraught with difficulty. After the cessation of the first agreement in December 1879, the Homeward Conference was allowed to lapse. This was caused largely by the intransigence of the Holt brothers. They were obstinate in their dislike of this agreement despite John Swire's apologia of its benefits. To Swire, the facts were undeniable. By the year ending July 1880, the Ocean Steam Ship Co. had not only carried on average an increased tonnage of cargo over that for the previous year, but had earned on average freight rates some $16\frac{2}{3}$ per cent higher.[1] When an analysis was made for the carriage of tea only, the figures were even more favourable, showing an increase of 65 per cent from Shanghai and 85 per cent from Hong Kong. A new homeward agreement was negotiated in 1881, but there were many difficulties affecting its efficient operation. In July 1882, Swire wrote 'I think we may now consider the Conference burst up temporarily'.[2] The agreement continued through 1883 but efforts to renew it failed. There was a short-lived compromise in 1884 but this broke up when Gellatlys demanded the admission of an outsider, Moguls, into the Conference, claiming that the 1881-82 agreement had not been legally dissoved.[3] By 1886, however, Holts' suspicions had given way to a freer acceptance of the principles underlying Conference arrangements and

[1] Holt MSS., Swire correspondence, Swire to A. Holt, 20 July 1880.
[2] Sheila Marriner and F. E. Hyde, *op. cit.*, p. 165.
[3] *Ibid.*

they were anxious that a new Homeward Conference should be negotiated. Unfortunately, this desire coincided with the beginning of litigation occasioned by the struggle between the Conference lines and Moguls, and it was not until the end of 1892 that there was any hope of a homeward agreement being signed. This agreement took effect from the end of January 1893. As we have seen, a new Outward Conference was negotiated at the same time and, as a result of the operation of the two agreements, freight rates began to rise. There was, however, still some apprehension as to the probable duration of this newly-won peace. In the event, outward agreements continued to operate for several years, though the homeward one was temporarily interrupted in 1897, when Holts withdrew because they alleged that they had been treated unfairly.[1] John Swire intervened with some speed and, in one of his last efforts in Holts' interests before he died, was able to negotiate new terms.[2] Thereafter, with only minor modifications, the principles of Conference agreements which had so far been worked out remained in operation, at least until 1914.

*

Within the general structure of Conference agreements as outlined above, there were pooling agreements between individual companies. The terms under which pools operated were normally kept secret and, indeed, S. G. Sturmey suggests that all Conferences are reluctant to divulge their nature and scope.[3] Before 1914, the importance of pools was, perhaps, less significant than in the years following the First World War, but it is clear from the shipping archives that such arrangements were numerous and, in the China trade, followed three distinct forms.

In the first place, there were steamship pools; as the name suggests they provided for a division of earnings per ship. Secondly, there were joint purse agreements, in which receipts were divided between participants in such a way that each registered ton of ship earned the same gross freight. Thirdly, there were cargo pools under which aggregate cargo was divided among members in stipulated proportions. Differences in the amounts

[1] Sheila Marriner and F. E. Hyde, *op. cit.*, p. 165.
[2] *Ibid.*
[3] S. G. Sturmey, *British Shipping and World Competition* (1962), pp. 325-7.

eventually carried by each company were adjusted at a standard of value specially agreed upon. The chief points in the operation of these distinctive pooling arrangements can be illustrated (at least for the China trade) by various examples.

A steamship pool was arranged at the time of the first China and Japan Conference. Under the provisions, it was agreed to pool 7 Glen ships, 3 Castles, 13 Oceans. This pool operated for four months and, when settlement was finally made, it transpired that between them the 23 ships had carried 52,400 tons of cargo, averaging 2,278¼ tons per ship. Each ship was entitled to carry this amount, and it was agreed that any ship carrying more than this amount should pay 24s per ton on the excess to those ships carrying less. The 7 Glens had exceeded their allowance by 3,586 tons, the 3 Castles by 538 tons, while Holts' Ocean ships had undercarried to the extent of 4,124 tons. Holts were, therefore, due to receive a total of £4,303 4s 0d from Glens and £645 12s 0d from Castles.[1] It became generally recognised that the most serious disadvantage of such a steamship pool was that it took no account of the size or speed of the ship. Swire was able to convince Holts and the other members of the Conference that the second type of pool, a common or joint purse agreement, gave a better and, on the whole, a fairer system of distribution. Eventually, in 1883, after prolonged negotiations, he managed to persuade Holts and Glens to enter into a common purse agreement.[2] This applied only to homeward voyages. All homeward earnings from the carriage of cargo, coolies, and pilgrims (though not first and second-class passengers) were paid into a common account.[3] This amount was then divided between the two lines in proportion to the gross tonnage of shipping sailing from Shanghai. Each company had the right, before contributing to the pool, to deduct charges for loading and discharging cargoes. A similar arrangement was entered into between Holts and the China Mutual in the 1890's.[4] On this occasion however, the allocation was concerned with the carriage of Manchester and Yorkshire goods. Holts' Ocean Steam Ship Co. and the China Mutual virtually monopolised the

[1] Sheila Marriner and F. E. Hyde, *op. cit.*, p. 168.
[2] *Ibid.*
[3] *Ibid.*
[4] Holt MSS., Minutes of China Mutual S.N. Co., 1890-1902; Minutes O.S.S. Co., 27 A.G.M., 17 Feb. 1892.

carriage of piece-goods and yarns to China and Japan.[1] By working together it was obvious that they could exert a dominant influence on the trade. The subsequent pooling agreement between the two companies aimed at equalising the freight earned per gross ton of shipping despatched. By 1895, this pooling arrangement had been strengthened by an implicit inclusion of Moguls, whereby tonnage was limited on the route. Whenever tenders were invited for the carriage of goods it was agreed that consultation should take place between the three companies; the line which obtained a contract was required to offer a share to the other two, the primary object being to prevent rate-cutting when special cargoes were available.

An excellent example of this third type of agreement, the cargo pool, is to be found in that which was operated between 1885 and 1887 by the P. and O., Holts, and Glens. These three companies were in a very strong position because they owned the majority of the Conference vessels.[2] By joining together to form a pool of homeward cargoes from China, Japan and the Straits, they were able to make a reasonable division of the trade. Of the China cargoes, Holts received a 30·5 per cent share, P. and O. 37 per cent and Glens 32·5 per cent; cargoes from Japan were allocated rather differently, Holts receiving a 25 per cent share, P. and O. 50 per cent, and Glens 25 per cent. Shipments from the Straits were shared thus: Holts 36 per cent, P. and O. 25 per cent, and Glens 39 per cent.[3]

The distinctive feature of this pool was that it operated on cargo, not on freight. Each line retained its own earnings and varied freight rates in such a way as to try to attract cargoes in the correct proportions. If any company exceeded its percentage share, it had to pay into the pool, on the excess tonnage carried, an amount equal to the average gross freight per ton earned by the Ocean Steam Ship Co. over the period as a whole. Holts were allowed to deduct one half to cover carrying costs and rebates to shippers. Accounts were settled quarterly and, for the quarter May to August 1885, the results were as follows: the P. and O. undercarried its quota and was paid on balance £9,981 and the

[1] Holt MSS., Minutes of China Mutual S.N. Co., 1890-1902; Minutes O.S.S. Co., 27 A.G.M., 17 Feb. 1892.

[2] Sheila Marriner and F. E. Hyde, *op. cit.*, pp. 169-70.

[3] *Ibid.*

Glen ships overcarried and had, therefore, to pay £7,611 into the pool; this amount was paid to the P. and O. as part of the £9,981 received by them, Holts making up the balance of £2,370 on their overcarriage of cargoes.[1] This pool was enlarged in 1886, when the Shires and Castles agreed with the other three companies on a limitation of cargoes. The main pool between the original three companies, however, worked well until 1887, the year in which the Conference system as a whole came under attack. Despite the suspension of agreements, Holts nevertheless attempted to secure a prolongation of the pooling arrangements, but they were unable to convince the Glens that it would be mutually advantageous to do so. There were other examples of cargo pools which could be cited, but enough has been said in this context to show that shipping companies engaged in the China and Japan trades had, under John Swire's leadership, worked out a variety of methods by which to overcome the damaging effects of competition, whether such competition arose from an over-supply of tonnage, from seasonal deficiencies in the volume of cargo on offer, or from adverse fluctuations in the level of freight rates.

Finally, one must mention the somewhat particular conditions obtaining in the Straits trade. Holts were involved in this trade, partly because of the activities of their agents, Mansfields in Singapore, and partly (as will be seen later) because of the enterprise of a member of the Mansfield firm, Theodore Cornelis Bogaardt. At an early date, Swire had expressed concern at the growth of competition in the trade. Despite their growing dependence on it, however, it was Holts who frustrated Swire's efforts to achieve a basis of agreement with the P. and O. and Glens, the two other companies interested in carrying from Singapore and other Straits ports. It was not until 1885, therefore, that a pooling agreement was arranged between the P. and O., Glens, and Holts, covering the Straits as well as China and Japan. This pool was given added significance when the other members of the Conference agreed to make returns to shippers on Straits cargoes, both outwards and homewards. In operation, this pool (which lasted until 1887) raised freight rates by as much as 50 per cent. Thereafter, the agreement lapsed, largely owing to opposition from the P. and O. to the renewal of discussion on the subject.

[1] *Ibid.*

Apart from Holts, the Straits trade was for most British companies engaged in Far Eastern trade residual to their main business. As far as Straits shippers were concerned, they had to rely on whatever shipping space was left over after the main line ships had called at Chinese and Japanese ports. Because shipping space was an uncertain factor, freight rates were liable to violent fluctuations, at times reaching very low levels. This overall situation was a serious embarrassment for Holts, particularly during the 1880's when their ships, in terms of speed and efficiency, became less able to compete with those of the other companies. They were forced back on Straits cargoes to fill holds which could not be filled in Chinese ports. The only serious rival to Holts in the Straits trade after 1884 was the China Mutual, though this rivalry was confined largely to the carriage of cargoes outwards. On the homeward runs the latter company relied for its main return on Chinese and Japanese sources, having, by the employment of more efficient ships, made inroads into Holts' hitherto entrenched position in these trades. Perhaps the best way of emphasising the situation is by a comparison of actual cargoes carried. Between September 1889 and September 1892, when no agreements were in operation, Holts carried 183,423 tons of yarns and Manchester bale and case goods compared with the China Mutual's 76,868 tons. Over the same period, Holts carried to the Straits 53,866 tons as compared with the Mutual's 6,807 tons. Also at this time, the P. and O., Ben, Shire and Glen Lines together only carried 1,874 tons of these goods to the Straits.[1]

John Swire, aware of the implications of the unbalancing effects of the Straits trade on Holts' general prosperity, worked ceaselessly for the establishment of a Straits Conference. In 1897, his hopes were realised; agreement was reached and, by the following year, was working well. Its success was, in large measure, due to the co-operation of a powerful body of freight agents who controlled a large proportion of the trade.[2] These agents were granted special commissions to maintain their loyalty. Many merchants were also strongly in favour of this Conference for, when in 1910 the Straits government passed legislation against the Conference, they were not prepared to forgo the benefits of regular sailings and more efficient services and wholeheartedly

[1] Swire MSS., Memo, 18 Nov. 1892.
[2] F. E. Hyde, *Blue Funnel, op. cit.*, p. 88.

supported the shipowners against their own government.[1] Even the Royal Commission on Shipping Rings could find little evidence on which to fault this agreement.

*

In these various ways order was established in shipping relationships. Without entering into a discussion on the merits or demerits of Conferences as a whole, it is clear from an examination of the Far Eastern shipping market that their operation raised freight rates, and generally maintained them in times of depression at levels higher than those which would have operated in a free market. In strictly economic terms this may have been a disservice to shippers, but there is little evidence to show that they were, thereby, placed in a worse position. On the contrary, if the deferred rebate is offset against the rise in freight rates, their final costs were often lower. This was so, because the regulation of trade by agreement not only ironed out the excessive range of fluctuations in freight rates, but the regularity of service brought increased trade to all the participants. Nevertheless, despite the relative success of most of the agreements, the Conference system as a whole had to sustain a vigorous assault during the 1880's against its very existence. We have already referred to the China Mutual and Mogul companies. In fact, the two companies became involved in litigation with other members of the China Conference, litigation which was not only concerned with a specific point of contention in the working of an agreement, but which eventually turned into an examination of the legality of Conference instruments as a whole.

Despite the undoubted success of the first Conference agreements, there were many instances when merchants and shipowners were in conflict over such matters as the payment of rebates and the general level of classified freight rates. On the whole, these difficulties were quickly resolved either by John Swire, acting in his capacity as chairman of the Conference, or by the intervention and decision of the Conference committee itself. In 1882, however, a new and complicating factor was introduced into the China trade. The foundation of the China Shippers Mutual Steam Navigation Co. (with a capital of £1 million) was based on a principle already used in insurance in China. As the title of the

[1] *Ibid.*, p. 133.

D

new company implied, the users of the ships (i.e. the merchants) were also mainly the shareholders; they were to receive *pro rata* dividends from the profits of the trade after allowances had been made for depreciation and reserves. Any surplus remaining was to be allocated under a precise formula to contributors of freights and shareholders. It was claimed that the main object of such an arrangement was to free merchants from domination by Conferences. Be that as it may, the coming of this powerful rival certainly threatened the position of the established shipping companies such as Holts.

John Swire, watchful of Holts' interests and annoyed at this challenge to the Conference system, argued that the trade was already over-supplied with tonnage and that existing companies could not put aside sufficient funds to cover depreciation.[1] Nevertheless, by 1884, the Mutual Co. was in operation and, for the next few years, as we have seen, maintained competitive services with the Blue Funnel Line in the China, Japan and Straits trades.[2] It was not, however, faithful to the purpose of its inception; it was forced to seek the protection of the Conference umbrella and accept the standard terms laid down for the classification of freight rates.[3]

Meanwhile, another set of circumstances was about to bring division rather than collaboration into the China trade. For some time, John Swire had been apprehensive about the inclusion of some members in the Conference. In particular, although among the signatories, Gellatly, Hankey and Sewell did not run cargo liners; but, in 1883, the Mogul Co. was formed for the purpose of taking over their interests, Mr E. Gellatly becoming manager of the new company which owned four ships. In the 1884 tea season, the Conference allowed two of these ships to load on the Hankow berth and carry cargoes to London, the only stipulation being that they conformed to Conference regulations.[4] In 1885, however, Moguls threatened rate warfare if they were not given full admission to the Conference. This admission was refused because Mogul ships did not provide a regular service to the Far East

[1] *The Times*, 30 Nov. 1882.
[2] For further details of this company see F. E. Hyde, *Blue Funnel*, *op. cit.*, and Sheila Marriner and F. E. Hyde, *op. cit.*, *passim*.
[3] F. E. Hyde, *Blue Funnel*, *op. cit.*, p. 72.
[4] Sheila Marriner and F. E. Hyde, *op. cit.*, p. 148.

hroughout the whole year; the ships were sailed to Australia and only participated in the China trade during the peak of the tea season.[1] The natural refusal of the Conference lines to allow Moguls to skim the cream of high rates during the tea season resulted in a rate war and, in 1885, in legal action. In May of that year, the Shanghai agents of the Conference issued a circular specifically stating that any shippers using Mogul ships would forfeit their rebates.[2] Swire immediately realised the implications of such a statement and when, in June, Moguls claimed that the Conference of 1884 (which had allowed them two sailings) had not lapsed, he prepared Holts and the other Conference members for legal battle. His intuition was right. In August 1885, Moguls applied for an injunction to stop the Conference discriminating against Mogul ships. This application was refused. Moguls thereupon sought other means to satisfy their ends, regarding the rebuff as a 'desperate culmination of a series of provocations'.[3] The legal arguments dragged on and were aggravated by the precipitate action of one of the Conference's own members, the China Mutual. This latter company had never been a willing member of the Conference. The terms of its foundation had been designed specifically to protect merchants against Conference rulings but, despite these intentions, the China Mutual had been forced, by pressure of circumstances, to enter the Conference. The directors had secretly supported the Mogul case and, in April 1887, they broke with the Conference and joined Moguls in a rival outside combination.[4] Gellatlys then took their case to court claiming that their ships had been restrained from carrying on normal trade, contending in support of their claim that the Conference members had conspired to prevent China merchants from using their ships for the carriage of cargo from Yangtse ports. Thus, the legal argument was widened and now included a charge of conspiracy, a charge which Swire and other members of the Conference strenuously denied.[5]

It is not necessary to trace the details of the protracted legal battle which followed. This has been done elsewhere.[6] It is

---

[1] Swire MSS., Memo, 10 Dec. 1887.
[2] Sheila Marriner and F. E. Hyde, *op. cit.*, p. 148.
[3] *Ibid.*, Swire MSS., Swire to Scott and Mackintosh, 6 Aug. 1885.
[4] F. E. Hyde, *Blue Funnel*, *op. cit.*, p. 72.
[5] Sheila Marriner and F. E. Hyde, *op. cit.*, p. 149.
[6] *Ibid.*, pp. 149-50; *China Mail*, 19 Aug. 1889.

sufficient to state that judgment went against Moguls and that their subsequent references to the Court of Appeal and to the House of Lords were equally unsuccessful. The essence of the final pronouncement on the validity of Conferences was that they were legitimate devices, under the terms of which shipping companies had a right to compete in the interests of their trade; such action did not constitute a conspiracy 'provided that there was never intimidation, obstruction or molestation'.[1] The inducement of higher freight rates or the prospect of return in the form of a rebate could also not be construed as interference with the course of trade.[2] So ended a struggle involving the legality and, by implication, the very existence of shipping Conferences. That this conflict should have arisen in the China trade is no fortuitous occurrence. It was precisely because problems inherent in the China trade seemed to be incapable of solution that the principles underlying the structure of Conferences were worked out and put into practice. Thereafter, apart from the great inquiry by the Royal Commission which reported in 1909, the complex system of Conference agreements in practically every trade and on every sea route has worked within the framework of the law.

Thus, between 1870 and 1890, British shipping companies had encountered and overcome a range of difficult problems. In the first place, primary mechanical problems of sending a steamship to China had been solved by the introduction of a scientifically designed ship made of iron and powered by compound-tandem (later triple-expansion) engines. In the second place, commercial problems were overcome through the creation and use of powerful steamship agents; while the logistical difficulties concerned with the supply of tonnage and the ill effects of unrestricted competition had come within the regulation of shipping Conferences. The undoubted success of these various ventures in the China trade was the outcome of Alfred Holt's mechanical skill and John Swire's organisational gifts. It will be seen later whether the foundations which these and other men laid were capable of supporting the considerable changes in the pattern of Far Eastern trade, and whether their efforts were successful in overcoming the rivalry of powerful foreign shipping lines which entered that trade after

---

[1] Sheila Marriner and F. E. Hyde, *op. cit.*, p. 150.
[2] *Ibid.*

1890. Up to that date, however, it is reasonably true that British enterprise (particularly in the field of shipping) had opened up a new area of the world to British capital. The resultant flow of trade was, at one and the same time, the reward of enterprise and the mainspring of future effort.

CHAPTER III

The Financial Organisation of the Traditional Produce Trades: Tea and Silk in China, 1860-1890

IN the carriage of bulk primary commodities from the Far East, there were three principal problems which continuously impeded freedom of movement. The first was involved in securing an unrestricted flow of such goods to the main Chinese ports, the second was concerned with standards of quality, and the third was in the all-important field of finance. The steamship provided the answer to the first of these problems. The second impediment, however, was rather more intractable, partly because of the inefficiency and inherent weakness of Chinese production methods and partly because of general obstruction by up-country producers to Western ideas, designed to give Chinese agriculture a more intensive and centrally organised system. Finally, if trade was to find a proper stimulation, it was essential not only to have an efficient system of financial organisation between producer, buying agent and shipowner, but also a generally acceptable form of currency with which to sponsor and undertake transactions. This problem of currency was only really overcome when bill markets were allowed to develop, when banking facilities were established and when the considerable resources of the steamship agents were given rein to function properly.

The ancient Chinese trade of tea is an example illustrative of the way in which Western enterprise encouraged expansion during the nineteenth century until, owing to the rise of highly competitive sources in India and Japan, decline set in to the considerable reduction of its former importance. In this context, however, the pressures upon development were exercised principally from the side of demand, very little opportunity being afforded to foreign capital to influence quality or methods of production. For one thing, the great distance separating the tea producing areas from the ports inhibited foreign influence. Another factor, namely the prohibition on the holding of land by foreigners (apart from that in Treaty ports), made it almost impossible to start tea plantations under a Western system of organisation. The converse was true in Japan, where centrally organised control welcomed such ideas and made it possible for capital from abroad to establish efficient production units. The weaknesses in the position governing the supply of China tea, however, need not be over-emphasised. As we shall see, the foreign merchant was, on occasion, able to modify some Chinese trade practices and certain methods of production and treatment. Nevertheless, his inability to control basic and traditional systems of production left him with a more narrowly defined role than in other lines of business. The relative decline in the export of China tea, in the face of competition from elsewhere, may be attributed in part to this fact.

It was usual for the foreign merchant in China to buy the tea from dealers at the ports. Apart from the Russian buyers who made direct contact with up-country producers, it was rare for merchants to conduct business outside the ports.[1] There was, therefore, no intermediate foreign contact at any point in the long channel of distribution. Between the peasant cultivator and the sales organisation in the port, there existed a chain of Chinese middlemen. These varied in number from area to area and in accordance with seasonal requirements but, on average, a normal estimate might be as many as ten.[2] The obvious result of this pattern of distribution was to add to final costs—a process which ultimately made China teas less competitive than those from other countries. The cultivator was usually responsible for the initial drying of the leaf. He then sold his crop to a dealer who manufactured it before passing it to a Chinese Hong. There were probably many other hands through which the tea passed from the dealer to the Hong, particularly if finance had to be found for the transmission of the product.[3] Only very rarely did foreign resources help in the

[1] G. C. Allen and Audrey G. Donnithorne, *China and Japan, op. cit.*, pp. 53 *et seq.*
[2] *Ibid.*
[3] Rathbone MSS., Correspondence, A. Smith to Rathbone Bros. and Co., 17 Nov. 1863.

financing of channels of distribution. It is not possible, however, to give such an assertion a degree of precision. There were instances when consignments of tea were financed by foreign merchant houses or by Chinese and foreign banks before they reached the ports.[1] This practice probably became more common after 1880. Even so, the extension of credit facilities remained rather obscure, as the evidence suggests that it was a two-way system. In fact, many foreign houses were in the habit of making annual settlement and there were periods when Chinese merchants were giving substantial credit facilities to foreign tea exporters.[2] This, however, was peculiar to the tea trade and differed from the practice in other commodities, especially those in which the export trade was not surplus to the needs of a large and long-established home market. Despite evidence in the Rathbone and Swire papers that Chinese houses were engaging in the export trade, the general conclusion must be that sales promotion was conducted by foreign merchants and, for many years, representatives of foreign houses made annual visits to the United Kingdom, Europe and America, for the purpose of increasing business.[3] In this process of establishing and maintaining contact with outside markets, the Chinese were inhibited by lack of finance; whereas the Chinese merchant had to pay high rates of interest to native banks in order to finance exports, his European and American counterpart had access to credit at low rates. The latter also had the advantage in understanding the taste and requirements of his consumers, an important advantage in a commodity which depended for its success on skilful blending and mixing.

The second great staple of Chinese trade with Western countries was silk. This commodity, like tea, provides an example of an ancient trade which was expanded during the nineteenth century under the stimulus of Western enterprise. As in the case of tea, this stimulation fell prey to outside competition towards the end of the century and silk ultimately declined in relative importance as an item in China's overseas trade. Though foreign merchants were able to procure improvement in quality so as to make Chinese silk acceptable in European markets, they were unable to effect lasting

[1] Rathbone MSS., Correspondence, A. Smith to Rathbone Bros. and Co., 17 Nov. 1863.
[2] G. C. Allen and Audrey G. Donnithorne, *op. cit.*, pp. 54 *et seq.*
[3] Sheila Marriner, *Rathbones of Liverpool* (1961), p. 63.

changes in traditional methods of production. As a consequence, the more efficiently organised industry in Japan coupled with the dynamic system of distribution there, undermined the extensive nature of the Chinese trade and eventually brought the industry in this latter country to virtual stagnation. There were two distinct types of raw silk exported from China during the nineteenth century. The first, and more traditional, was produced from worms fed on mulberry leaves. This type of silk came from central and south China. The second (designated tussore or pongee) came from worms fed on oak leaves and was produced in north China. The bulk of the trade was in the hands of Western merchants, though there were a few Chinese houses participating in the export of raw silk. There are some references to Chinese producers of tussore trading on their own account through export agents in the Treaty ports, but they invariably dealt in poorer quality silk which had been rejected by established foreign houses.[1]

The foreign firms dealing in silk varied greatly in the scope of their operations. Some were general merchants such as Jardine Matheson, Rathbone, Worthington and Co., and Birley and Co; others specialised in the handling of silk and silk products, many of them being direct branches of houses in Lyons, Macclesfield, and in the United States. The manufacturers of Lyons found distinct advantages in setting up purchasing houses in China in order that the quality of their supplies might be ensured.[2] On occasion, retail stores in Britain opened buying branches for silk fabrics at Chefoo. Such a development, however, was not a feature of the nineteenth century; it began towards the end of the period dealt with in this volume and was extended after the end of the First World War.[3] The constant concern about quality induced foreign merchants to make repeated attempts to influence production methods. The pressure increased as European manufacture became increasingly mechanised, for mechanical processes could only be successful if silk of a uniform quality was used. Despite persistent efforts on the part of Western merchants, the problem remained virtually unsolved. The Chinese producers were organised in small units. In order to overcome lack of uniformity in production, therefore, foreign merchants had to concern

[1] G. C. Allen and Audrey G. Donnithorne, *op. cit.*, pp. 61 *et seq.*
[2] *Ibid.*
[3] *Ibid.*

themselves with two main branches of the industry: cocoon production and reeling. The first of these, cocoon production, was extremely difficult to organise as it was dispersed over wide areas and located in districts where supplies of mulberry leaves were plentiful. By contrast, in Japan, where the problem was tackled with firmness and with efficiency, improvement in quality was brought about by controlling silkworm eggs. Egg producers in Japan were licensed and were required to maintain official standards of quality before their products could be sold. Thus, the whole production system was subject to strict government control —a factor which could not be applied in China.[1] As a consequence, a high proportion of Chinese eggs and cocoons were either diseased or lacking in uniformity. Foreign dealers attempted to overcome this problem and until recent times it was they, rather than the Chinese producers, who effected change. From 1880 onwards, there is evidence that Chinese customs officers were taking part in a process of regulation.[2] At Ningpo, for example, these officials, after making a survey of the reel silk industry, drew up proposals for the eradication of disease in silk worms.[3] This initiative led eventually to a wider acceptance of control and was, in fact, responsible for the introduction of the Pasteur system of treatment for diseased silkworms. A school of sericulture was opened in the 1890's employing Japanese teachers. Although this institution provided good cocoons and made a wide distribution of eggs, the influence on the dispersed industry as a whole was only marginal. The extent of China's failure to overcome the problem of disease was given emphasis in a report of the International Committee for the Improvement of Sericulture (established in 1917).[4] Their findings merely emphasised the growing difference between Chinese and Japanese methods and underlined the reasons for the growing strength of competition from Japan.

The second important problem was concerned with the supply of a uniform quality of thread to the European silk weavers. There is evidence that, from an early date, foreigners had made attempts to improve the reeling process. In fact, during the early 1840's,

[1] G. C. Allen and Audrey G. Donnithorne, op. cit., pp. 61 et seq.

[2] Chinese Customs Decennial Reports 1882-91 for specified ports, quoted by G. C. Allen and Audrey G. Donnithorne, op. cit., p. 63.

[3] Ibid., Ningpo, p. 382.

[4] G. C. Allen and Audrey G. Donnithorne, op. cit., p. 63.

serious efforts had been made to secure a better preparation of raw silk for the market. Up to that time the silk had been wound by hand; but the introduction of a semi-mechanical process, whereby reels were put on to a winding frame, together with methods of classifying sizes of thread, helped in some measure towards the securing of uniformity. Unfortunately, however, the majority of the Chinese producers refused to use these new methods, though there is some evidence that the ideas involved had some effect on their own primitive techniques.[1] In general, there was some improvement in the quality of thread in the Canton area and, later, in Manchuria. During the 1870's and 1880's, there were further and persistent efforts by European and American business men to secure a greater measure of control over the reeling process. Filatures, or reeling factories, began to be established, but they were not generally welcomed by the Chinese and most of the early filature companies had a short life.[2] Foreign enterprise was, however, more successful in the 1880's. Several new filatures were opened, including one owned by Jardine Matheson. Together these employed several hundred Chinese workers, and used the same methods as those operating in France and Italy. The product was more uniform than the traditionally-reeled silk and, under the stimulus of European management, Chinese filature silk began at length to compete more successfully with that of the Western manufacturing centres. The impact of this success led to the formation of Chinese and Anglo-Chinese ventures, skilled workmen from the Rhône Valley being brought out to provide the labour force.[3]

In spite of these efforts, the movement towards standardisation in reeling was painfully slow. As G. C. Allen and Audrey Donnithorne have pointed out, foreign-owned filatures were only responsible for 1,500 bales of raw silk in 1891 out of a total of 61,000 bales exported from Shanghai.[4] Four years later filature silk amounted to about one-quarter of all silk exported, the remainder being hand

---

[1] F. R. Mason, *The American Silk Industry and the Tariff* (1910), pp. 15 *et seq.*
[2] *Ibid.*
[3] Swire MSS., Memo on Silk, Jan. 1881; A. R. Colquhoun, *The Opening of China* (1884), p. 28.
[4] G. C. Allen and Audrey G. Donnithorne, *op. cit.*, p. 66, quoting *British Diplomatic and Consular Reports on Trade*, No. 1101, Shanghai, 1891, p. 13.

reeled. Thereafter, the number of filatures began to increase rapidly. By 1901, there were twenty-eight filatures in Shanghai and three at Foochow. Most of them were owned by Chinese, although they were generally under European (i.e. Italian) managers. This pattern was repeated in the rapid expansion which took place after the Revolution of 1911. The mills were usually financed by syndicates and were quite small, having an average capital of 50,000 Mexican dollars.[1] The silk thus produced was sold by brokers who, more often than not, had a financial interest in the manufacture. These brokers, in turn, depended on advances from Chinese banks which were also interested in the marketing of cocoons. In relative terms, these variations in traditional behaviour represented a considerable degree of change in Chinese attitudes towards the foreigner; but they were, by comparison with what was happening in Japan, not sufficiently widespread to effect changes in the pattern of trade. The Japanese producers were quick to realise that, if large volumes of silk were to be provided at uniform quality to suit the needs of a mechanised factory process, there must be centralised control over specific stages of production. Accordingly, this control was exercised in two ways: by the licensing of egg production and by the establishment of close relations between groups of silk raisers and particular filatures. The strength of supervisory functions at various points in both the production of eggs and cocoons ensured uniform quality. At the same time, centralised authority at the ports secured an efficient channel for the flow of Japanese silk into overseas markets.[2] In China, on the other hand, it was not possible to exercise such a closely integrated system of control. The Chinese government, for a variety of reasons, lacked the power and organisational ability to institute effective authority and it was largely for this reason that China lost so much of the silk trade.

*

Although the relative importance of silk and tea in China's export trade declined from decade to decade, these two commodities retained the largest share of the trade as a whole. In the returns for 1868, the first year in which complete figures are available, tea

[1] J. Dautremer, *La Grande Artère de la Chine: le Yangtseu* (1911), p. 66.
[2] Swire MSS., Swire to A. Holt, 20 Nov. 1895.

and silk together constituted nearly 95 per cent of all Chinese exports. This percentage share, however, dropped from 84 in 1880 to 46 in 1900. By 1913, the percentage had diminished to 34. In order of priority, tea had held first place in the list of exports up to the 1890's, but thereafter silk became China's premier export commodity by value. Just before the outbreak of war in 1914, China was exporting three times as much silk as it had shipped in 1868 and this amount comprised about one-quarter of China's total exports.

The above facts have to be set against a fairly continuous expansion of trade generally; as traditional staples lost ground in relative terms, other products assumed a greater degree of importance in the list. With the improvement of internal communications after the turn of the century, soya beans, vegetable seeds and oils began to acquire a more significant proportion of China's export trade; by 1913, for example, these comparatively new products totalled 55 million Haikwan taels and amounted to about 14 per cent of exports by value. Other products, such as cotton, coal, wool, hides and skins, eggs and egg products, rapidly increased their share both in volume and value of the total export trade. A similar pattern is discernible in the import trade. Up to about 1890, the most important item in the trade was opium amounting to an annual value of between 30 and 40 million Haikwan taels. Opium, however, gave way to cotton goods and cotton yarns, the former rising from 20 million Haikwan taels in 1868 to 110 million in 1913[1] and accounting for approximately 23 per cent of total imports. Cotton yarn registered an even greater increase; in 1868 only some 54,000 piculs were imported; by 1913, this volume had grown to 2,685,000 piculs. Opium, cotton goods and cotton yarn accounted for just under 70 per cent of total imports in the years before 1900; in the decade before 1913 they still constituted as much as 40 per cent, though other important products such as rice and wheat flour began to acquire an increasing share as the years went on. Sugar, tobacco, coal (for bunkering ships) and kerosene were also increasing in both volume and value and were thus to some extent replacing the gaps caused by the diminishing proportion of the older staples. We shall examine the changing source, distribution and general pattern of

[1] Yu-Kwei Cheng, *Foreign Trade and Industrial Development of China* (1956), p. 16.

these trades in a subsequent chapter. It is sufficient here to note the relative importance of the change in the traditional commodity trades and, in general terms, relate these changes to the wider background of expansion in trade as a whole.

It is extremely difficult to obtain a reliable measurement of the growth of China's export and import trades. If value in Haikwan taels is taken as a basis of measurement, the annual average rate of growth of China's exports was 6·3 per cent for the period 1882 to 1921. Within this period, however, there was a faster rate of growth at 7·9 per cent per annum between 1882-86 and 1902-06, growth in the latter period being at 4·2 per cent per annum. Apart from this, exports remained steady over the whole period at 6 per cent per annum. Obviously, these figures do not give an accurate indication of measurement as they are drawn from uncorrected values. They do, however, reflect change in the demand for tea and silk and the corrective increase in demand for other export products such as bean-cake, oilseeds, egg products and skins and furs. A sharper definition can be obtained by taking volumes of specific exports. Exports of tea and silk by value show a growth rate of approximately 4 per cent per annum between 1887 and 1921, but if the same calculation is made for volume, the rate is 2·9 per cent per annum. This latter figure would probably be a rather better indicator of growth for China's exports as a whole, though there would be obvious variations for specific products.

*

Before the coming of the steamship to the Far East, Western merchant houses had to battle with persistent and obstructive problems in the financing of such commodities as tea and silk. The basic cause of these problems stemmed from the lack of a uniform currency. Before 1840, the East India Co. had financed a considerable proportion of foreign trade with China by the use of Mexican dollars[1]; but, with the opening up of both China and Japan to Western commercial enterprise, the differences in exchange between the wide range of currencies on offer became more marked. As a result, merchant houses found great difficulty in supplying acceptable media for the purchase of produce and were often

[1] Rathbone MSS., W. S. Brown to S. G. Rathbone, 4 May 1852.

placed in embarrassing situations arising from shortage of cash. What exchange rates there were between the various forms of currency became subject to wide fluctuations—a phenomenon which might account for the difference between a profit and a loss over a wide range of transactions. Furthermore, this particular problem for Western traders was aggravated by the fact that a banking system (as Western merchants understood it) was barely established. It was, therefore, a question of time before the currency problem could be resolved by the institution of Western banking methods—a process which, as we shall see later, was advanced by the opening of speedier systems of communication with the Far East.

Broadly speaking, there were, before 1880, two ways in which a merchant might pay for deliveries of tea and silk from China. In the first place, the traders could provide exchange facilities following the importation of Western manufactured goods. These goods could be exchanged in the Treaty ports for some form of currency acceptable to the tea or silk merchants. Secondly, trade could be effectively sponsored through the use of a variety of financial instruments such as dollars, East India Co. bills, letters of credit and precious metals. Whichever form or combination was chosen, there were likely to be difficulties in the way of a direct settlement. Spanish or Mexican dollars, for example, bore no uniformity of value from one Treaty port to another.[1] East India Co. bills, as Dr Sheila Marriner has shown in her study of Rathbone Bros. and Co., were originally used for the transmission of funds from India to Britain; but up to 1858, when the Crown assumed responsibility for Indian finances, they had been increasingly used by merchants trading with China as a convenient form of exchange.[2] Like most currencies, however, they fluctuated in value and thereby involved merchants in speculative transactions. In the use of precious metals there was, again, considerable difficulty in maintaining levels of value. The prospect of a shortage of bullion usually led to an increase in shipment, a factor which could, and often did, lead to gluts and shortages. Superimposed upon this type of ebb and flow was that caused by crises in the manufacturing economies of the West. In 1847 and 1857, silver

---

[1] *Ibid.*, Birley Worthington and Co. to Rathbones, 11 March 1854; Sheila Marriner, *op. cit.*, p. 176.
[2] Sheila Marriner, *op. cit.*, pp. 176 *et seq.*

flowed outwards from Europe.[1] At other times, countries based on a silver standard exhausted the world supply—a situation not amenable to relief in China where the peasant cultivator had a natural propensity to hoard silver. The profitability of shipping precious metals to China, therefore, was likely to vary from time to time and in accordance with a complex set of circumstances.

The export of manufactured goods from Britain, Europe and America to China was but another facet of the exchange situation. Some consignments were genuine exports, that is to say, they were shipped by manufacturers wishing to find markets for their products in Asia. The proceeds from the sale of these cargoes would normally be returned in the form of tea and silk; but if tea or silk prices were considered to be too high for a transaction, these proceeds would often finance the trade of other correspondents.[2] This was certainly the practice followed by such firms as Rathbones, Dents, Ashtons and Balfours. Nevertheless, in addition to this genuine two-way trade, cargoes of manufactured goods were frequently sent out with the express purpose of providing some form of exchange. There was, however, some difference of opinion as to the economic value of such a procedure. There were times when British merchants in China were not eager or willing to receive manufactured goods because the commercial climate might be such that they would be difficult to sell and yield little profit.[3] This view, however is not supported by the many references in the Rathbone correspondence during the 1850's and 1860's, nor by equally pertinent references in the Holt, Swire and Brocklebank papers at a later date.[4] Perhaps the safest method used by merchant houses for sending funds to China was by means of letters of credit. These originated from a merchant house or from a bank, and under them bills of exchange were able to be drawn, though up to the 1860's their volume was small. It was not until bill markets had been developed in China that this became one of the most important channels for the financing of trade.

Finally, we must mention the all-embracing part which opium

---

[1] Rathbone MSS., Birley Worthington and Co. to Rathbones, 27 Oct. 1853; Sheila Marriner, op. cit., p. 177.

[2] Ibid., p. 177.

[3] G. Wingrove Cooke, China 1857-8 (1858), p. 200.

[4] Sheila Marriner, op. cit., p. 178; also Holt MSS., Minutes of O.S.S. Co., and Swire MSS., Correspondence with Chinese Merchants contains continuous and pertinent references.

played in the exchange of tea and silk. Up to 1870, a large part of Britain's imports of these commodities was financed either directly, or indirectly, by sales of opium to China *via* Hong Kong. Some British houses, such as Dents and Birleys, imported opium direct from India and used it both as a means of exchange and as a profit-making item in their trading list.[1] It was more common, however, for such trade to be undertaken by Indian agency houses controlled very largely by Parsees. They sent back to India the proceeds from the sale of opium in the form of bills purchased from traders in China. The insidious threads of this trade enmeshed an increasing area of commercial activity. An increasing number of merchants who, on moral grounds, would have forborne to use opium as a trade commodity, had perforce to accept bills drawn against opium sales and in return sell their own bills to Parsees. To many Western houses this traffic in opium was distasteful and resistance to its use began to grow. The Rathbones and the Holts, staunch Unitarians, undoubtedly helped in shaping opinion but, if the experience of the Rathbones be taken as a guide to events, the difficulties of trading in China without opium as a means of exchange were almost insurmountable. In spite of their good intentions (which were written into their Articles of Association) Rathbones only partially succeeded in upholding their resolutions.[2] They were forced from time to time to rely on the Parsees for the sale of their bills and found, like so many other merchants, that the need for exchange facilities could not be divorced from opium. Nevertheless, credit must be given to them for the effort which accompanied their attempt to sustain their self-imposed restriction. Because of their refusal to deal in opium, their Canton house eventually became unable to serve their Shanghai house adequately. They thereupon closed the house at Canton and concentrated their business in Shanghai where 'our not being in opium will not be such a drawback to us'.[3] This was but one example of intention translated into practice. It was a gesture which helped to harden opinion. By the 1870's, the new steamship agents were in a much

---

[1] Holt MSS., Correspondence from A. Holt to J. Swire, 1868-72, contains frequent references to opium finance, also Rathbone MSS., as Dr Sheila Marriner has shown, contains many lengthy letters on this subject.

[2] Sheila Marriner, *op. cit.*, p. 180.

[3] Rathbone MSS., S. G. Rathbone to A. G. Lathom, 19 June 1850, quoted Sheila Marriner, *op. cit.*, p. 181.

E

stronger position to offer alternative sources of credit acceptable to Chinese dealers in the financing of produce transactions. The multiplication of new credit facilities eventually brought about change in traditional attitudes and customary practice; thus the relative importance of opium as a currency was undermined and its use as an instrument of trade began to decline.

If firms such as Rathbones did not wish to use opium or bills drawn on opium sales, they had to find some other acceptable medium. As a result, the role of the bill of exchange assumed a greater degree of significance and its use a greater measure of acceptance. The effects of this were two-fold: as a means of exchange these bills led directly to a simplification of the currency problem which had, for so long, bedevilled the financing of Chinese trade; they also, through the provision of standardised terms of credit, strengthened the links between China and the outside world. In this latter respect, the increasing use of the bill of exchange was of vital importance in expanding trading connections between India and China. In the 1840's, bill markets in the Far East were not well-developed, apart from being the prime source for the remittance of bills to India. Because of this link with India, it became necessary for any merchant house wishing to establish credit-worthiness in China to create a sound financial reputation in India. The corollary to this was the foundation of a number of reputable and well-organised agencies in the latter country. Among such firms were Ewart, Lyon and Co., and later, Hoare Miller and Co. They acted on behalf of many China houses sending shipments of cotton to Canton. The shippers of this cotton drew bills on the China houses and, by such means, a flow of credit was built up. It was through Ewart, Lyon and Co., and Hoare Miller and Co., that many British houses established their reputation by giving their bills circulation in India.[1] As confidence in their paper increased, it was possible to sell the bills of the China houses on Ewart, Lyon and Co. for remittance to India at very good rates. Once reputations had been established, the position had to be secured by an increasing flow of business. Only by such means could a house's name become familiar in both India and China. As Dr Marriner has shown, this was precisely the course followed by Rathbones and they, in turn, acted as a model for other houses at a somewhat later date.

[1] Rathbone MSS., S. G. Rathbone to W. Rathbone, 27 Dec. 1849.

In the newly emerging code of commercial practice, the effectiveness of bill-broking operations depended both on the flow of paper and upon the control of its volume. A balance had to be struck between the number of bills drawn to finance a house's financial needs and those drawn under credits to other houses. If too many credits were issued, the rate of discount would rise and transactions would, as a consequence, be curtailed.[1] The success of the whole structure, so based on credit, depended on goodwill. If we may again cite Rathbones as an example, their acceptances by 1885 were somewhat under £25,000 a month.[2] When the crisis of 1857 broke, their credit was so well-established that they managed to honour their commitments, despite the fact that numbers of other houses extensively engaged in the American trade got into serious difficulties.[3] By the 1860's Rathbones were granting large credits (sometimes as much as £60,000) to their correspondents for the purchase of teas and silks.[4] A few other British firms had achieved a comparable reputation and, in 1870, bills were being sold in considerable quantity at very little above the rates ruling for 'the very best paper'.[5] With the coming of steamship agents and more highly organised banking, finance for day-to-day produce transactions became systematic and less circuitous. This, in turn, helped in regulating the flow of goods to the ports and in adjusting volume more closely to the shipping space on offer. In other words, China was given a more highly integrated commercial framework within which the tempo of future expansion could be regulated, less in accordance with tradition and more in the interests of its own economic needs.

*

For the purpose of this present narrative, however, it is necessary to trace the inception of exchange banks in the Far East and examine some of the factors affecting their business operations and the growth of their influence before 1914. Arising from the exercise

---

[1] *Ibid.*, S. G. Rathbone to W. Rathbone, 13 May 1850, quoted Sheila Marriner, *op. cit.*, p. 190.
[2] Rathbone MSS., H. W. Gair to W. Rathbone, 2 Jan. 1855; *ibid.*, p. 190.
[3] Sheila Marriner, *op. cit.*, p. 190.
[4] Rathbone MSS., W. Lidderdale to S. G. Rathbone, 11 Mar. 1868.
[5] Sheila Marriner, *op. cit.*, p. 191; also G. C. Allen and Audrey G. Donnithorne, *op. cit.*, pp. 31-51, *passim*.

of its powerful monopoly, the East India Co. had opposed the
institution of banks in the Far Eastern territories within its control. This broad generalisation, however, needs some qualification.
In practice, the opposition from the company was directed against
banks promoted in England. Local banks, some of which had been
established under its auspices or set up privately by exchange
houses, were given protection. In this context, Indian agency
houses which had been in the habit of providing banking facilities
tended, with the growth of business, to separate this specialised
function from their other commercial activities and to form private
banks. Many of these banks did not survive the crash of Barretto
and Co. of Calcutta in 1828, and the provision of services very
largely became concentrated in the hands of the Presidency banks,
the first of which was the Bank of Bengal.[1] After a somewhat
shaky start, this bank achieved a sufficient degree of stability to
enable it to act as a model for the creation, in 1840 and 1843
respectively, of the two other Presidency banks of Bombay and
Madras. Though the East India Co. made every effort to protect
the Presidency banks from overseas competition, the restrictions
which such protection imposed, and their exclusion from exchange
business, left scope for rival concerns to offer alternative services
with profit to themselves. Nevertheless, it is generally true that,
up to the middle of the nineteenth century, India as one of the
territories under British control had not come within the scope
of an incorporated British banking system. It was not until 1851
that the Oriental Bank Corporation received its charter.

The Oriental Bank Corporation was originally a co-partnership
under the title of the Bank of Western India, founded in Bombay
in 1842. Its function had been to provide exchange and such other
banking facilities from which the Bank of Bombay, under the
terms of its charter, had been excluded. Branches of the Oriental
Bank were soon established at Calcutta, Colombo, Singapore and
Hong Kong and, with the removal of the head office to London in
1845, the name was changed to that of the Oriental Bank Corporation.[2] In 1849 there was an amalgamation with the Bank of
Ceylon (incorporated in 1841) and a royal charter was sought to
enable this expanded enterprise to operate 'anywhere east of the

---

[1] J. Leighton-Boyce, 'The British Eastern Exchange Banks', C. D.
Cowan (ed.), *The Economic Development of South-East Asia* (1964), p. 20.
[2] *Ibid.*, p. 21.

Cape of Good Hope'.[1] As Leighton Boyce has pointed out, the East India Co., owing to a mistake on the part of government departments, was not consulted about the Oriental Bank's proposed charter. Consequently, no serious opposition emerged and the charter was granted.[2] A rapid extension of the bank's business began forthwith with the opening of branches in Mauritius, South Africa, Australia and New Zealand. Success bred success and a spate of similar banks followed in the wake of the Oriental's promotional effort. Among these new formations were the Chartered Bank of India, Australia and China, founded in 1853, and the Chartered Mercantile Bank of India, London and China, founded in 1858.

These new banks were essentially patterned on British banks in that they were conservative in management and circumscribed by sanctions. They were authorised to issue notes, but reserves in specie had to be guaranteed to the equivalent of at least one-third of the notes in circulation. The Treasury retained a rigid control over note issue, limiting circulation to an amount not exceeding the paid-up capital of the bank. Any addition to this amount required new sanction from the Treasury, involving protracted and inhibiting procedures.[3] The banks' total liabilities at any given time were restricted to an amount not exceeding three times the paid-up capital including deposits. In other words, the seal and form of a Western banking system was imposed on India and through India, because of its trading and commercial contacts, ultimately on the Far East.

Until the opening of the Suez Canal, however, trade with the East did not grow with any degree of consistency and, as alternative sources for the financing of trade were reasonably adequate, banking business as such was strictly limited. The result was the growth of intense competition between the newly established banking houses. The reckoning came with the collapse of the cotton boom during the American Civil War. Exchange banks tumbled like ninepins; out of a total of fifty-one such banks in existence in Calcutta, Bombay and Hong Kong at the beginning of 1886, only twelve had survived a year later; among the survivors

[1] *Ibid.*
[2] *Ibid.*
[3] *Ibid.*; also Swire MSS., Memo by John Swire on Far Eastern banking operations, 8 Dec. 1880.

were the Chartered Bank of India, the Oriental Bank Corporation, the Chartered Bank of India, London and China, and the Hong Kong and Shanghai Banking Corporation. To this extent, the securely based banks had weathered the storm and remained as evidence of the triumph of sound, though conservative, principles in the conduct of financial affairs.

Of all the banks which were created in the 1860's to serve Far Eastern business, the Hong Kong and Shanghai Banking Corporation was perhaps the most significant. According to Sir Thomas Sutherland, later chairman of P. and O., the bank originated as the result of an after-dinner conversation amongst a few well-known Eastern merchants. It started at a time when commercial conditions were generally unpropitious; as already stated, the cotton boom in Bombay was coming to an end and inferior short staple cotton exported from Shanghai, Hong Kong and Ningpo was about to become unsaleable on a falling market. Furthermore, the Overend and Gurney crisis in 1866 had serious repercussions in the Far East, bringing down a large number of Eastern banks in its wake. The fact that the new Hong Kong and Shanghai Bank could survive these events is proof not only of the careful preparation preceding its establishment, but of the need for an efficient organisation capable of serving the interests of an expanding trade in China and Japan.

The new bank was founded in 1864 and began business simultaneously in Hong Kong and Shanghai on 3 April 1865. It was incorporated by the Hong Kong Legislative Council in 1886 and opened branches in Calcutta in 1867 and Bombay in 1869, and an agency in Singapore in 1870. Having a capital of 5 million dollars (half-paid up), the Hong Kong Bank was the result of a desire by Hong Kong merchants to have a bank of their own. 'The banks in China', so ran the prospectus, 'being merely branches of English or Indian corporations formed chiefly to do exchange operations with their home centres, were not in a position to deal satisfactorily with the extensive local Chinese trade.'[1] It was confidently anticipated that the Hong Kong Bank would meet this need and, by virtue of its management and situation, 'take the same position in the Colony as the Presidency banks did in India'. As most of the shares were taken up by Hong Kong mer-

[1] Quoted in A. S. J. Baster, *The International Banks* (1935), pp. 165 et seq.

chants and institutions concerned with the China trade the bank was from its inception, therefore, a local foundation. In this respect it was the first of its kind.

At first, there were many difficulties to be overcome. The Taiping Rebellion had interfered with the normal flow of trade, serious losses were incurred from exchange fluctuations during the Franco-Prussian War and there were many costly experiences with the bank's first compradores. In addition, there was some involvement with bad debts falling due from local industrial and commercial concerns. In 1875, the London managers, by making unauthorised investments, lost the bank £171,000. As a result of mounting difficulties, therefore, the London directors decided to appoint a London committee of experienced bankers to supervise transactions in the London office. This might have led to an extension of control from Britain; but the Hong Hong Bank, despite obstruction, maintained its independence. As evidence of this, it successfully opposed the pressure from London banks to reduce the usance of bills on China from six to four months' sight. Two further points need to be emphasised, points arising from the active policy pursued by Thomas Jackson who had become general manager in 1875. By maintaining its silver capital in China during the period when silver was falling in value, the bank was able to make substantial profits from the high money rates in all the Far Eastern markets while its competitors, capitalised in sterling, were reducing their silver investments to a minimum, thereby causing a money scarcity. The second point, involving the profitable use of the bank's resources, sprang from its loan policy with the Pekin government. From 1875, early loan business had been on a silver basis. In 1885, however, it was decided (on a falling silver market) that borrowings in future should be repaid in sterling. This decision effectively protected the bank from long-term exchange risk. Throughout the years from 1880 to 1914, the bank grew steadily in size and prestige and, although occasional heavy losses were sustained, the general strength of the Corporation's assets was sufficient to meet and overcome such short-term embarrassments. In general, the bank showed consistent growth and vitality and became a central link in the financial and trading structures of the Far East.

In some respects the banking network described above constituted an enclosed ring. As we have seen, this ring included the chartered banks, but there were, in addition, the Agra Bank Ltd., a reconstruction of the Agra and Masterman's, the National Bank of India Ltd., the Oriental Bank Corporation, the Comptoir Nationale d'Escompte de Paris, and the Hong Kong and Shanghai Banking Corporation. By the end of the century, changes had taken place in the composition of this group, the Agra and Oriental Banks having ceased to function and the Comptoir and Chartered Mercantile banks having been reconstructed. It was, nevertheless, extremely difficult for a new bank to break into the field and make headway against established rivals. The only chance of success involved a policy fraught with risk and danger, the entertainment of business of a speculative nature. The most prudent course was for such a bank to find a new territory for its operations. This, however, was not easy of realisation because banking operations could not be successfully undertaken until an area was in the process of growth and trade was expanding. Nevertheless, despite the disasters of 1866 and the difficulties imposed by the devaluation of silver in the later years of the century, the British exchange banks steadily increased and improved their branch organisations. By 1900, they were represented in all of the more important commercial centres in the East, at first confining their branches to the ports but later, as trade developed, extending to the up-country districts and the very interior of China itself. Finally, as China became drawn increasingly within the political and acquisitive grasp of Europe, new and nationally sponsored exchange banks such as the Deutsche-Asiatische Bank and the Russo-Chinese Bank were opened in competition with British banks. One of their main functions was in the financing of Chinese government loans. By contrast with British exchange banks they tended to confine business within the limits of their own national interests. Under the protection of their own governments, they enjoyed advantages not open to other commercial banks and often engaged in speculative operations in an endeavour (or so it seemed) to secure business at any cost.[1] British banks, on the other hand, conducted their affairs on a broad basis, accepting clients of any nationality against due assurance of financial stability. In these circumstances, therefore, it is a little surprising that, despite the

[1] See especially A. S. J. Baster, 'The Origins of the British Exchange Banks in China', *Economic History*, Jan. 1934, pp. 148 *et seq.*; also F. E. Lee, *Currency, Banking and Finance in China* (1926), pp. 85 *et seq.*

growth in Far Eastern trade especially after 1890, only one new British bank, the Eastern, should have been established during the twenty years before 1914.

How did these exchange banks organise their daily business in the interests of tea and silk exporters? In so far as they were instrumental in arranging foreign loans to the Chinese government, they were indirectly responsible for an extension of Western authority (particularly in the form of territorial concessions and railway construction) exacted by foreign governments as a *quid pro quo* for financial aid; but in the provision of adequate funds for normal business requirements they directly touched the lives of China's merchant classes and, through them, the well-being of the peasant population.

During the 1860's and 1870's, it was usual for chartered banks to allow their branches to set aside a specific sum which could be used as working capital in support of exchange operations. As a further support, branches were given credit facilities in London 'under which they could draw sterling drafts, provided that cover in the shape of equivalent remittances was furnished within three months'.[1] Such credit extension was usually limited to an amount not exceeding the branch's capital, the object of such dispensation being to ensure liquidity in preparation for the shipping season. At such times, when tea or silk cargoes were piled upon the wharves at Shanghai, Foochow and Tientsin, the demand for paper increased phenomenally. As Leighton Boyce has stated, it was precisely at such periods that the rate of exchange in London was low, thus enabling profits to be made from a rise in rates and so offset overdrafts in London through the purchase of sterling remittances on more favourable terms.[2] Another way in which a China bank could supplement its resources was by attracting local fixed and current deposits, though in the case of fixed deposits, these could not be retained longer than one year. In reality, it was through the use of fixed deposits for exchange operations that profitable business could be built up.[3] Before the coming of exchange banks, British and Indian firms in China had made their returns to Calcutta and Bombay partly in bullion but more generally in first-class bills on London. This procedure was

---

[1] J. Leighton-Boyce, *op. cit.*, p. 23.
[2] *Ibid.*
[3] *Ibid.*

established and comprehended a large proportion of the exchange business of Eastern ports; but with the growth of trade and with the emergence of a more acceptable form of currency, the volume of bills increased every year. Thus, by the time exchange banks had become operative in China they were a ready and convenient channel for the active flow of bills. As a result, there was a narrowing of the gap between buying and selling rates.[1] There were periods, however, when the new banks experienced difficulty in covering their Indian drawings on London by direct remittance. In order to meet such a difficulty, they were often forced to sell Chinese drafts drawn on their Indian offices against goods imported into China, the proceeds of these sales in China being invested in sterling bills on London. This is a single example of how the institutional mechanism became involved in the older pattern of settlement between India, China and Britain. The sterling bills were, in turn, used for sterling drawings of the branches of the various Indian banks. The process was not without profit, though in order to maintain profitabilty it was necessary for the Indian branches to make continuous flows of funds available for meeting the drafts from China. Moreover, such funds had to be provided at cheaper rates than the equivalent in rupees of the sterling remittances from China. Thus, by these intrinsically Western devices, the Chinese exporters of tea and silk were given surety that payment would be made for goods received. Confidence grew in the validity and effectiveness of the bill and the bank draft and, as a consequence, the financing of both imports and exports became standardised in practice and bound by all due safeguards.

In course of time procedures continued to be improved. The extension of the telegraph to the East in 1870 caused something of a revolution in the financial operations of the tea and silk exporters. Banks in China were henceforth able to sell telegraphic transfers on London and India, thus superseding the old method of making drafts on Bombay or Calcutta. This fact, coupled with the use of other bills, led to a decline in acceptance business among Eastern banks. It was obviously of greater advantage for a tea or silk merchant to use a telegraphic transfer than involve himself in protracted and, on occasion, hazardous bank operations. Under the new system he could be sure that the money would be paid over in

[1] Evidence from finance operations in Rathbone and Swire MSS.

London within twenty-four hours. Apart from this, however, the speed of the new form of communication helped in safeguarding the value of proceeds and investments against the continuous fall in the value of silver.

Although it had long been the practice in London to arrange for bills to be drawn against the shipment of goods from Britain to India, there were no transactions in bills on China until after 1886. Again, according to Leighton-Boyce and A. S. J. Baster, the banks proceeded 'on the assumption that their business lay in buying exchange in China, but not upon that country'.[1] It was only at a somewhat later date that it became common usage for shipments to be financed by drafts on China; though, as risks increased because of depreciation in the value of silver, sterling drafts were made payable in local currencies at ruling London rates.[2] In this way, risk to the merchant was diminished while, at the same time, exchange banks making purchases of sterling in China could protect themselves from loss either on current or future delivery. This new practice had a marked and lasting effect upon the financing of outward cargoes; the old process of covering shipments by loans was almost entirely replaced by the currency draft.

Thus, in the course of some sixty years before 1914, vast changes had taken place in the production, distribution and financing of the traditional commodities of tea and silk. With the opening up of both China and Japan to Western ideas and Western enterprise, there had been a shift in supply. China's entrenched position as a tea and silk producer had been gradually undermined by the more intensively capitalised and centrally controlled methods adopted by Japan. By the use of superior techniques, the Japanese producer was able to compete on more than favourable terms in both the quality and price of product. As a consequence he captured the United States market for silk from his Chinese rival. In much the same way Indian competition captured the United Kingdom market for tea. China was left, therefore, with a relatively declining export trade in these two staples and was eventually forced into an acceptance of change in both the composition and pattern of its trade.

Parallel with these changes came equally important new procedures in the financing of trade which, in turn, resulted from the

[1] J. Leighton-Boyce, *op. cit.*, p. 24.
[2] *Ibid.*, p. 25.

impact of Western technology and the linking of Europe and the Far East with speedier systems of communication. The telegraph, no less than the steamship, was a powerful stimulus in this respect. Archaic and disorganised systems of exchange yielded in some way to Western ideas which were able to effect a degree of stability and uniformity in the currency media and, later, with the creation of banks, of systematic practice in commercial relationships. In this respect, therefore, there was created a better regulated and sounder based commercial system for the promotion of newer commodity industries which were to play an increasingly important role in the trade between the West and the East after 1880. Though the traditional commodities of tea and silk were subject to declining trends in China, the increasing value of tin, rubber, tobacco, sugar and copra to the Far East as a whole was more than sufficient to offset such decline. Thus, as some trade links were weakened, others of a stronger and more vital character were formed. Western enterprise and finance increased in scope, gaining a new role and a new direction.

CHAPTER IV

The Products of Indonesia—
Coffee, Sugar, Tea and Tobacco

THE principal commodity trades with the East Indian Islands before 1890 were in coffee, sugar, tea and tobacco. In the competitive structure of these trades, the strength of Dutch interests was historically based, the focus of enterprise being centred in Java with Batavia as the chief port. In large measure, the growth of new ideas spread by Western capital and enterprise, and their application to traditional forms of peasant agriculture, was reflected in changing relationships between Dutch government administrators and native cultivators and, in particular, in the changing pattern of production consequent upon the stimulation of new trades. Before 1865, Britain had only a marginal interest in such trade but, with the coming of the steamship, active competition developed between Dutch and British shipping companies. In the course of the struggle, Singapore and Hong Kong developed vast *entrepot* trades and became alternative bases to Batavia for the distribution of produce from the Islands.

Following the repossession of territory by the Dutch after the Raffles period, the Dutch government found that the peasant cultivator in Java and the adjacent islands had not profited from the inducements of a money income which free cultivation for an open market had offered to him. New methods had, therefore, to be devised to increase the growth and export of produce and to secure its carriage in Dutch rather than in British ships. Accordingly, a reaction against economic liberalism set in and regulation replaced *laissez-faire* as a guiding principle of policy. State intervention was initiated in 1825 with the establishment of

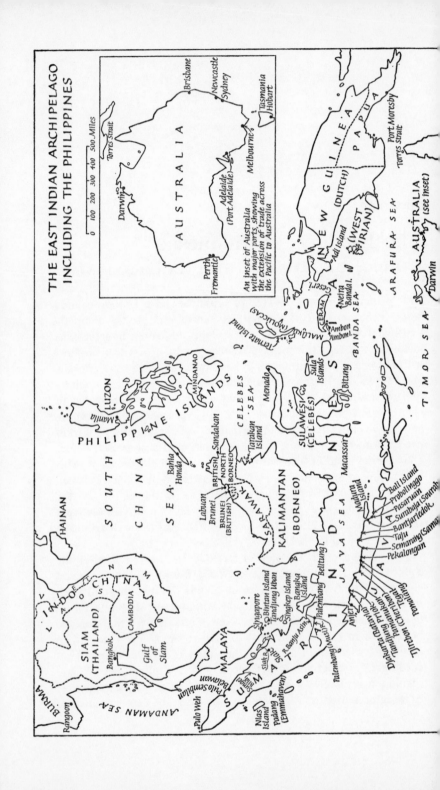

THE EAST INDIAN ARCHIPELAGO
INCLUDING THE PHILIPPINES

An inset of Australia
with major ports, showing
the extension of trade across
the Pacific to Australia

the Nederlandse Handel Maatschappij (N.H.M.), an import-export agency. It had a capital of 37 million florins, the king of the Netherlands being the principal shareholder and guaranteeing from his own privy purse a dividend of 4½ per cent.[1] The advent of this agency was followed, three years later, by the creation of the Java Bank with a capital subscribed by the Netherlands government and the N.H.M.[2] Finally, the institutional framework of this new economic policy was completed by the introduction of the 'culture system'—a system under which the native cultivators, instead of paying a proportion of their crop to the government as rent, were required to set aside a proportion of their land (usually one-fifth) for the production of prescribed crops such as coffee, sugar, tea and tobacco. The advantages of this system were two-fold, admittedly in the interests of the government. In the first place, the produce was bought at basic prices and shipped by N.H.M. to the Netherlands where it was sold with profit. In the second place, it induced the government itself to take a more active part in agricultural production, not only in the development of new techniques, but also in the provision of better communications and work on irrigation and drainage schemes. The net effect of these policies was to increase production and export of agricultural products, the latter rising from 12·9 million florins in 1830 to 74·2 million florins in 1840.[3] As we shall see later, the production of commercial crops was vastly expanded and compensated the rapid decline in the old and traditional spice trades. Allen and Donni-thorne have emphasised a third advantage accruing to the government from this system, namely the regular subvention from the Indies representing a surplus of the colonial government revenues (called *batig slot*) and assuming the form of a tribute payment. This averaged 3·9 million florins a year in the 1840's and rose to 14 million florins by the 1850's.[4] In all this development, the N.H.M. held a monopoly position, having control of consignments of government produce to the Netherlands and handling much of the exports of private planters who were being encouraged to enter into active promotion of particular agricultural products. The

[1] G. C. Allen and Audrey G. Donnithorne, *Western Enterprise in Indonesia and Malaya* (1957), p. 23.
[2] *Ibid.*
[3] Calculated by G. C. Allen and Audrey G. Donnithorne, *op. cit.*, p. 23.
[4] *Ibid.*, p. 24.

extent of the N.H.M.'s control of trade is shown by the fact that in 1840 two-thirds of all exports from Java was controlled by this agency.

There were many other complementary factors influencing the changing pattern of economic growth in the East Indies. These were mainly non-economic in character but nevertheless reacted upon the general profitability of economic enterprise. In 1848, for example, the Dutch colonies were brought under the authority of the States-General, and the government was made responsible for the submission of annual reports on economic progress in overseas territories. This had the immediate effect of exposing colonial administration to criticism from a growing body of Dutch liberals who had, for some time past, been active in opposing the 'culture system'. The struggle between conservative and reformist factions in Holland over colonial policies was protracted but, eventually, the upholders of authoritarian state control had to give way before the persistent efforts of powerful liberal groups. With the abolition of slavery in the Islands in 1860, a more liberal spirit began to prevail; during the next ten years cultivation on behalf of the state was abandoned in the case of pepper, cloves, indigo, tea and tobacco. Though this left two of the chief crops, coffee and sugar, under the old system, a law passed in 1870 provided for its termination as applied to sugar, within the next twenty years.[1] Thus, by the beginning of the twentieth century, coffee was the only crop under the 'culture system'.

A major liberalising influence came in 1870 with the passing of the Agrarian Law. Under its provisions, leases were granted for periods of up to seventy-five years to Dutch and colonial farmers and also to companies registered in the Islands. Production and trade were thus thrown open to development by private Western enterprise. Furthermore, in 1871, legal sanction was given for the hiring of land from natives for a limited period: namely five years for land held on customary tenure and twenty years for freeholds.[2] Side by side with these land reforms went a corresponding liberalisation of the taxation system and the farming out of poll taxes was abolished. Import duties were lowered and preferences

---

[1] See J. S. Furnivall, *Netherlands India: a Study of a Plural Economy* (1944), pp. 135 *et seq.*

[2] *Ibid.*, pp. 177-80; also G. C. Allen and Audrey G. Donnithorne, *op. cit.*, p. 25.

in favour of Dutch imports and Dutch ships were either reduced or rescinded. At a later date, however, state aid had to be given to shipping, and new lines were created to cope with the increasing competition from British steamship companies.[1]

In short, a revolution had taken place in the administration and economic policy governing the production of primary products in the Netherlands East Indies. The way had been opened for private capital and economic individualism to expand. That private enterprise could so readily take over functions exercised by the state was undoubtedly attributable to the effectiveness of the N.H.M. in identifying itself with the needs of the new economy. Having been a mainstay of the 'culture system', it now began to finance productive enterprise on a large number of estates, such finance being made available either from its own resources, or from government funds entrusted to it. By such means, the N.H.M. became the first of the Cultuurbanken, the prototype of the finance houses which were to assume such an influential role in the development of Western-type agriculture in the Islands. The prime function of these institutions was in the granting of long-term capital to private estate owners, while the Java Bank and other commercial banks made credit available for the financing of produce shipped to Europe.[2] It was a gradual process of transformation, the state continuing to own vast areas of land and, in the matter of communications, retaining an overall authority. In spite of this, however, the generating spirit of Western capitalism had begun to open up new and lucrative trades and the economy of the whole area was given new strength and impetus.

*

From what has already been said, it will have become obvious that the Netherlands East Indies provides an example of a rapidly expanding area of agricultural production during the second half of the nineteenth century. In the 1830's, the principal export commodity was coffee, with sugar and indigo in second and third places. By the middle of the century, sugar had replaced coffee as the chief crop, a position which it held for the next thirty years, while coffee and indigo continued to decline absolutely as well as

[1] I. J. Brugmans, *Tachtig Jaren Varen met de Nederland, 1870-1950*, pp. 21-2.
[2] J. S. Furnivall, *op. cit.*, pp. 180 *et seq.*

F

relatively, and tobacco had appeared as a leading export. This changing pattern of agricultural production was accentuated by a series of crises in the 1880's (particularly that in sugar) which led planters to seek alternative forms of production and raise new crops for which there was a growing demand. In this context, the rise of tea and rubber as relatively new types of agricultural enterprise have to be noticed; and, by the beginning of the twentieth century, the older types of agricultural produce, with the exception of sugar, declined in importance and were replaced by other more profitable ones such as palm oil and copra.

The cultivation and production of coffee was long-established, coffee being the principal commodity introduced by Dutch settlers. The fact that it survived for so many centuries, despite vicissitudes, was largely the result of Western ideas and enterprise. During the greater part of the nineteenth century, coffee was the major export crop and, up to the 1890's, the value of coffee exports was greater than that of sugar.[1] Although there was a decline in the present century, the trade continued to be relatively important until the outbreak of the Second World War. In organisation of production after 1830, coffee may be regarded as an example of the successful application of the 'culture system'. Since coffee beans required very little preparation before they were exported, government contractors were not needed to exercise supervisory control. As a consequence, the organisation of the industry remained comparatively simple in structure and relatively efficient in management.

The growth of demand for coffee led to an expansion of production outside Java. After 1847, for example, local chieftains in certain areas in Sumatra were required to supply the government with fixed amounts of the produce, and in Celebes, where the coffee bean was introduced at a comparatively late date, the government had a monopoly of export cargoes. Nevertheless, even in Java, coffee was not entirely under government sponsorship. In the heyday of the 'culture system', coffee was grown and shipped to Holland by privately owned concerns. As J. A. M. Caldwell has calculated, by 1870, production from private estates amounted to about 14 per cent of the total; by 1914, this percentage was 88.[2]

[1] G. C. Allen and Audrey G. Donnithorne, op. cit., Appendix IV, p. 291.

[2] J. A. M. Caldwell, op. cit., p. 82, 'Indonesian Export and Production from the Decline of the Culture System to the First World War', C. D. Cowan (ed.), The Economic Development of South-East Asia (1964).

Thus, within four decades, private enterprise had become responsible for nearly the whole of coffee production and, consequently, the bulk of the export trade.

The encroachment of private capital upon the entrenched position of the 'culture system' in the production of coffee was not, however, effected without difficulty. In 1878, a plant disease which had previously been rampant on the coffee plantations in Ceylon was carried to the East Indies. This caused an immediate loss of production and a fall in exports, a situation which might have resolved itself had it not been for a coincidental and contemporaneous flood of coffee on to the world market from Brazil and other South American countries. The result was that within six years after 1877 the export price of Indonesian coffee was almost halved; by contrast, the world price of coffee remained buoyant in response to rising demands.[1] New strains of plant (*caffea robusta*), resistant to disease, were, however, introduced from the Congo; as substitution increased, the danger of fluctuation in supply was consequently removed. Henceforth, levels of production were affected only by seasonal considerations. One other important result of falling prices was that many of the estates which had formerly been under coffee cultivation were turned over to more profitable crops such as tea and, at a later date, rubber. There was, however, no set pattern of fluctuation in aggregate terms. If coffee production declined in Java, it was, more often than not, restarted in the Outer Provinces as a countervailing influence to a fall in price of locally grown staples.[2] Thus, when tobacco prices fell and the Sumatran industry was badly hit, coffee planting was introduced there as a possible counter device. In general, the estate cultivation of coffee declined after 1890 and native cash crop production increased; by 1929, native grown coffee amounted to about one-half the total output and some three-quarters of total exports.[3] Before 1914, Java was the principal exporter, but by 1930 the Outer Provinces were shipping well over 50 per cent of total exports. This changing pattern of production and trade did not imply a lessening of interest or of active support from Western merchants. The latter simply shifted the centre of their activity

[1] J. A. M. Caldwell, *op. cit., loc. cit.*
[2] W. H. Daukes, *The P. and T. Lands* (1943), pp. 40-4.
[3] J. H. Boeke, *The Evolution of the Netherlands Indies Economy* (1946), pp. 16-18.

from estate to native cultivation, handling increasing volumes of cargo and, on occasion, entering into direct methods by organising native production. This was especially the case in Celebes, where a new type of bean was introduced and a flourishing trade in it developed with Germany and Scandinavia. Merchants from Macassar worked through the intermediary of Chinese dealers and, as contacts increased, the native producer was linked to Western markets by well organised and efficiently run agencies controlling the distribution of his product.

The following table gives some indication of the range in the production, and the value and volume of the export trade in this particular crop:

Production and Export of Indonesian Coffee

Year	Annual average coffee production (ooo metric tons)	Annual average coffee export weight (ooo metric tons)	Annual average coffee export value (ooo florins)
1865-69	79	59	36,339
1870-74	78	68	45,617
1875-79	89	81	72,025
1880-84	94	115	54,364
1885-89	69	64	37,623
1890-94	51	51	43,860
1895-99	56	53	41,687
1900-04	48	44	25,904
1905-09	32	28	16,184
1910-14	35	28	22,552

Source: J. A. M. Caldwell, *op. cit.*, p. 82.

It will be seen that the value and volume of exports followed a downward trend after 1890. A more detailed analysis would have shown wide year to year fluctuations. By the early 1930's, when world depression led to a steep decline in prices, there was a reversal of the tendency for the share of peasant-grown coffee to increase. There was a recovery in both prices and volume after 1936, and this lasted without undue fluctuation until the outbreak of war in 1939. Within the time-span of this book, however, production rose between 1865-69 and 1880-84 at a rate of 1·2 per cent per annum; but thereafter a cumulative decline set in at a rate of 2·9 per cent per annum. Exports by volume show a similar trend if one excludes the somewhat dubious figures at the beginning of the 1880's; the initial rise was steeper at 4·5 per cent per annum and the cumulative decline after 1885 was sharper at 4·8 per cent per annum. Prices on the other hand were more buoyant, rising at 7·1 per cent per annum for the period 1865 to 1879 and declining thereafter at a cumulative rate of 3·4 per cent per annum.

Apart from the impact of economic fluctuations upon the progress and prosperity of agriculture however, the above figures also reflect the damaging effects of disease which, as we have stated, attacked coffee plantations during the 1880's. Coffee was not unique in this respect; sugar was equally affected. In this case, the widespread incidence of disease in the sugar-cane coincided with an economic recession in the middle years of the 1880's and with the introduction and stimulation of beet sugar production in Europe. The consequences flowing from these underlying causes of depression were serious and enduring. The individual sugar planter gave place to the limited company, and the Cultuurbanken acquired a greater degree of control over the individual units which they were financing. As these banks, in turn, passed under the control of financial institutions in the Netherlands, the exercise of authority over the economic growth of the East Indies was given a European rather than, as hitherto, a local source of direction. Major decisions were increasingly made in Holland, a fact which helps to explain the rapid introduction of more scientific techniques in the production, harvesting and the distribution of various crops.

Sugar profited greatly from these changing circumstances. Production nearly doubled between 1885 and 1900 and exports, stimulated by increasing demand and a reduction in the sugar export duties, showed a comparable buoyancy.[1] There were many interwoven threads of a causal nature maintaining the position of sugar as a principal product of East Indian agriculture. Not least of these were changes in the system of land tenure and in the laws affecting the employment of labour. Of equal importance were financial factors affecting the reallocation of resources through the medium of the Java Bank and other institutions. There was also an extension of planting in the Outer Provinces and, as a consequence, a redisposition of acreage under production, a fact which assumes significance following the decline in Java's erstwhile predominant place as a source of supply.

From the beginning of the nineteenth century, it was usual for

[1] J. A. M. Caldwell, *op. cit.*, pp. 79-80. Figures of production and export compiled from a wide range of sources.

Dutch colonial sugar planters to rent land from native proprietors on short-term leases. Some standardisation was achieved by the Rent Ordnance of 1871 which fixed a maximum of five years for land held by natives on customary tenure and twenty years for land under private ownership. The maximum term for leases was eventually changed to twenty-one and a half years.[1] The result was that on short-lease land Western capital was used for the promotion of crops similar in all respects to those planted by native labour. The growing of sugar admirably conformed to this agricultural pattern and, consequently, a large proportion of rented land was turned over to this crop.

Up to 1860, the majority of workers engaged in the production of sugar were unfree. In fact, various forms of compulsory service were in existence until comparatively recent times; but, although outright slavery had been abolished and debtor bondage prohibited in Java, many labour contract systems continued to enforce legal sanctions against defaulters. The law was rigorously applied throughout the Islands during the middle years of the century and the penal system was not breached until 1879 when sanctions were abolished in Java. By this latter date, new circumstances had been created by the establishment of plantations in the Outer Provinces, the sugar and tobacco estates in eastern Sumatra being dependent upon labour from other countries and consequently not subject to Dutch labour laws.[2]

In Java, the sugar workers employed by Western firms usually received a cash income for their services and, in consequence, were brought under the influence of Western capitalistic enterprise. Furthermore, the whole restrictive pattern of agricultural life was given new prospects of freer development through the inception of a gold exchange standard. This enabled the Bank of Java to extend credit facilities and thus make resources available for private, as distinct from state, schemes for the stimulation of primary production. In 1875, for example, the Bank of Java was given permission to issue notes virtually without limit, apart from the sole proviso that it should maintain a specie reserve amounting to 40 per cent of the issue and fiduciary reserve. Security against the remaining 60 per cent was held in short usance drafts on other financial

[1] G. C. Allen and Audrey G. Donnithorne, op. cit., p. 70.
[2] Holt MSS., Minutes O.S.S. Co., 1879-1885; Personal memoranda by Alfred Holt, 1885.

institutions.[1] Thus greater flexibility in the issuing of notes was of assistance to both industrial and agricultural producers. Through such media the bank was able to restore confidence in times of depression (especially in the sugar crisis of 1883-84), and at other times helped to stimulate production by making direct advances towards the building of sugar and tea factories. After 1900, however, the provision of funds for this particular type of business was restricted in the interests of liquidity, other more recently established financial institutions in the East Indies taking over this function.[2]

Thus, within the changing pattern of agriculture, sugar had attracted resources and had become the most important and highly lucrative of East Indian products. While it had continued to expand both in production and in exports, the other traditionally-based commodities such as coffee and indigo had declined. The disasters of the 1880's had been overcome although, as we shall see, the impact of these disasters led to diversification in the use of land and funds, and sugar henceforth had to compete for resources with newer products such as tea, rubber and tobacco. For the most part, however, sugar continued to hold a dominant place within the economy. It was not until the 1930's that sugar lost its predominance to such products as mineral oil. The following figures give some indication of the volume and value of the export trade, a trade in which British shipping companies participated increasingly after 1890:

Production and Export of Indonesian Sugar

Year	Annual average sugar production (000 metric tons)	Annual average sugar export weight (000 metric tons)	Annual average sugar export value (000 florins)
1865-69	153	151	34,269
1870-74	189	185	45,107
1875-79	230	217	56,741
1880-84	307	292	59,463
1885-89	388	367	63,547
1890-94	469	436	61,042
1895-99	638	627	67,264
1900-04	889	848	73,698
1905-09	1,160	1,156	121,720
1910-14	1,405	1,436	150,832

Source: J. A. M. Caldwell, op. cit., p. 79.

[1] G. C. Allen and Audrey G. Donnithorne, op. cit., p. 184.
[2] L. de Bree, Nederlandsch-India in de Twintigste Eeuw: Het Bankwezen (1918), pp. 52-3, cited Allen and Donnithorne, op. cit., p. 185.

In general terms, sugar production increased at an average annual rate of 5·1 per cent over the period 1865 to 1914. Exports by volume increased at an annual rate of 5·3 per cent, though there is evidence of the effects of disease and depression in the 1880's in a fall to 3·8 per cent, followed by acceleration to a rate of 6·4 per cent from 1890 to 1914. If value is made the basis of calculation, correlation with price movements is discernible. Over the whole period there was a growth rate of 3·4 per cent per annum reflecting falls in price. From 1865 to 1879, growth was 5·2 per cent per annum. Between 1875 and 1904, however, growth was reduced to 1 per cent per annum, though if the period be extended to 1914 the annual average rate of growth was 7·4 per cent. This latter period (1900-1914) was one in which volume rose some 69 per cent at relatively stable prices.

*

The crises in the production and distribution of the principal agricultural staples of coffee and sugar in the 1880's led, as already stated, to a diversion of resources into new enterprise. This took the form of estate production of such commodities as tea, rubber and tobacco. Although tea had been grown in Java since the beginning of the nineteenth century, some ninety years were to elapse before it became a major product in the export list. Whatever government assistance had been given to tea production in the early years of the century, the results had proved to be disappointing. Following the decision to encourage tea planting as an alternative crop in Java and as a new one in the Outer Provinces, private enterprise was given greater scope and initiative.

Hitherto, the main achievement of government intervention in the tea industry had been in the field of experimentation. In 1824, a German, von Siebold, was sent to Japan under government auspices. He collected plants for naturalisation in the Indies. Under state sponsorship, tea seeds were planted in experimental gardens at Buitenzorg[1] and skilled labour from Chinese tea-growing districts was employed in an attempt to establish the processing of the leaf. Chinese managers were also given responsibility for the organisation and direction of the first tea factories. These early efforts, however, were not a commercial success and state control was superseded by a system of production under

[1] G. C. Allen and Audrey G. Donnithorne, *op. cit.*, p. 101.

contractors, a system similar to that currently in practice for the production of sugar and other crops. These contractors were supplied with funds to cover fixed and working capital in return for working the estates and delivering the tea to government agencies at fixed prices.[1] Unfortunately, the product of this state management was neither competitive in price nor uniform in quality. Large deficits on both production and trading account began to accumulate and, in the end, the whole government-aided scheme collapsed. Tea production, thereafter, was developed by private enterprise, the majority of the estates being leased either to individuals or to companies.

The planting of the tea soon spread beyond the limit of these leased estates; though rapid expansion was inhibited, first by the spread of rust disease, and secondly by the scarcity of land at an altitude suitable for the cultivation. In fact, it was only when cinchona and coffee prices fell so drastically in the last decade of the century that tea production increased, very largely because land became available as less profitable forms of cultivation were abandoned. Even so, the Javanese tea planters had to overcome many obstacles before they could command a market large enough for them to make a profitable return on capital. In order to improve quality, they were forced to enlist the services of men skilled in the cultivation and blending of teas. In this quest, they turned to the expertise of Indian tea growers, a British business man named John Peet being one of the first to go to Java and give Dutch growers the benefit of his wide experience.[2] The consequence was that Assam seed, which grew successfully in the Javanese habitat, gradually superseded the China plant. No less revolutionary were the changes which were introduced into the factory side of the industry. By the beginning of the twentieth century, mechanical processes and techniques for withering the leaf, long-established in India and Ceylon, were being widely used. New inventions such as the Hobel wet leaf shifter machines for eliminating stalks, as well as those for sorting teas, were all successfully put into operation on a large number of estates.[3] Continuous research, much of which was financed by private companies and to a lesser

---

[1] J. A. M. Caldwell, *op. cit.*, p. 84; Proefstation voor Thee, *Gedenboek der Nederlandsch-Indische Theecultuur, 1824-1924* (1924), p. 5.
[2] G. C. Allen and Audrey G. Donnithorne, *op. cit.*, p. 102.
[3] *Ibid.*

extent by government institutions, was applied and directed towards the solution of problems affecting growth and quality. Finally, the opening of government nurseries and the setting up of tea-testing bureaux, such as that sponsored by Dunlop and Kolff in 1905, freed planters from dependence on Indian sources of supply by ensuring high uniform standards of quality in locally produced seed.[1] All these efforts were responsible for the increasing importance of tea both as a source of livelihood in the Islands and as a commercial product in international trade. As such it became a chief source of export income and provided lucrative cargoes for Dutch and British ships serving Far Eastern ports.

The flow of capital into this industry came from a variety of sources, from the co-operative efforts of the planters, from the personal savings of estate managers and from Britain and Europe. British capital was certainly attracted into Indonesian tea production after 1909. The links in the chain of interest are easily discernible. Noel Bingley, a pioneer British tea and rubber planter in Java, persuaded Arthur Lampard of Harrison and Crosfield to sponsor the flotation of Javanese tea companies on the London market.[2] This was quickly followed by the opening of Harrison and Crosfield's own office in Batavia, which ensured them direct supervision over the production on their own estates. The same firm also became interested in the prospect of growing tea in Sumatra where both government and private enterprise co-existed. After some initial experimentation in south Sumatra, the main development became centred upon the higher land of the east coast region. Tea plantations were laid out in 1910 by Harrison and Crosfield and other Dutch companies with similar interests in Java. As a result, capital began to flow in, and both development and organisation in the production of Sumatran tea were given stimulation. A brief picture of the rapid, but late, growth of tea exports is given in the figures on the opposite page.

The figures exhibit a growth rate of 6·4 per cent per annum for production for the period as a whole. Between 1865 and 1899, however, the rate was only 3·9 per cent but there was a rapid acceleration to 11·7 per cent in the following years, showing a complete correspondence with the promotional activity outlined

---

[1] G. C. Allen and Audrey G. Donnithorne, *op. cit.*, pp. 102-3.
[2] Harrison and Crosfield Ltd., *One Hundred Years as East India Merchants 1844-1943* (1943) pp. 47-8.

above. In fact, production doubled between 1905 and 1914. Exports by volume follow the same pattern if one excludes the first observation. Receipts from exports, however, showed an initial rate of growth at 23·4 per cent per annum between 1865-69 and 1870-74; thereafter, growth ceased to 1895-99; from 1895-99 to 1910-14, receipts rose at a rate of 12·9 per cent per annum, rising prices corresponding with a virtual five-fold increase in the volume of exports.

Production and Export of Indonesian Tea

Year	Annual average tea production (000 metric tons)	Annual average tea export weight (000 metric tons)	value (000 florins)
1865-69	1·5	1·0	748
1870-74	1·7	2·0	2,140
1875-79	2·5	2·5	2,183
1880-84	2·5	2·5	1,768
1885-89	3·3	3·2	2,152
1890-94	4·0	3·0	2,018
1895-99	4·7	4·4	2,442
1900-04	8·5	8·8	5,210
1905-09	12·5	13·9	8,360
1910-14	24·7	24·3	19,394

Source: J. A. M. Caldwell, *op. cit.*, p. 85.

The other two estate crops of importance, rubber and tobacco, were comparatively new commodities in the range of East Indian agricultural production. Within the chronological limit of this volume, tobacco had a somewhat longer history than rubber, the latter product being of little significance in the exports from the Islands before 1914. It is for this reason, therefore, that we do not propose to enter upon an account of its production, apart from making the point that, like tobacco, its promotion as an export crop depended upon the stimulation of Western capital and ideas. Of all the changes so far mentioned, however, none was more profound in its effect than that exemplified in the production of tobacco; for it was in this particular form of cultivation that Western ideas in the use of land, labour, capital and managerial skill had free rein. Such was the force of this enterprise that, in organisation, the growing of tobacco eventually became a model for much future development in agricultural patterns throughout the East.

Tobacco was a product in growing demand from Western markets, but the conditions of sale were highly specialised in both range and quality. A prerequisite of commercial success was the skill which could be applied to the preparatory processes. As the best type of leaf could only be grown in a limited number of areas and required strict systems of rotation, production from the start had to be intensively capitalised and organised in accordance with the best current scientific practice.

In the application of Western capital one has to take account of two factors: the first was the distinctive difference between the type and quality of tobacco grown in Java and that grown in the Outer Provinces; the second was that government control over production was relinquished at a comparatively early date, thus leaving the way clear for development under various forms of private enterprise. During the operation of the 'culture system', the organisation of tobacco cultivation in Java was almost identical with that governing the sugar industry, though tobacco was never considered to be as important a crop as sugar. The government did not promote measures to monopolise supply and, as a consequence, many private firms began to undertake production. With the abandonment of the last vestiges of the 'culture system', however, a divergence of interests became apparent though, as far as Java was concerned, this was not of significance as the centre of gravity had begun to swing away from Java to the Outer Provinces.

With the abandonment of state control over tobacco, many private firms began to exercise authority by taking over agreements previously contracted between native cultivators and the government for the supply of the product. Other privately owned concerns obtained land on concession from native states, and a wide variety of methods of producing the crop gave distinctive regional differences in both the organisation of the industry and in the quality of the finished product for export. In east Java, for example, planters leased land from village landholders, paid the land tax, supplied the seedling plants and prepared the leaf for shipment.[1] This proved to be a reasonably efficient procedure as it ensured a sharing of risk between the native cultivator and the Western firm. This, at least, was true until the pressure for finer

---

[1] W. M. F. Mansvelt, *Geschiedenis van de Nederlandsche Handel-Maatschappij* (n.d. Vol. II), pp. 11-15.

quality tobacco began to make more insistent demands on the producer. As a result of commercial pressure, therefore, planters were impelled to take a more active interest in the processes of cultivation. This, in turn, led to the organisation of production through the delegation of authority. Allen and Donnithorne cite the case of one George Birnie, a tobacco planter and exporter, who was, at first, responsible only for the buying of the crop. He subsequently became involved in the leasing of the land and finally, in the planting of the seedlings. His business expanded rapidly and, by the beginning of the twentieth century, he was employing a European staff of sixty, in addition to five hundred East Indian *mandours* who supervised some thirty-five thousand natives under contract to him.[1] The assets of this large-scale enterprise consisted of a large capital stock in the form of equipment used in the preparation of the tobacco for the European market. The commercial side of the business was secured by agents in close association with British and Dutch shipowners. In short, the whole system was highly integrated and was a model for subsequent development in all Java.

The employment of Western capital was also the initiator of highly integrated forms of production in the Outer Provinces. In this promotional effort there was a direct link between the employment of Dutch capital and British and German shipping enterprise. Jacob Nienhuys, after a somewhat unsuccessful start in Java, went to east Sumatra where he found natives already growing tobacco. The leaf was particularly suitable as a cigar wrapper and, in conjunction with P. van den Ahrend, he started to ship quantities to Amsterdam.[2] The latter also engaged in trade with Singapore where, as we shall see later, a flourishing connection was established through the Mansfield agency with Holts' Blue Funnel ships. The strength of the Sumatran tobacco growers was increased through the foundation in 1869 of the Deli Mij, an organisation financed largely by N.H.M.[3] Shortly after its promotion, the company obtained the services of Jacob Cremer, a man of outstanding personality and business acumen. He introduced administrative methods and an organisational structure which became the

---

[1] G. C. Allen and Audrey G. Donnithorne, *op. cit.*, p. 97.
[2] F. E. Hyde, *Blue Funnel*, *op. cit.*, p. 50; also Allen and Donnithorne, *op. cit.*, p. 97.
[3] W. Brandt, *De Aarde van Deli* (1948), pp. 139-40.

prototype for nearly every other tobacco company. It was this organisation which won the unstinted praise of Arthur Lampard when he visited the Deli region in the early 1900's; but Alfred Holt, John Swire and Cornelis Bogaardt could have informed him of the excellence of Sumatran tobacco some twenty years earlier, for they had been actively engaged in a profitable association with the Deli tobacco growers since the 1880's.

Success in the production of the Deli wrapper leaf, however, was not attained without the surmounting of many difficulties. Cropping on any given acreage had to be restricted to one year in eight, the land having to lie fallow for the intervening seven years. It was necessary, therefore, to have large tracts of land available for cultivation with the additional surety that such land would be free from restrictive legislation. In fact, most of the tobacco land had been acquired under concession from the sultan of Deli under conditions which virtually transferred sovereignty to the companies. The need to produce a high-grade leaf called for elaborate preparatory processes and a large pool of labour. The land itself required intensive cultivation before the seedlings were planted and, when planted, the essential leaves of the maturing bushes had to be protected against pests and disease. Finally, as only two leaves could be harvested from each plant, the labour involved in collection was hard and tedious. The ultimate stages of the tobacco process, drying, fomenting, curing and sorting, required a high degree of skill and experience. To meet the exacting labour demands from the industry, the Deli Planters' Association brought indentured Chinese labourers in Holt ships from Penang and Singapore. At a later date, they tapped the reserves of labour in China itself. The laxity of government control over east Sumatra, however, led to the prolongation of abuses in this system and eventually the whole matter of labour supply and labour rights had to be regulated by the Dutch parliament. Eventually, Javanese labour replaced Chinese and, by 1909, kampongs of free labour were in existence.[1] This was but another step along the road towards the realisation of an identity of interests between East and West, between employer and employed.

Not all the tobacco companies in Sumatra were as successful as the Deli Mij. It took some time for the new promoters to realise

---

[1] G. C. Allen and Audrey G. Donnithorne, *op. cit.*, p. 98.

that the area suitable for the growing of good quality tobacco was comparatively small. Nevertheless, the flood of company flotations continued until there were upwards of one hundred in the Deli region alone. The inevitable process of attrition by bankruptcy or by amalgamation ultimately reduced this number; by the outbreak of war in 1914, there were only four units of importance left. These controlled more than 90 per cent of production and virtually the whole of the export trade. The following figures attempt to give an impression of the growth of this trade by volume and value:

Production and Export of Indonesian Tobacco

Year	Annual average tobacco production (000 metric tons)	Annual average tobacco export weight (000 metric tons)	value (000 florins)
1865-69	8·5	7·6	3,601
1870-74	14·0	13·0	8,357
1875-79	12·8	17·3	19,316
1880-84	15·0	16·8	17,497
1885-89	23·0	24·4	24,377
1890-94	28·0	32·8	32,664
1895-99	36·0	39·3	39,200
1900-04	43·0	51·1	38,203
1905-09	53·0	66·6	52,613
1910-14	65·0	75·0	73,059

Source: J. A. M. Caldwell, *op. cit.*, p. 83.

It will be noticed that figures for exports after 1875 are larger than those given for production. This is explained by the fact that the production figures do not include tobacco grown by Indonesians, production which, though mainly for the home market, was sold in relatively small quantities to estates for export. In any case, estimates of Indonesian tobacco production are highly speculative and, therefore, are not reliable for purposes of measurement. The average annual rate of growth for export volumes was 5·0 per cent for the period as a whole, though if the period 1865-69 is excluded from the calculation, the rate was 4·5 per cent. On the whole prices were well maintained; from 1865-69 to 1875-79, receipts rose by no less than 18 per cent per annum, the apparent price increase from 0·472 florins per kilo to 1·111 florins per kilo being the obvious cause. Thereafter the growth rate averaged 3·9 per cent. This is less than the increase in export volume because of some price decline. From 1900-04 to 1910-14, when prices were increasing, growth by value became 6·7 per cent per annum.

*

We have examined four of Indonesia's agricultural products. Apart from the organisational changes which these commodities exhibit in the use of resources, their relative importance may be judged from their function as export commodities. Before 1860, the receipts from the sale of coffee and sugar were undoubtedly the mainstay of the 'culture system'; but exports of coffee, sugar, tea and tobacco continued to hold a predominant place in Indonesia's total trade until the end of the century. These four commodities had accounted for 82 per cent of the volume and 78 per cent of the value of total exports in 1875.[1] By 1914, however, these proportions had respectively fallen to 47 and 45. As these staples declined in relative importance, other 'newer' commodities such as copra, rubber, tin and petroleum steadily increased their share of total exports; so much so that, on the outbreak of war in 1914, they were credited with about 32 per cent of Indonesia's export income.[2] In this changing composition of trade, the salient point to notice is that coffee exports fell consistently from 1880 onwards, the share of total trade by value dropping from 34 per cent in 1880 to 2·3 per cent in 1920.[3] Sugar, on the other hand, remained relatively stable (apart from 1913) and increased its share of total exports to 47 per cent by 1920. The rising trend for the 'newer' commodities after 1900 was, as must be obvious, the result of a later development in the application and use of resources.

If we now turn to the changes in volume of the four principal agricultural products, the Islands sent 75,000 metric tons of coffee and 99,000 metric tons of sugar abroad in 1855; by 1890, coffee exports had fallen to 38,000 metric tons whereas sugar had risen to 367,000 metric tons. These trends had been further strengthened by 1913, coffee exports having fallen to 29,000 metric tons and sugar having reached the record figure of 1,471,000 metric tons.[4] Exports of tobacco rose from 11,000 metric tons in 1880 to 87,000

[1] J. A. M. Caldwell, *op. cit.*, p. 79.
[2] *Ibid.*, pp. 87-91.
[3] J. S. Furnivall, *op. cit.*, p. 337; *Statistical Pocket Book of Indonesia*, 1941; J. H. Boeke, *The Evolution of the Netherlands Indies Economy*, pp. 22-4; League of Nations, *International Trade Statistics 1930*.
[4] J. A. M. Caldwell, *op. cit.*, pp. 79, 82.

THE PRODUCTS OF INDONESIA 85

metric tons in 1913[1]; while those for tea rose from 3,000 metric tons in 1890 to 27,000 metric tons in 1913. Of the so-called 'newer' commodities, exports of copra increased from 67,000 metric tons in 1900 to 229,000 metric tons in 1913, and tin and tin ore from 16,000 metric tons to 21,000 metric tons for the same period.

This somewhat boring catalogue of figures can, perhaps, be given relevance if we attempt an estimate of the markets for such products and give some indication of the part played by British shipping companies in the carriage of such cargoes. Unfortunately, figures for this kind of analysis are not readily available, though information for some commodities is more precise than for others. For this reason, it is only possible to say that Britain was receiving about one-third of Indonesia's output of tea in 1911 and that about 70 per cent of the cargoes were being carried in British ships.[2] On the other hand, figures for Javanese sugar exports are more informative. If we take an average for the years 1890-95, Europe absorbed 164,000 tons per annum (41 per cent), America 106,600 (27 per cent), British India 5,308 tons (1 per cent) and China, Japan and Hong Kong, 122,550 tons (31 per cent).[3] A similar average for the years 1905-10, however, shows a surprising change, average annual intakes being as follows: Europe, 17,500 tons (2 per cent), America, 136,450 tons (19 per cent), British India, 235,380 tons (33 per cent), China, Japan and Hong Kong 327,670 tons (46 per cent). The sharp fall in the export of sugar to Europe can be explained by the growing competition from beet sugar production. The consequence was that Indonesian supplies were diverted to meet the rising demand from Indian, Chinese and Japanese markets, a trade in which Holt ships participated. As the evidence from their voyage accounts shows, however, the direct trade between Java and Britain remained depressed between 1905 and 1912.[4] On the other hand, the Swire organisation profited in two ways: first, from the increasing cargoes carried to Hong Kong in their China Navigation Co. ships and secondly, from the rising receipts from their Taikoo Sugar Refinery.[5]

[1] *Ibid.*, p. 83.
[2] Holt MSS., R. D. Holt Diary and Personal memoranda, 1904-1914. An examination of the shipping trade with the Netherlands East Indies.
[3] J. A. M. Caldwell, *op. cit.*, p. 81.
[4] F. E. Hyde, *Blue Funnel, op. cit.*, p. 126.
[5] Sheila Marriner and F. E. Hyde, *The Senior, op. cit.*, pp. 98-112.

G

In the carriage of tobacco, there was a somewhat different emphasis. Of the 32,000 metric tons lifted in 1890, some 20,000 metric tons were carried in Holts' feeder ships to Singapore and thence by main line ships to Britain. Thereafter, such trans-shipment cargoes declined in favour of the direct line services instituted by N.S.M.O.[1] By 1914, Holt ships (including those belonging to associated companies) were engaged in the carriage of about 75 per cent of all tobacco sent from Indonesia to the European market. In the tin and rubber trades the same pattern is discernible, British ships (i.e. mainly Holts') carrying homewards about one-half of total exports by 1914. Finally, one may make an interesting and, at the same time, a curious comparison. According to Richard Holt, the share of Indonesian produce carried in British ships rose from 20 per cent in 1870 to 45 per cent in 1912[2]; whereas that in Dutch ships to Holland declined from 57 per cent to 28 per cent for the same period.[3] This occurred despite the fact that the Dutch made strenuous efforts in the 1880's and 1890's to capture the carrying trade.

Among Indonesia's principal imports, textiles from Western markets and rice from Burma and Siam were the most important. These trades were almost wholly dependent on foreign shipping, even when Dutch companies are excluded from the calculation. The rice trade, in particular, was so dependent; exports from Burma being controlled by British ships and those from Siam almost equally divided between British and Chinese services. Whereas the bulk of Burmese rice exports went to Europe (especially after the Suez Canal was opened), the greater part of Siam's exports went to China and to Singapore. Chinese millers in Bangkok dealt directly with Chinese merchants in both Singapore and Hong Kong instead of using British merchant houses as middlemen. In course of time, the former port became the distribution centre for the Islands whilst the latter performed a similar service for China and Japan. In 1875, roughly 60 per cent (2,420,000 piculs) of Siamese rice exports went to China and Hong Kong and 27 per cent (1,140,000 piculs) to Singapore. By 1911-12, China and Hong Kong's share (7,545,000 piculs) had fallen to 43 per cent,

---

[1] Holt MSS., Minutes O.S.S. Co., 1890-1900.
[2] Holt MSS., R. D. Holt Diary and Personal memoranda, 1904-1914.
[3] J. A. M. Caldwell, *op. cit.*, p. 96.

while that of Singapore (5,975,000 piculs) had risen to 34.[1] The impact of Bogaardt's rice ships can be judged from the fact that, in 1890, imports of rice to Singapore had risen to 1,990,000 piculs, an increase of nearly 80 per cent on the figure for 1875. Some 65 per cent of all the rice carried from Bangkok to Singapore between 1885 and 1899 was undertaken by Holts and Mansfields. The distribution from Singapore to the Islands was in the hands of nearly every shipping company based in Singapore, including Holts' East India Ocean Steam Ship Co. and their direct services by N.S.M.O. After 1899, however, Holts' transhipment services were taken over by North German Lloyd, though some cargoes of rice continued to be shipped in main line ships from Singapore to Hong Kong, despite a steady encroachment into this trade by local and Chinese-owned companies. Holts' rice ships trading to the Islands had to meet ruthless competition from Dutch feeder services, from the Straits Steam Ship Co. and from German direct line incursions on the berth. The profitability of the East India Ocean Steam Ship Co. was put in jeopardy and, as a consequence, the company was sold in 1899 to North German Lloyd. Thereafter, until 1914, Holts relied on this latter company to undertake the transhipment of their cargoes to East Indian ports.

Enough has been said to indicate the nature and extent of the change in East Indian agriculture to give due emphasis to the part played by Western capital. Production in traditional commodities was transformed under the stimulus of an expanding market. New crops, organised in accordance with Western ideas, were introduced as new demands arose. The steamship company, the steamship agent and the Western merchant controlled and regulated the carriage of rich cargoes from the East. Some of these merchants such as Harrison and Crosfield and George Wehry and Son, as well as agents such as Walter Mansfield and Butterfield and Swire, performed a variety of functions as financier, producer, shipper and shipowner. They supplied the main stream of exports to the West, but they also engaged in the cross-service trades of the Islands. In this, they were unconsciously taking part in a struggle for power between the two ports of Singapore and Batavia for the economic and commercial domination of the south-east Asian

[1] J. C. Ingram, 'Thailand's Rice Trade and the Allocation of Resources', C. D. Cowan (ed.), *The Economic Development of South-East Asia* (1964), p. 107.

region. This was a struggle mainly of relevance to the *entrepot* trade of the area but, at a later date, it involved the direction of main line cargoes and changes in the pattern of trade. In the last resort, the demands from an expanding world trade stimulated the flow of resources into agricultural development. This, in turn, created the need for shipping services and commercial machinery to sustain the flow of cargoes. Singapore, Batavia, Shanghai, Hong Kong and Yokohama became the focal points of the newly-sprung commercial enterprise and were, henceforth, the regulating links between the West and the emergent economies of the East.

CHAPTER V

Competition and Change in Local Shipping Services, 1860-1914

IN 1859, George Mansfield had sailed out to Singapore to start in business as a ships' chandler. He was moderately successful and when he died in 1863, his brother Walter had already taken over the business. Walter was joined in 1865 by George's son, George John Mansfield, a boy of fifteen. This was not a particularly propitious beginning for a firm which was to become one of Singapore's most powerful agency houses, with an influence extending far beyond the port itself to the whole of south-east Asia and ultimately across the Torres Straits to Australia.[1]

A turning point in the firm's history came with the advent of Holts' Blue Funnel steamships to Singapore. Alfred Holt had used the old-established firm of Symes and Co. as his agent. Being more conversant with the sailing ship, they were not aware of the more pressing economic needs of the new steamships, needs which required the ordering of cargo, the quick turn-round of the ship and a watchful regard for costs. Holt was less than satisfied with the handling of his first voyages and decided to change his agent. It was at this precise juncture that Walter Mansfield returned to England with the express purpose of securing the Blue Funnel agency. He was successful in his quest and, in 1868, he returned to Singapore in one of Holts' ships with the contract in his pocket. So began one of the most profitable associations in the history of British shipping. The original ships' chandlery business was converted into a company, Walter Mansfield and Co., and in due

[1] See A. Jackson and C. E. Wurtzburg, *The History of Mansfield and Company*, Part I, *1868-1924* (1953), pp. 1-2.

course George John Mansfield became a partner.[1] After Walter Mansfield's death in 1873, George Mansfield carried on the agency with the assistance of a shrewd Dutchman, Theodore Cornelis Bogaardt. With something of the buccaneer in his make-up Bogaardt had originally gone out to Java, but had eventually found employment in Singapore as a shipping clerk in the Europe Hotel. By a wise investment of his small savings in various steamship lines, he managed to acquire capital and influence. Joining Mansfields in 1872, he put his considerable administrative gifts to work and took over control of the firm after the retirement of George Mansfield in 1883.[2] Under his forceful direction, Mansfields' business grew in scope and magnitude. The two-fold purpose which Bogaardt pursued with relentless energy was determined by Singapore's position as a port. The first objective was to capture the steamship trade with the Malayan peninsula and the second to control as much as possible of the trade between Singapore and the ports of the island archipelago. In order to implement this idea, a branch office was opened in Penang in 1878, under the title of Mansfield, Bogaardt and Co., Bogaardt himself taking charge of this office until 1882. Penang was a port in the strategic chain between Suez and the Far East; it tapped the trades of western Malaya and controlled the routes to the eastern coast of Sumatra. In 1890, another branch office was opened at Sandakan in British North Borneo. Thus, under the inspiration of this leadership, Mansfields' activities had begun to embrace a wider field of new enterprise. Apart from the Blue Funnel agency they had, by 1890, acquired the management of Holts' ships sailing to Deli, Bangkok, Borneo and western Australia and undertook work for Swire's China Navigation Co. and for certain Spanish ships sailing between Singapore and the Philippines.[3] In addition to this diverse range of business, they carried on a large shipping and forwarding service on their own behalf and acted as agents for the carriage of Muslim pilgrims between the Straits and Jeddah, as well as being suppliers of indentured labour to the rice lands of Siam and the tobacco estates of Sumatra.[4] Most of these activities were conducted on behalf of the Ocean Steam Ship Co. but, in

[1] See A. Jackson and C. E. Wurtzburg, *The History of Mansfield and Company*, Part I, *1868-1924* (1953), pp. 1-2.
[2] F. E. Hyde, *Blue Funnel, op. cit.*, p. 35.
[3] *Ibid.*, p. 36.   [4] *Ibid.* pp. 36-7.

1891, Bogaardt and two other Mansfield partners joined with some of the principal Chinese merchant houses in Singapore in founding the Straits Steam Ship Co.[1] This company ran a small fleet of ships between Singapore and west coast Malayan ports for the carriage of local produce and, in particular, rich cargoes of tin ore from the newly producing areas in Perak. In short, Mansfields acquired a strategic importance in both the local and the international trade of the area and became a microcosm of south-east Asian development.

*

The attention of the Holt brothers had been drawn to the possibilities of engaging in the Deli tobacco trade by George Mansfield. Philip Holt had visited Singapore in 1879 and had been struck not only by the size and nature of the trade but also by the potential for its expansion.[2] On his return to England Philip persuaded Alfred Holt that the Ocean Steam Ship Co. ought to take part in it, either as a direct service or through their agents in Singapore. At the annual meeting of the company in 1880, the managers were instructed to make facilities available in the tobacco carrying trade 'beyond what their competitors could offer'.[3] This directive proved to be the start of a highly profitable business based on Singapore, with Mansfields taking over the control of the shipping interests in the trade.

Holts had already ordered a small ship called *Ganymede* of 405 tons gr. This ship was put directly into the service of carrying tobacco from Deli to Singapore, where the cargoes could be loaded on to the main line ships steaming between Liverpool and Shanghai. A hulk was also fitted out and moored at Belawan (the port of Deli) for storage purposes. The venture was profitable because the tobacco came forward at the off-peak season for China tea. The hope that 'this investment of the Company's funds might prove to be remunerative' was, therefore, fulfilled.[4] A second ship, *Ascanius*, was added in 1880 and a second hulk placed at Penang to help in the development of the tobacco trade with the rapidly

---

[1] K. G. Tregonning, *Home Port Singapore: A History of Straits Steam Ship Co. Ltd., 1890-1965* (1967), pp. 13 *et seq.*
[2] Holt MSS., Memo by Philip Holt on Sumatran Trade, 1885.
[3] Holt MSS., Minutes O.S.S. Co., Feb. 1880.
[4] F. E. Hyde, *Blue Funnel, op. cit.*, p. 51.

growing port of Langkat. In the following year, two small screw
steamers were put into the tobacco fleet; sheds, together with an
agent's house, were also built at Deli.[1] For an extension of the
trade between Belawan and the Straits, *Hebe* and *Calypso* were put
into service, to be replaced subsequently by *Circe* and *Medusa*.
Thus Holts, by a wise employment of resources (amounting to
£50,000) had secured a virtual monopoly of the trade in Deli
tobacco to Britain. So great was the support which this trade gave
to the main line ships, annual average profits approximating
£25,000, that the managers were determined not to 'allow opposition boats to get a footing if they can help it'.[2] Alas for their hopes!
In the very next year, subsidised German mail steamships broke
Holts' monopoly and, as a necessary consequence, freight rates
had to be reduced, thereby cutting earnings by nearly 50 per cent.
Thereafter, though tobacco continued to be a major item in Blue
Funnel cargo lists, Holts' position in the trade was never without
challenge even though they supplied the British market with the
bulk of its supply from this source.

In 1882, Holts undertook a second venture with their agents in
Singapore. The growing importance of the rice trade in Burma,
Siam and Indo-China had already attracted Chinese, French and
Dutch ships, but it was particularly in the trade from Bangkok
that Holts were interested, believing that the employment of small
steamships might prove to be profitable in operation. It was a
much more highly competitive trade than that in tobacco and the
requirements were different. If cargoes of rice were not readily
on offer, there were usually large numbers of passengers who
needed transport. Consequently, the ships in this trade had to be
built to perform a dual function. *Hecuba*, a steamship of 1,000
tons, was the first Holt ship to take part in this trade, followed by
Hecate in 1884 and *Medusa* in 1885. A fourth ship, *Hydra*, was
added in 1889.[3] *Hecuba* had earned an average annual net profit
of £10,000 and it was the successful working of this ship that
persuaded the Holt management to embark further capital in the
trade. They did not own the Singapore-Bangkok line outright,
although they held a controlling interest and on occasion lent
money to Mansfields to cover their share in the venture. 'It may

---

[1] F. E. Hyde, *Blue Funnel, op. cit.*, p. 51.
[2] Holt MSS., Memo by Philip Holt on Sumatran Trade, 1885.
[3] Holt MSS., Minutes of O.S.S. Co., 1880-1885.

be mentioned', stated the report of the annual meeting in 1886, 'that Mr Bogaardt who, with Mansfields, represents this Company's interests (in this trade) at Singapore, has considerable shares in all three steamers and can be trusted to do the best with them that can be done.'[1] In the carriage of passengers this trust was well founded. In 1876, nine-tenths of the emigrants from Swatow to Singapore and Bangkok were carried in steamships, about half in Chinese-owned boats. By 1885, nearly one-third of them were taking passage in Holt ships.[2] The rice trade was perhaps less lucrative, though in terms of quantity Holts carried some 40 per cent of all Siamese rice exported to Britain.

If these extensions of trade from Singapore were of importance to Holts' earning capacity, they were more so to Mansfields' position as steamship owners and agents. In particular, these operations brought nearer the realisation of Bogaardt's dream for an extensive steamship service from Singapore northwards to Burma, Siam and the China coast and south-eastwards to the Islands. The practical steps which he took towards realising his ambition, however, were not always acceptable to the Holt brothers. In 1884, he purchased the steamer *Pyah Pekhet* on the company's behalf, apparently without authority to do so. His action met with objection and Holts refused to sanction the purchase. Thereupon Bogaardt borrowed the purchase price and managed the ship himself.[3] In later years, the Holts were induced to buy outright or take partnerships in several ships in the trade to and from Singapore, among which were *Memnon* and *Ranee* (totalling £21,000) for trade with North Borneo.[4] Bogaardt's persistent efforts led to the formation of a small fleet, the trading interests of which were directed outwards from the Borneo run to the other ports in the East Indies, including Menado and Ternate. Finally, some eight ships were acquired to trade in the Java Seas and the Moluccas area.

As far as British shipping was concerned, the general pattern of trade with the Islands before 1880 had been based on miscellaneous cargoes outwards in return for such products as tin, arrack, sugar, pepper, gum benzoine, cassiavera (low quality

---

[1] *Ibid.*, Minutes O.S.S. Co., 1886.
[2] Holt MSS., Personal memoranda by Alfred Holt, 1885.
[3] Holt MSS., Minutes O.S.S. Co., 1 Feb. 1884.
[4] F. E. Hyde, *op. cit.*, p. 53.

cinnamon) and dry hides. The new steamship services from Singapore were based on the supply of cotton and woollen piece-goods and rice in return for the more lucrative cargoes of sugar, tea, rubber and tobacco. As these trades developed, Java assumed a more important position on the export side, the outlet for supply being Batavia, rather than as hitherto the smaller ports of Probolinggo, Tegal, Cheribon, Klakah and Pekalongan. Demand for shipping services increased, freight rates remained relatively high and the prospects for the establishment of steamship routes with the Islands were excellent, provided that competition with Dutch shipping companies could be regulated on terms of equality.

Dutch shipping had been protected by preferential duties against foreign competition in the years before 1865. Consequently, it was relieved of the necessity of making technical improvements, and when protection was relaxed it failed to meet the competitive challenge from British, French, German and American lines. It was with the object of redressing the competitive balance that, in 1870, Prince Henry of the Netherlands took the initiative in the establishment of the Nederland Line. Nevertheless, in the early years of its existence, this new company was not successful as it had to purchase its ships abroad and employ foreigners to run them.[1] The relative position of the Dutch in maritime affairs improved after 1883, the year in which the Rotterdam Lloyd had been founded, to take over the shipping interests of Willem Ruijs and Son. A few years later, in 1888, a Dutch syndicate subscribed capital for the foundation of a third major company, Koninklijke Paketvaart Mij. (K.P.M.), to trade between the islands of the archipelago and provide feeder services (based on Batavia) for the two main line companies. In other ways, too, the central government gave support to shipping companies and local authorities in providing resources for the improvement of ports and harbours; the channels at Belawan and Macassar, for example, were deepened to allow ocean-going vessels to load on berth and thus avoid the necessity of having to call at Singapore or Penang to pick up cargoes of produce from the Islands. Thus, there was a shift in emphasis, Singapore losing some of its *entrepot* trade to direct-line ships and also some of the cross-service trades, which were henceforth taken over by the feeder ships of the K.P.M. In

[1] I. J. Brugmans, *op. cit.*, pp. 10-20.

other words, Batavia became a rival port to Singapore in the steamship trades of south-east Asia.

The growing strength of the new Dutch shipping interests was brought home to Holts when they were driven out of the rice carrying trade which they had started between Singapore and Padang.[1] The nature of the opposition on this route was a presage of future events and convinced them, if indeed they needed convincing, that equally resolute measures would have to be put into effect if they were to maintain their position in the cross-service trades. As we have already stated, it was greatly to the advantage of the Nederland and Rotterdam Lloyd lines to have a feeder service which would bring the products of the East Indies to Java, where they could then be conveniently loaded on to their main line ships. The K.P.M., by establishing such a service, provided an alternative channel to Holts' feeder services *via* Singapore. To strengthen the growing volume of through traffic, the three Dutch companies entered into an agreement in 1891 concerning the calculation of through freights and the division of the freight between the first and second carriers.[2] This was a challenge which Holts, as the chief British company concerned with the Island's trades, could not ignore. The Dutch feeder services not only threatened their subsidiary lines but, indirectly, affected the carriage and capacity of the main line steamships homeward bound for London and Liverpool. At first, the Dutch sent their ships through the Sunda Straits and only occasionally (and always under protest from Alfred Holt) did they use the coast of Sumatra. The K.P.M., however, was obliged by its contract to call at Deli where tobacco was loaded *en route* for Batavia. This was a further threat to Holts' interests and the cumulative effects of Dutch encroachment into the various trades, hitherto largely controlled by British steamship companies, led Holts to take measures for their protection.

Believing that attack was the best form of defence, Holts created two new companies. The first of these companies was founded in Amsterdam in 1891 in conjunction with the Dutch firm of J. B. Meyer; it had a capital of 2 million guilders of which Holts subscribed three-quarters.[3] Under the title of Nederlandsche Stoomvaart

---

[1] F. E. Hyde, *Blue Funnel, op. cit.*, p. 86.
[2] *Ibid.*, p. 83.
[3] *Ibid.*, p. 84; Holt MSS., papers relating to the firm of J. B. Meyer; N.S.M.O. papers, 13 Aug. 1891.

Maatschappij Oceaan (N.S.M.O.) it managed a fleet largely consisting of older Blue Funnel ships put under the Dutch flag. By this device Holts obtained freedom of entry into Javanese ports where their ships, now under the Dutch flag, could compete on equal terms with those of the Nederland and Rotterdam Lloyd. The service which this new company inaugurated was a direct one between Amsterdam and Batavia, and a principal item in the cargo list was sugar. The second company was called the East India Ocean Steam Ship Co. and was capitalised at just under £100,000. Its fleet consisted of a portion of Bogaardt's original fleet, together with a number of those ships which had been purchased specifically for the Moluccas trade. Though the management of the company was retained in Liverpool, the working of the ships was undertaken from Singapore. It was anticipated that Holts would be able to provide a service in the insular trades as efficient as that provided by the K.P.M. This hope, however, was not realised. The competitive struggle in the coastal and insular trades continued. Holts were driven out of the rice trade between Singapore, Penang and Padang: the profits from their Deli tobacco trade dwindled in face of determined opposition from Dutch and German lines and, in the Borneo trade (rice from Singapore and tobacco in return), their cargoes were captured by the more forceful enterprise of North German Lloyd. It was realised that the remoteness of control from Liverpool was highly disadvantageous to the successful running of ships in such competitive conditions and, in 1899, Holts dissolved the company and sold the ships to North German Lloyd. This latter company agreed to maintain transhipment services for Holt cargoes, a state of affairs which lasted until the outbreak of war in 1914 when North German Lloyd ceased to function, and the Straits Steam Ship Co. took over these services on Holts' behalf.[1]

In the direct Java trade, there was a better prospect for a working arrangement with competing lines. After a short but sharp rate-cutting episode, both Holts and the Dutch companies sought compromise and agreement. In February 1892, therefore, an agreement was concluded with the Dutch mail lines for an equitable working of the Java trade. In political terms, this was a vindication of common sense for thereafter the two sides worked

---

[1] K. G. Tregonning, op. cit., pp. 45-6; also F. E. Hyde, Blue Funnel, op. cit., p. 158.

together in reasonable harmony. In economic terms, however, the situation was less propitious. The Java trade continued to be depressed throughout the early 1890's. To make matters worse there was a considerable wastage of resources arising from the routing of cargoes, a process which accentuated the sensitivities of merchants and shipowners in both Singapore and Batavia. 'In 1893, a temporary solution of this problem was achieved by a further agreement, whereby the K.P.M. was given a monopoly of the inter-insular traffic under certain guarantees to the N.S.M.O.[1] It was not until 1900 that an agreement satisfactory to all sides could be concluded. By the beginning of the present century, the insistent pressure of competition had forced Holts into a large capital expenditure on new fast ships which they ran direct from Suez to Padang and Java, thus by-passing Singapore. This shortened voyage times and led to earlier delivery of cargo, factors which, in turn, induced merchants to use these Holt services for their higher value produce and merchandise.[2] As opportunity offered, the strength of this Java line was maintained by the replacement of old compound-tandem engined ships, with larger faster vessels powered by triple expansion engines. The competitive balance swung in Holts' favour and made the Dutch companies more amenable to persuasion. Accordingly, in 1900, the Batavia Vrachten Conference was instituted, under the terms of which the Nederland, Rotterdam Lloyd and N.S.M.O. came to an agreement about the control of shipping space. The Conference was, in reality, a Conference of agents controlling the disposal of cargoes, the despatch of through traffic from the K.P.M., the remuneration of freight and other functions of a like organisational character.[3] It was not, however, able to take decisions on matters of freight policy without first consulting the principals. It was but a logical step from this to the establishment of a Conference of the controlling firms in Europe and, in 1904, the Principals Homeward Freight Conference came into being.[4] This Conference created a cargo pool involving all cargoes brought

---

[1] F. E. Hyde, *Blue Funnel, op. cit.*, p. 94; N.S.M.O. MSS., Correspondence between J. Swire and J. B. Mayer, 1893; also Holt MSS., Swire to Robert Holt, 6 Dec. 1894.

[2] Holt MSS., Minutes of O.S.S. Co., 1896-1905; see especially Minutes 20 Feb. 1901.

[3] F. E. Hyde, *Blue Funnel, op. cit.*, p. 95.

[4] *Ibid.*

homewards to Europe with the sole exception of that from the Deli coast. The Agents Conference was extended by the inclusion of the Deutsche-Australische Dampschiffs-Gesselschaft and, in 1907, by Messagéries Maritimes.[1]

Thus, as far as Holts were concerned, though the profits from the Java trade were subject to fluctuations from several influences, the persistent causes of depressed earning capacity, including uncontrolled competition from the Dutch lines and the technical inferiority of their own ships, had been very largely eliminated. The Ocean Steam Ship Co. had obtained a much firmer hold on this trade and had formulated a much surer policy by which its operations could be kept at a profitable level. We shall see later how the pattern of the Java and other Island trades changed during the whole period under review.

*

Meanwhile, on the China coast, developments were taking place at Shanghai no less important than those which have just been described at Singapore. These events were stimulated by the application of Western enterprise and capital to the needs of trade. Such enterprise was largely channelled through the steamship and was activated by the intense rivalry of British, American and Chinese companies which wanted to secure to themselves as large a share of the carrying trade as possible.

Before 1870, British interests had been served by numerous merchant houses relying upon local Chinese shipping companies for the movement of cargo. The steamships of the Ben Line and the Blue Funnel Line had begun to establish contact with the principal seaports along the coast and the P. and O. had its mail service to Hong Kong; but for river trade and coastal traffic, the principal steamship services were in the hands of the British firm of Jardine Matheson and the American firm of Russell and Co.[2] These two companies operated from Shanghai and had loose agreements for the share of trade on the Yangtse, as well as links with Tientsin to the north, and Ningpo, Wenchow and Foochow to the south. Jardines also had strong connections with Hong Kong.

[1] F. E. Hyde, *Blue Funnel, op. cit.,* p. 95.
[2] George Blake, *The Ben Line* (1956), pp. 45 *et seq.*; K. C. Liu, *op. cit.,* pp. 79-80; Sheila Marriner and F. E. Hyde, *The Senior, op. cit.* c.IV, pp. 58 *et seq.*

Further south still, on the Canton River, the ships of the Hong Kong, Canton and Macao Steamboat Co. performed similar functions in their acquisition of an increasing share of the tea and opium trades. It was into this comparatively stable situation that the forceful personality of John Samuel Swire burst like a bombshell in 1867.

The firm of John Swire and Sons was a Liverpool house which traded for some forty years in general merchandise. Growth was restricted and little innovation was effected. Nevertheless, in the 1850's, some expansion began to take shape; agents were established in Australia and there was a strengthening of connections with America.[1] It was in the ten years from 1865 to 1875, however, that a great burst of activity transformed this firm from a local and provincial organisation into one of international importance. The fiery genius of John Samuel Swire was responsible for this revolution.

The textiles consigned to Swires for sale in China were handled for them in that country by the firms of Augustine Heard and Co. and Preston, Bruell and Co. Swires were, however, dissatisfied with the financial standing of the latter company and they thereupon established their own house in the East under the title of Butterfield and Swire with their first office in Shanghai. The full story of this venture has been written elsewhere[2]; all that is necessary, in this present context, is to state that this new house secured the Holt agency and by 1870, under the stimulus of Holts' expanding steamship services, there were branch houses in Yokohama, Hong Kong and Foochow. Eventually other branches were established at Swatow, Tientsin, Hankow, Kobe, Amoy and Chefoo. In 1872, the China Navigation Co. was formed and, in the following year, Swire Bros., New York, came into existence; in 1874, the Coast Boats Ownery was created, in 1875, the Manchester House was opened and, in 1881, the Taikoo Sugar Refinery was formed in Hong Kong.[3] This, by any measure, was a significant scale of achievement; a considerable impact on the shipping and economy of the China coast and Yangtse River was implicit in every extension of Swires' activity and has now become a matter of history. Apart from the forceful energy and entrepreneurial skill of John

---

[1] Sheila Marriner and F. E. Hyde, *The Senior, op. cit.*, pp. 13 *et seq.*
[2] *Ibid.*, pp. 17 *et seq.*
[3] *Ibid.*, pp. 20-2, pp. 58 *et seq.*, pp. 79 *et seq.*, pp. 98 *et seq.*

Swire himself, much of the early success and importance of these ventures in the life of China must be attributed to the efficiency and skill of the firm's local partners. William Lang, who was Swire's Eastern manager, was a specialist in Lancashire cotton goods. F. R. Gamwell was Swire's right-hand man in London. James Henry Scott, son of C. C. Scott of the Greenock ship-building firm, began his career in the humble position of book-keeper and general factotum, but by the mid-1870's had become a partner in Butterfield and Swire.[1] The fourth of Swire's lieuten-ants was Edward Mackintosh who managed the Hong Kong branch from 1879 and became a partner in the firm. Thus ably assisted, Swire himself kept control of the whole business simply because he controlled the capital. This capital increased over the years as the Swire brothers allowed a good deal of their profits, and the interest accruing to them, to remain in the firm. These accumulating resources were not only a source of strength to Butterfield and Swire, especially in periods of adverse trade fluctuations, but also to the development of shipping activity, following the founding of the China Navigation Co. and the Coast Boats Ownery. By the 1890's, a strong financial position had been built up and the problems affecting the organisation as a whole were less concerned with finance than with the efficiency of management in the various sectors of Swires' expanding interests.[2]

As each new branch of Butterfield and Swire was established, a careful assessment was made of its potential contribution to the enlargement of steamship services, as well as of its ability to engage in produce transactions. Thus, a branch in Yokohama was considered essential not merely for the handling of Japanese produce but as a potential base of the extension of trans-Pacific sea routes; equally, the house at Hong Kong would benefit their shipping interests in a variety of ways. Writing to William Lang in 1869, Swire stated, 'Mr Holt, anxious to augment his fleet of China Steamers to commence the coasting trade and dissatisfied with the management of Birley and Co., has requested us to open in Hong Kong: and, after mature consideration we have consented, firmly believing that his agency alone authorises this important step. Besides which, other business to and from England and the Australian colonies will add largely to our commission account.

---

[1] Sheila Marriner and F. E. Hyde, *The Senior*, *op. cit.*, p. 22.
[2] *Ibid.*, Chapter 10, p. 185.

48705

The Singapore agent is to be under your authority. We think that Holts' line is only in its infancy and that Hong Kong is by far the most important station in the East for the future of the steam trade—also that the specie, passenger and intermediate business is nothing to what it will be. There is another point worthy of consideration. The owners of the White Star Line of Australian packets, for which we are agents in the colonies, are contracting for six steamers each 3,500 tons register and about 420 feet long. We don't believe that the trade will be able profitably to employ them—certainly not homewards even if outwards—but in time a return voyage may be made with coals to Hong Kong, coolies for San Francisco and/or Panama, grain for San Francisco to Liverpool, calling at the west coast ports for passengers and light freight. We want to be established in Hong Kong for chance of this business.'[1] The working of these agencies was, however, only the preliminary to a vast expansion of enterprise by Swire. His foresight enabled him to calculate with accuracy the potential range of demand for new shipping services in Chinese waters and his initiative provided the mainspring of action in this sphere of development. The China Navigation Co. came into existence in London in 1872 with a nominal capital of £360,000, of which £300,000 was paid up.[2] Two of the principal shareholders were John Swire and his brother, William Hudson Swire, but the Holts and the Rathbones were also subscribers, together with other well-known shipping families such as Ismay, Imrie, Dale, Barlow, Harrison, and John Scott of the Greenock ship-building firm.[3] Butterfield and Swire were appointed managers of the new company.

The original intention had been to open up trade on the Yangtse with three new ships specially built for the purpose. There was an expansive thrust to this intention in 1873, when the Union Steam Navigation Co. was purchased, thereby adding two fully operational ships some time before the ships of the China Navigation Co. were completed. This purchase also gave the China Navigation Co. valuable properties (including wharves and go-downs) in the principal river ports. Concurrently with this

[1] Swire MSS., Swire to William Lang, 20 Sept. 1869.
[2] Sheila Marriner and F. E. Hyde, *The Senior, op. cit.*, p. 60; also Swire MSS., Swire to H. J. Butterfield, 22 Feb. 1883.
[3] *Ibid.*

H

incursion into the river trade, Swire made every effort to engage in coastal shipping. Though short of capital, he persuaded John Scott that three ships, built in 1873 for the Spanish trade but unable to participate in it because of civil disturbances in that country, could be a profitable investment in the China coasting trade. H. J. Butterfield was also persuaded to become a co-owner in this venture with John Scott, and the Coast Boats Ownery established in 1874.[1] Up to 1882, the China Navigation Co. and the Coast Boats Ownery were operated as separate units, but on 1 January 1883 they were amalgamated. Thus began a collaboration which helped to change the history of shipping and trade on the Yangtse and along the China coast.

During the first ten years of its existence, the China Navigation Co. waged a bitter struggle against powerful competitors. Although originally created to develop the lower Yangtse trade, the company was endeavouring by the mid-1870's to enter the Canton trade and, by the end of the decade, it was trying to penetrate both the Shanghai to Ningpo and the Shanghai to Tientsin routes. Every new effort was hotly contested by rival shipping concerns and it was only possible to make progress by acquiring shares of trade already in the hands of established firms. In so doing, it had further to compete with the newly founded China Merchants Steam Navigation Co., which was also claiming its right to enter these trades.[2] The record is one of continuous battle with the American interests managed by Russells, with the Hong Kong, Canton and Macao Steamboat Co., with Jardine Matheson's steamship interests and with the China Merchants' government-sponsored company.

There were in being a number of agreements which had attempted to allocate shares of trade and areas of operation. Russells, Dents and Jardines had signed a ten-year contract demarcating their respective spheres of influence,[3] Dents and Jardines agreeing to leave the Yangtse to Russells while the latter refrained from working the coast southward from Shanghai. Russells and Jardines shared the Shanghai to Tientsin route, Jardines were given a monopoly of the Shanghai to Foochow trade and the Hong Kong, Canton and Macao Steamboat Co.

---

[1] Swire MSS., Swire to John Scott, 6 Nov. 1874.
[2] Sheila Marriner and F. E. Hyde, *The Senior, op. cit.*, p. 61.
[3] K. C. Liu, *op. cit.*, Chapter IV.

had a monopoly of the Canton River trade. Russells had allowed the small Union Co. to run two ships on the Yangtse, but when Swires purchased this company, they immediately came face to face with the entrenched position of Russell's Shanghai Steam Navigation Co. The details of the ensuing struggle between the China Navigation Co. and Russells have already been published and it is not necessary to repeat them here.[1] Briefly, Swire met force with force, rate-cutting with rate-cutting, until eventually in August 1873, the two sides were weary of conflict and an understanding was reached whereby the lower Yangtse trade was divided equally between the two companies.[2] As a *quid pro quo*, the China Navigation Co. promised not to send ships to Ningpo for five years. In the following year a pooling agreement was put into operation—an agreement which, during the years from 1874 to 1876, worked in Swires' favour.[3]

Having thus established themselves, Swires had to meet the growing threat from the China Merchants Steam Navigation Co. This company was determined to force an entry into the trade and, as an earnest of their intention, began to force freight rates downwards. Almost at the same time Swires began a long, costly and unsatisfactory war with the Hong Kong, Canton and Macao Steamboat Co. on the Canton River. The only peaceful area of operation was in working the coastal trades where the Coast Boats Ownery was becoming established within the terms of the five-year agreement. In 1877, however, the situation changed. The China Merchants Co. purchased Russells' Shanghai Steam Navigation Co., a move which threatened Swires' interests both on the Yangtse and along the China coast. Rates collapsed and, by way of retaliation, Swires invaded the Shanghai to Ningpo route. Again, it is not necessary to go into the details of this protracted and somewhat unedifying story of conflict. In the end, common sense prevailed and agreement for the working of the various trades was reached.[4] The Yangtse trade was divided in the proportion of 45 per cent to the China Navigation Co., and 55 per cent to the China Merchants; the Ningpo trade was equally divided. This, at least, brought some peace into the river trade but it sparked off

[1] *Ibid.*, pp. 112-20.
[2] Sheila Marriner and F. E. Hyde, *The Senior, op. cit.*, p. 62.
[3] K. C. Liu, *op. cit.*, pp. 132-3.
[4] K. C. Liu, *op. cit.*, pp. 63 *et seq.*

further contention in the coast trade. The ten-year agreement which Jardines had concluded with Russells and Dents in 1867 (under which Jardines had promised not to send ships on to the Yangtse) had come to an end. Jardines accordingly felt that they now had the right to enter the Yangtse trade and they regarded the agreement between Swire and the China Merchants as a deliberate affront. Though Swire was taken by surprise at Jardines' reaction, he regarded the fact that they were building two ships for the Yangtse trade as an open declaration of war.[1] By 1879, therefore, the prospects of a further period of intense competitive warfare were real and imminent. There is evidence, however, that Swire tried to avoid an open conflict. Having at length reached agreement on the Canton River, where a joint purse arrangement had been concluded giving Swires three-eighths and the Hong Kong, Canton and Macao Steamboat Co. five-eighths of the trade, he planned to extend a common purse or pool to the whole of the China coast trade. This would have embraced all the vessels engaged in the coastal trades, including the six ships of the Coast Boats Ownery, Jardines' five ships, five belonging to the firm of Siemssens and some of the China Merchants' ships.[2] Unfortunately, this combination did not come into effect because of the antagonism of the other companies; but, eventually, Jardines' interests were drawn together in the Indo-China Steam Navigation Co., a formidable competitor as it took over three ships on the China to Calcutta run together with the assets of the China Coast Steam Navigation Co. and the Yangtse Steamer Co. Swire's reply was to negotiate for the merging of the China Navigation Co. and the Coast Boats Ownery. Before this was concluded, however, Jardines and Swires had arranged the terms of an agreement, a *via media*, which had to await effective sanction until they could persuade the China Merchants to join them. The China Merchants finally joined in 1882, and two pooling agreements were signed by which the Yangtse trade was divided: 42 per cent to the China Merchants, 38 per cent to Swires' China Navigation Co. and 20 per cent to Jardines.[3] On the Shanghai to Tientsin route, Jardines and Swires had 28 per cent each and the China Merchants 34 per cent. In addition, each company promised not to enter certain

[1] Sheila Marriner and F. E. Hyde, *The Senior, op. cit.*, p. 69.
[2] *Ibid.*, p. 72.
[3] Swire MSS., Swire to W. Lang *et al.*, 17 Feb. 1882.

trades at all; the China Navigation vessels were not to sail from Shanghai to Foochow or to Wenchow, both the China Navigation Co. and the China Merchants agreed to keep off Jardines' Hong Kong to Calcutta route, while Jardines promised not to sail from Shanghai either to Ningpo or Wenchow, or from Hong Kong to Canton.

These agreements marked the end of the formative struggles in which Swire broke into established monopolies, struggles which were won at great financial cost to his whole organisation, particularly as they had been conducted during a period in which there had been depression in the China trade and general financial stringency.[1] Furthermore, the background had been made more complicated by the fact that ocean vessels were also competing for business with river and coastal steamers. To offset these difficulties Swire had excellent managers at his command, a factor of considerable importance in his ultimate success. If these episodes in the cross-service trades be set against the wider agreements already referred to in the ocean trades, it will be readily appreciated that the whole trade with China and south-east Asia had been given a formal system of regulation and a degree of precision. The steamship did not have to wait upon the elements as did the sailing ship; consequently voyage times were exact and cargo needed to be so ordered that its flow met the requirements of the ship. This, in turn, led to a quickening of commercial tempo and a consequent reaction upon merchants and producers in the interior. The economic penetration of the Islands, of Japan and of the heart of China itself was a phenomenon peculiar to the spirit of Western enterprise. It remained to be seen how it touched the lives of the millions whom it purported to serve.

*

We must now endeavour to relate the various steamship activities outlined above to the actual lifting of produce in and from Chinese ports and the return of cargoes in the form of manufactured goods. Apart from general import and export figures, the sources for detailed analysis are not readily available; therefore, it is not possible to give a precise picture. Nevertheless, it is clear that, by using shipping company records and relating them to official statistics, certain assessments of a general nature can be made.

[1] Sheila Marriner and F. E. Hyde, *The Senior, op. cit.,* pp. 74-5.

In the general disposition of trade, during the period 1860 to 1914, changes had taken place in the links between China and south-east Asia which, in magnitude, were no less important than those between China and Western markets. Though Britain, Europe and the United States took an increasing share of trade in Indonesian agricultural products such as coffee, tea and tobacco and, after 1900, exercised a virtual monopoly over the supply of rubber and tin, China turned to south-east Asia for the food staples of sugar and rice. In the distribution of rice from Siam, China, as we have seen, received the bulk of her imports by direct shipment, though Singapore did act as *entrepot* for part of China's supplies. The main destinations of Singapore's rice shipments, however, were the ports of the Indonesian Islands. Sugar, on the other hand, was exported from Batavia either direct or *via* Singapore to Hong Kong where, after refinement, cargoes were transhipped to other Chinese ports and to Japan. In such context, it is perhaps of relevance to attempt analysis of the complex inter-relationships developing in the trade between China's principal ports and the outside world.

Before the Opium War (1839-42) Canton had been the only port open to foreign trade. At the end of hostilities, however, the Treaty of Nanking sanctioned the accessibility of four other ports to foreign shipping; of these Shanghai, which served the rich Yangtse Valley, was the most important. Flourishing local trade connections were built up between Shanghai and Chinkiang, Kiukiang, Tientsin and Hankow. The opening up of China not only accentuated the importance of Shanghai as a centre for river and coastal trade, but gave it international status. According to available trade returns in the 1870's, Shanghai handled about 60 per cent of China's total trade. It is true that, after 1878, the share was diminished but, despite the opening of many other ports and despite the development of new trades in which Shanghai did not participate, it still controlled over 40 per cent of total trade by 1914. Canton's share also declined over the same period. The inference is, therefore, that the trade of these two major ports was not increasing in proportion with the growth of China's trade as a whole. On the other hand, Tientsin and Hankow not only increased the absolute value of their trade by twenty to thirty times, but their respective shares also increased from less than 2 per cent in the 1870's to about 6 per cent by 1913. The Manchurian port of

Dairen also acquired a growing proportion of China's trade after 1907, mainly because of its control over the growing export trade in soya beans. If we take a general average of the trade of these ports for the years 1911 to 1914, Shanghai serving central China accounted for nearly half of total imports and exports; south China (largely through Canton) accounted for 27·0 per cent; Hankow, Tientsin and Dairen serving north China and Manchuria controlled 23·5 per cent.

Against this background, one may set a rather more detailed examination of flows in particular commodities. After 1870, a large transhipment business developed between Shanghai, Chinkiang, Kiukiang and Tientsin. In return for cargoes of sugar, pea-oil and black dates, Chinkiang sent to Shanghai valuable shipments of hemp, wood oil, vegetable tallow and tobacco.[1] In the Kiukiang trade, Shanghai transhipped textiles, lead and opium, the greater part of such cargoes being consigned by Chinese merchants.[2] The return trade was principally in black and green teas, some 60 per cent of the volume passing through Chinese hands.[3]

Apart from Shanghai, there was an increasing volume of cross-trades with the ports of Tientsin and Hankow, trades which were undoubtedly stimulated by the advent of river and coastal steamships. Up to 1875, about one-half of Tientsin's imports consisted of cottons, woollens and opium though, by 1880, the share had fallen in face of a growing importation of Chinese produce.[4] In relative terms, Tientsin's export trade was not large and, while there was some re-export of Western products, the bulk of the trade consisted of cargoes of Chinese commodities. By contrast, the trade to and from Hankow (passing *via* Shanghai) was, in the years before 1870, almost entirely dependent for its stimulus on the river steamships. In 1867, Hankow's import trade was almost equally divided between overseas goods (cottons, woollens and opium, 44 per cent) and Chinese produce (principally tea, amounting to 42 per cent).[5] These proportions were not substantially

[1] K. C. Liu, *op. cit.*, pp. 64, 65. From figures drawn from Imperial Maritime Customs: *Reports on Trade, 1866-1874*.
[2] *Ibid.*
[3] *Ibid.*
[4] *Ibid.*, pp. 109 *et seq.* quoting Imperial Maritime Customs, *Statistics of Trade at Port of Tientsin, 1863-1872*, pp. 10-17.
[5] *Ibid.*, pp. 107 *et seq.*

altered until the 1880's when the tea trade began to show signs of
decline. Between 1867 and 1874, however, there was a change in
the magnitude of Hankow's re-export trade.[1] In the latter year,
tea accounted for 51 per cent, a figure which was not very different
from that in 1867 though the trade as a whole had grown, re-
exports of Chinese produce (as distinct from overseas produce)
rising from 32,000 Hankow taels to 777,000 taels in seven years.
The bulk of this re-export trade was to Shanghai for transhipment
and was carried in river steamships.

In general, one has the impression confirmed that the Chinese
merchant body was much more active in the control of trade than
were the native merchants in the Netherlands East Indies. This
was undoubtedly the result of a much wider control which the
Chinese had over the financing and distribution of local produce
and also over the varying degrees of specialisation required in their
handling. The comparative strength of such enterprise resulted
from a relaxation of government control, particularly in the
Treaty ports where compradores were steadily increasing their
power. As resources grew, more and more of the import trade fell
into Chinese hands. This applied particularly to textiles, the value
and volume of which assumed a premier place in China's import
list by the late 1870's. At first (i.e. before 1860) the textile business
was controlled by the large Western merchant houses who bought
and sold on their own account. Such imports remained the pro-
perty of the foreign merchants until they were sold to the Chinese
dealers. By the late 1860's, however, these dealers, with their local
experience and low distribution costs, were superseding the
foreigners in all parts of the trade which did not require contacts
abroad, that is to say, in all stages apart from the actual business
of importing. It was because of this that transhipment business
passed largely into Chinese hands. Perhaps the best description
of the whole situation is given in a report dated 31 January 1870,
written by H. E. Hobson of the Hankow Customs, in which are
enumerated the various groups of Chinese merchants at Hankow.
'The chief dealers in opium', Hobson wrote, 'are Cantonese, those
in cotton and silk piece goods Chekiang people, the crockery and
medicine trade is done by Kiangse merchants, the tobacconists are
all Fukien men, whilst tea, oil, tallow, furs and miscellaneous goods

[1] *Ibid.*

are dealt in by natives from almost every province.'[1] These were all beneficiaries of steamship transport and their transactions increased in direct proportion to the increase in steamship traffic during the last quarter of the nineteenth century.

In the trade between Shanghai and Tientsin there was a predominance of imported goods. Of the foreign trade between Tientsin and other Treaty ports, some 60·7 per cent was carried in foreign vessels in 1867; by 1872 this percentage had dropped to 55·9. Nevertheless, by the mid-1870's there had been a substantial increase in Chinese produce shipped to and from the Treaty ports. As Dr K. C. Liu has shown, there were twenty Chinese firms at Tientsin all of which were branches of firms at Canton and Hong Kong, together with seven which were branches of firms at Swatow and three which were branches of firms at Foochow. 'The Cantonese firms dealt in cotton piece-goods as well as in sugar and tobacco, while among the Swatow firms, there were two that specialised in opium.'[2] There was also an increasing practice for Chinese merchants in Tientsin to buy direct from foreign merchants in Shanghai and, by 1867, there is evidence that Chinese merchants had their own agents there to arrange for deliveries by steamship. As far as steamship services in the cross-trades were concerned, the position was much easier during the 1860's in Singapore and the Islands than in China. Because of the high cost of operation, steamship services in Chinese waters were at first restricted to a part of the trade between the Treaty ports. Again, according to Dr K. C. Liu, 'this trade consisted of merchandise of high value which constituted a demand of comparatively low elasticity in a certain range of freight rates'.[3]

We have now seen, by way of illustration, how the coming of Walter Mansfield and John Swire helped in the creation of new enterprise. In so doing, they brought greater flexibility to the merchant and increased his resources. As a result, the commercial tempo of the Islands and the China coast was quickened and Western capital was able to bring fresh vitality to an area which, for centuries, had remained fast in the grip of tradition and history. While the strength of some Western merchant houses increased, it is generally true that greater power was given to the initiative

[1] H. E. Hobson, *Reports on Trade, 1869* (Shanghai, 1870), p. 28.
[2] K. C. Liu, *op. cit.*, p. 109.
[3] *Ibid.*, p. 110.

and enterprise of local merchants, particularly those whose business was conducted in ports along the China coast. The general impact of Western enterprise, especially that concerned with steamship services, had, therefore, a two-edged effect. It opened up vast areas in the Pacific to foreign trade and, at the same time, stimulated native resourcefulness in the methods and techniques of highly complex forms of trading organisation.

BURMA, SIAM, INDO-
CHINA, AND MALAYA
WITH MAJOR PORTS

0   100   200   300 Miles

CHINA

BURMA

River Kaladan

River Irrawaddy

Bay
of
Bengal

Yabu

Basseín

Rangoon

Maulmain
(Moulmein)

Amherst

SIAM
(THAILAND)

TONKIN

Hanoi

Diemdien

Haiphong

Gulf
of
Tonkin

HAINAN
ISLAND

INDO

Da-Nang
(Touräne)

Tenasserim R.

Bangkok

Tenasserim

CAMBODIA

Phnom-
Penh

River Mekong

CHINA

Gulf
of
Siam

ANDAMAN

SEA

COCHIN CHINA

Saigon

ANNAM

SOUTH CHINA SEA

SUMATRA

Kedah R.
Georgetown

Penang
Island

Port Weld

Sembilan Is.

Kuala
Selangor

Port
Swettenham

Klang

Port Dickson

Malacca

Johore Bahru

Tumpat

Kelantan R.

Kuala Trengganu

MALAYA

Kuantan

Str. of Malacca

Bintan I.

Seletar

Tanjong Rhu & Tanjong Penjuru

Singapore

Tanjong Pagar

CHAPTER VI

The Allocation of Resources: Siamese Rice, Malayan Rubber and Tin

HAVING dealt, albeit in a somewhat cursory fashion, with the stimulation of a new means of transport on traditionally-based cultures, we must now retrace our steps in order to understand the nature of Western enterprise in the Far Eastern region so far under review. Leaving aside for the moment the all-important revitalising influences within the Japanese economy, the most obvious sources for investigation lie in the production of Siamese rice and Malayan rubber and tin. The reason for this particular choice is based on the simple facts that the development of all three primary products did much to foster Singapore's position as a major port in south-east Asia, and that it is possible to arrive at certain conclusions concerning the allocation of resources within specific areas of enterprise and within precise limits defined by geography. From such an exercise it is hoped that conclusions may be drawn concerning the changes which Western capital, in its search for trade and in its exploitation of natural resources, made in the lives of selected communities—conclusions which might well apply to other regions of Asia similarly endowed with agricultural and mining potentialities.

To understand the full implication of the development of the Siamese rice trade, one must first establish that, from the end of the seventeenth century to the middle of the nineteenth century, Siam, like China and Japan, was completely cut off from the outside world. Rice was a staple of livelihood and food supply; its production fluctuated with the seasons and the necessities of the state's revenues. What trade there was outside national boundaries was carried on by Chinese junks and financed by Chinese merchants.[1] By the end of the reign of Rama III (1851) it was becoming apparent that Siam could not continue its policy of isolation. The implications of the British approach in Burma, and the opening up of China, made a change of policy necessary in the interests of the economy and in the acceptance of new ideas. The British government had already negotiated a treaty following the missions of Crawfurd (1821) and Burney (1825), and contact had been established with the United States through the Roberts mission in 1833; but the treaties negotiated by Burney and Roberts were not broad enough in scope to establish trading links. In fact, the terms of the Burney Treaty prohibited the export of rice by British merchants. With the accession to the throne of Rama IV (King Mongkut) in 1851, a radical change in outlook took place, Mongkut being convinced that if Siam were to remain an independent state, it had to become part of the international economy. Mongkut began by abolishing many impediments to trade and entered into a new agreement with Sir John Bowring in 1855, from which ensued a second treaty sweeping away all restrictions on imports and exports and giving British merchants the right to trade freely in all Siamese ports.[2] It was a direct result of this freedom that the Holt rice ships could initiate and eventually expand their trade between Bangkok and Singapore. A revenue tariff in the shape of a 3 per cent export duty was levied on the export of rice, and other duties were charged on the carriage of specified commodities, the duty on rice being fixed at 0.16 baht per picul.[3] By this change of policy Siam was admitted to the competitive arena of world trade and, apart from a small number of duties levied for revenue purposes, entered this arena as a free trade nation.

Under the stimulus of a growing demand for rice, production was increased. This production had been centred on the plain lands around Bangkok where a network of canals permitted easy transport; but, in due course, the thrusting enterprise created by foreign capital gradually penetrated (with the aid of railways) into

[1] James C. Ingram, 'Thailand's Rice Trade and the Allocation of Resources', C. D. Cowan (ed.), *The Economic Development of South-East Asia* (1964), p. 102.
[2] James C. Ingram, *Economic Change in Thailand since 1850* (1955), Chapters I and II, *passim*.
[3] *Ibid.*; also Holt MSS., Observations on the Rice Trade by Philip Holt, in an assessment of the need for tonnage, 1882-83.

the interior provinces. The area under rice cultivation expanded rapidly and traditional employment in handicrafts, so long the mainstay of up-country districts, declined in the face of the country's main agricultural product, the export of which brought in return a flood of textile piece-goods and other Western manufactures. Thus, as Professor J. C. Ingram has stated, 'a degree of specialisation appeared in response to the opportunities provided by world trade'.[1]

There was an increasing, upward trend in the volume of rice exports during the latter half of the nineteenth century, though this was achieved notwithstanding fairly wide short-term fluctuations. After a somewhat slow and erratic progress up to 1870 (1·8 million piculs), exports rose to a peak of an annual average of 25·7 million piculs in the period 1930-34. Set against this growth in trade was the equally remarkable phenomenon of a doubling of population. This combination of increasing supply and demand schedules, both in the home and world markets, represented the major economic change in Siam since 1855. The following figures speak for themselves:

Volume and Value of Siamese Rice Exports

Year	(000 piculs average)	(000 baht average)	Average price per picul
1857-59	990	—	—
1860-64	1,840	—	—
1865-69	1,630	—	—
1870-74	1,870	5,110	2·70
1875-79	3,530	10,110	2·90
1880-84	3,580	9,610	2·70
1885-89	5,320	15,080	2·80
1890-94	7,250	23,780	3·30
1895-99	8,000	36,410	4·60
1900-04	11,130	61,280	5·50
1905-09	14,760	81,020	5·50
1910-14	15,220	81,230	5·30

Source: J. C. Ingram, *op. cit.*, p. 105.

These figures include paddy, though this was a small part of the whole, as, until 1915, nearly all the exported rice was milled at Bangkok. These rice mills, established after the 1855 Treaty, were largely financed by British and American capital; by 1899, as

[1] James C. Ingram, 'Thailand's Rice Trade', *op. cit.*, p. 103.

Ingram has shown, three-quarters of the total number of mills had passed into Chinese hands. It is not surprising, therefore, that British traders should have encountered difficulty in the export of rice, having to compete with an increasingly severe competition from the Chinese. Apart from exports to Europe, which constituted only a small proportion of the whole, Chinese merchants controlled most of the Asian trade in the years before 1914. This control extended from the milling of the rice in Bangkok to the sale in Singapore or Hong Kong.[1] In the trade with Europe, the impact of the feeder services to the Holt main line ships can be seen from the following figures:

Exports of Siamese Rice carried by Holts and Associates
(000 piculs)

Year	Total exports	Carried by Holts and Associates To Singapore	To Europe (tons)
1875	3,920	—	—
1890	8,090	980	31,000
1900- 1904 average	11,130	2,460	34,000
1911-12	17,550	3,010	87,000

These mounting export figures were accomplished by an increasing area under production and by improved methods of cultivation leading to increasing yields. Jungle land was cleared and irrigation canals were dug, greatly extending the area of crop land; in fact, some 90 per cent of available crop land was put under rice in the period 1850 to 1914. It was a peasant small-holding economy in which a single staple supported a growing population under the stimulus of government encouragement. For example, tax laws contained incentive provisions designed to effect an expansion of the area under cultivation; the land tax (which, in any case, was low) was waived for the first few years of new planting.[2] In the second place, irrigation work and the construction of railways were undertaken directly by the government to serve the main centres of production in the delta and, later, the new areas of rice production in the north and north-east. Furthermore, a Land Act, passed in

[1] Swire MSS., An Examination of some trades along the China Coast—Memo by John Swire, 18 Nov. 1882; also J. C. Ingram, *op. cit.*, p. 104.
[2] J. C. Ingram, *op. cit.*, p. 110.

1908, gave to the individual the right to acquire virtually as much unused land as he could profitably cultivate. Finally, the institutions of a former feudal autonomy were discarded by the abolition of slavery and the substitution of a money-tax for forced labour, such restrictions on the liberty of the subject being abolished by law and proclamation in the latter half of the nineteenth century. In place of the feudal enforcements of labour, Chinese immigrants were increasingly employed as wage labourers to undertake manual and construction work. Thus, the emergence of a free labour force, an abundant supply of land and the right to own and cultivate it led to a diversion of native labour into agriculture and to a rapid expansion in rice production. The whole movement towards such production was given further impetus by rising prices of rice, under the stimulation of an increasing demand from all parts of the world. The net effect of these various factors on the export trade was reflected in rates of growth. Over the whole period from 1857 to 1924, there was an average annual rate of growth of 4·6 per cent. There was, however, a break in trend after 1905-09; from 1857-59 to 1905-09, growth was at 5·6 per cent per annum, while that for the remaining years up to 1924 was at 1·2 per cent per annum.

If the production and export of rice was the mainstay of the Siamese economy, the attraction of so large a proportion of the country's resources into the promotion of a single staple crop led to an inherent weakness. The extension of agriculture as a prime source of occupation caused an acute shortage of labour and personnel for industrial and commercial activity. As a result, shortages in non-agricultural employment had to be made good by immigration (chiefly Chinese), and this labour force eventually supplied the major part of the wage-earning class in the country. The growing specialisation and demarcation of function made it possible for the Chinese merchant and industrialist to secure particular advantages and helped them in acquiring control over commercial and other services. Against such a background it becomes a matter of conjecture why the Siamese government allowed the economic welfare of the native to rest upon the prosperity of a single product. According to Ingram, the answer might be found in the level of real wages which the system as a whole sustained. The price of rice was rising in terms of baht because this was still a silver currency and was depreciating in terms of gold. The depreciation of the baht reached a maximum in

1902, 'while the real wage, of course, involves more than rice, the baht prices of other exported goods and of imports tended to rise in the same proportion as the baht depreciated'.[1] From these facts Ingram concluded that changes in the rice wage-rate were sufficient to cover changes in real wages. By comparison, wage-rates for imported labour remained fixed within fairly rigid limits and at low levels, a fact which affected Chinese labour, but which scarcely touched the bulk of the Siamese population.[2]

The willingness of Chinese labour to work for low wages is reflected in the fact that the bulk of Chinese immigration took place at a time when real wages were falling sharply; but this fact does not, in turn, necessarily explain why such immigrants engaged in industrial and commercial occupations rather than in more lucrative agriculture. We need not elaborate upon the complexities of the Chinese labour market. All that need be said is that commercial employment was more suitable for the particular needs of Chinese labour at this time. Thus it happened that there was every incentive for the Siamese to use their resources in agriculture—an occupation which gave the population a steady standard of living, while imported labour was left to the performance of manual tasks and other less remunerative forms of work. The implication is that a given quantity of imported consumer goods could continue to be exchanged for a given quantity of rice with less effort than the production of those goods by indigenous labour. The economic sense of such a situation depended on the significance of the movement in the terms of trade for or against the rice producer. By taking a weighted index of import prices adjusted to new products and changes in quality, it would be possible to make such an assessment. Unfortunately, however, such an index is not available. Nevertheless, Ingram constructed a workable form of measurement by calculating the trend of rice exports in terms of textiles. As textiles formed a major item in Siam's import list, it is possible to obtain fairly consistent figures and Ingram was able to show an interesting exchange rate. From the 1860's until the end of the century, a picul of rice could be exchanged for an increasing volume of grey shirting, rising from 2 kilos to 9 kilos. 'The rise in white shirting per picul of rice was smaller, from 1·4 to 2·3 kilos in the 1860's to 4·5 kilos in 1898.[3] As the factor costs of

---

[1] J. C. Ingram, *op. cit.*, p. 113.   [2] *Ibid.*   [3] *Ibid.*, p. 118.

I

a unit of rice remained the same, the conclusions from Ingram's index must be that the real income of rice growers was rising, a further point strengthening the previous conclusion that wage labour was far less attractive than farming rice. After 1900, however, the terms of trade became less favourable for the rice grower; but, until 1910, it was of economic advantage to the Siamese state to pursue this single-minded purpose of allocating the greater proportion of its resources to the production of a single primary product. From it was derived the wealth to finance essential imports and the income to support an increasing population. Foreign capital provided the services necessary for trade and, in this way, there was an equable division of effort. The secondary effects were every whit as important: in the *entrepot* trade of Singapore, in the supply of an essential foodstuff to the Islands, in the import trade of China and in the export of manufactured goods from the West. Here was a classic example of economic liberalism at its best.

*

The history of natural rubber production in Malaya is well documented and needs only a brief mention in this present context. We are principally concerned with the impact of this implanted industry on Malaya's economy as a whole and, in particular, the effectiveness of rubber as a primary export commodity in the peninsula's overseas trade after 1895.

The inception of rubber planting in Malaya sprang from a series of experiments in the botanical gardens of Kew and Singapore, and the gardens of the British Residency at Kuala Kangsa in Perak.[1] The successful development of seedlings capable of systematic and organised production was as much the result of persistent pioneering work by government officials as of the natural advantages of habitat. Men such as N. H. Ridley, head of the botanical gardens at Singapore, supported by Hooker of Kew and many others, gave themselves wholeheartedly to the problem of introducing a rubber industry to south-east Asia. It was not until 1897, however, that a satisfactory system of tapping was discovered which made estate

[1] O. F. Cook, 'The Beginnings of Rubber Culture', *India-Rubber Journal* (April, 1933), pp. 450-2; R. O. Jenkins, 'Rubber: Introduction and Expansion with Special Reference to Malaya', *The Planter*, Feb.-Mar. 1955.

production a viable economic proposition. Even so, it was some little time before sizeable areas were put under production, even though the government was willing to grant up to 1,000 acres to any planter who might wish to embark upon such an enterprise. At the same time, there was a curious and contradictory attitude in official circles to this new product, born of suspicion and fear of the potential diversion of resources into, as yet, an untried venture. For a time, in the 1890's, even Ridley was reprimanded by the governor for growing 'exotics'.[1] Nevertheless, the process of rubber planting, once having begun, could not be checked. 200 acres were put under cultivation in 1897 by Stephens and McGillivray on their coffee estate; by 1904, this estate was exporting rubber to the value of 4,000 Straits dollars.[2] This was the beginning of a commercial organisation for the rubber industry in Perak. In Selangor, the brothers Kindersley, who had started the Inch Kenneth Coffee Estate in 1894, planted rubber on a small scale. Then followed the planting of 40,000 rubber trees on the Pataling Estate between 1897 and 1900.[3] So far, these individual pioneering efforts had taken place on coffee plantations; their sponsors had, therefore, not committed their resources entirely to the new crop but had hedged their risks with an alternative commodity—in this case, a traditional one for which there was a known demand. In this way, plantation rubber was developed within an existing cost structure, a structure which allowed the coverage of the seven-year period which, perforce, had to elapse between the planting of the rubber trees and their maturity.

The proprietary estate was, however, not the only form of undertaking in these early years. Among the early pioneers was the Oriental Estate Co. Ltd., owning the Bukit Rajah Estate in Selangor, and in Pahang the first rubber estate was planted by the manager of the Liang Exploration Syndicate Ltd.[4] As Allen and Donnithorne have shown, there was considerable initiative in the laying-out of estates by government and district officials, who were

---

[1] G. C. Allen and Audrey G. Donnithorne, *Western Enterprise in Indonesia and Malaya* (1957), p. 110.
[2] *Ibid.*
[3] Harrison and Crosfield Ltd., p. 20; also G. C. Allen and Audrey G. Donnithorne, *op. cit.*, p. 110.
[4] O. Marks, 'The Pioneers of Para Rubber Planting in British Malaya'. *British Malaya*, Vol. I., Feb. 1927, pp. 284-5.

familiar with up-country local conditions.[1] Apart from Guthries, and perhaps one or two others, few Singapore merchant firms risked their capital in these early pioneering efforts. Their enterprise waited upon events and they did not enter this new field of development until the first and second decades of the present century.

As capital flowed into the new production, companies were formed to establish rubber plantations to meet a growing demand from the new motor-car industry—a demand from the United States and Europe which became increasingly insistent. Conditions of production, however, made supply inelastic as rubber trees take seven years to mature. Prices of rubber began to increase sharply, from 4s per lb. at the beginning of the century to 12s 9d per lb. at the peak of the boom in 1910.[2] In general, there was a well defined relationship between costs and revenue, the sharpest rise in costs taking place during the first seven years after planting; thereafter there was an increasing return on capital as trees attained a maximum state of output. The larger estates were better able to keep costs within limits and thus achieve positions of maximisation; the smaller estates, largely because of inability to expand production rapidly in periods of boom or to survive periods of low prices, were not so financially successful in covering overheads. Whereas the smaller units of production rarely paid a dividend of more than 25 per cent in the early period, the larger units such as, for example, the Pataling Rubber Estates Syndicate, paid 45 per cent in 1908 and 325 per cent in 1910.[3] Nevertheless, individual enterprise continued to promote new production despite relatively unfavourable competitive conditions. With the passing of the boom, however, such enterprise dwindled and, more especially after restrictions were placed on the alienation of land, the opportunities for private development were greatly diminished. A new turn was given to investment after 1900 when the great merchant houses of Singapore called upon the resources of the London capital market for means to promote an expansion of production. These houses formed an essential link between the estate planters in Malaya and the investors at home; they were thus in a position to moderate the flow of funds in accordance with the

---

[1] G. C. Allen and Audrey G. Donnithorne, *op. cit.*, p. 111.
[2] *Ibid.*
[3] *Ibid.*; Harrison and Crosfield Ltd., pp. 20-2.

requirements of trade and the general state of demand for the product.

Unlike the growing of rice in Siam, the production of rubber was, therefore, an implanted industry very largely directed and controlled by external agencies and financed from external sources. The initiatory procedure assumed a standard practice. A proprietary concern or a small plantation company would seek the backing of one of the merchant houses in Singapore in the flotation of a new company in London, the additional capital usually being made up partly by proprietors' shares, partly by capital from the merchant houses and partly by new subscriptions from the money market.[1] In most cases the Singapore house was created the managing agent and secretary of the new company. Sometimes the merchant house would purchase a number of estates before promoting a new company. It is evident that they found it more expedient to establish investment trusts for the purpose of advancing loans secured by mortgages on existing estates in association with their own agency, such loans carrying the option of conversion into shares after a specified time.[2] Investors in the West, reassured by the reputation and first-hand knowledge of local conditions possessed by the Singapore houses, were ready to make capital available for a rapid expansion of the rubber industry in Malaya. Furthermore, the agency houses, having interested the financial centres of the West and having secured flows of capital, had themselves to safeguard their own position by establishing an administrative control and an organisational pattern in the management of new estates. By these means, capable men with technical experience and administrative skill were appointed to run the plantations, while the agencies provided trained accountants from their own offices to keep a check upon the profitability of individual units of production. In other words, this newly promoted industry was given precise direction in the ordering of its resources, and thereby assumed degrees of efficiency unparalleled in the other rubber growing areas of south-east Asia.

There were, nevertheless, sources of fairly large-scale capital formation outside the general pattern so far described. One such

[1] G. C. Allen and Audrey G. Donnithorne, *op. cit.*, p. 112; also Swire MSS., box containing documents on rubber planting and investment, 1895-1905.
[2] *Ibid.*

example was that of the Duff Development Co. in the state of
Kelantan. This company assumed a role of major importance in
the area bordering Siam. Robert W. Duff, pioneer and founder
of the company, received a concession of 3,000 square miles from
the Sultan of Kelantan 'together with commercial rights of every
description and extensive administrative and fiscal powers'.[1]
There were initial and frustrating delays to the development of this
concession, and the transfer of Kelantan to British administration
in 1909 did nothing to alleviate long-standing legal complications
concerning rights and title.[2] Ultimately the company was forced to
accept the status of ordinary landowner in return for substantial
compensation.[3] Meanwhile, however, the company had directed its
activities to the exploitation of mineral resources, rivers had been
dredged and a transport system organised. In 1906, rubber planting
began both on company-owned estates and on land leased to other
companies for such purpose. Eventually, rubber became a major
part of production within the framework of a virtual independence
from external sources. The company had control of a large initial
capital and this was augmented by the considerable compensation
received for the abrogation of its original concession.

Among the larger companies, owned by non-British or Asiatic
capital, the most important was the Franco-Belgian Société
Financière des Caoutchoucs which acquired extensive properties in
Malaya and Indonesia as well as Indo-China. The local Malayan
Chinese were also substantial investors though eventually many of
their holdings passed under British control. The Malacca Rubber
Estate, for example, was originally founded by Chinese capital and,
by 1900, was one of the largest producers; but the company was
later taken over by Guthries of Singapore.[4] Furthermore, the great
manufacturing concerns in the West were also providers of capital.
Stimulated by an increasing demand for their products, they found
it advantageous to secure control over their sources of supply. In
1910, the Dunlop Rubber Co. entered the field and, by 1915, when
Dunlop Rubber Plantations was founded, their holdings amounted

[1] G. C. Allen and Audrey G. Donnithorne, *op. cit.*, p. 113.
[2] *Ibid.*
[3] A. Wright and J. H. Reid, *The Malay Peninsula* (1912), pp. 152-65;
R. Emerson, *Malaysia* (1937), pp. 227, 252-60.
[4] Song Ong Siang, *One Hundred Years History of the Chinese in
Singapore* (1923), pp. 290-4, 449.

to the largest group under single ownership in Malaya.[1] The United States Rubber Co., through its subsidiary, Malayan American Plantations Ltd., also opened up extensive areas for production. As a corollary to this successful attraction of capital resources, the Malayans themselves began to plant seedlings and produce rubber on small-holdings of something less than 20 acres. As the boom developed, they were increasingly drawn into the occupation of rubber-growing particularly in Perak and Kelantan and, by the second and third decades of the century, their effort was contributing approximately one-half of Malaya's total supply. The very fact that their enterprise was not handicapped by heavy overhead costs enabled them to compete in terms of price, if not always in terms of quality, with the large estates and secure to themselves a large profitable return.

In the organisation and control of the second factor of production, namely land, there were distinctive differences from that existent in Siam. As a consequence of the establishment of British rule in Malaya, the authorities were forced to provide a legal basis for the holding of land which would, at one and the same time, protect the rights of native cultivators and permit the extension of European enterprise. Sir William Maxwell, following his appointment as Resident in Selangor in 1889, had laid down a system of land administration based on the Torrens principles.[2] This system, which was widely adopted in Malaya apart from the Straits Settlements, required the registration of all land transactions at a local land office. Hitherto, land could be transferred under a perpetual lease, but under the new code the rights of the local population were safeguarded. After 1911, it was enacted that terms of all leases should be subject to revision after the lapse of thirty years, while other provisions made it necessary for specified areas to be brought into cultivation within a given time span. Two years later, there was a further enactment which authorised the separate States of the Federation to set aside areas for use by Malays. Thereafter, there was a much more rigid control imposed upon the granting of land to European companies for development. Though this was of economic and social importance to the indigenous population, the prescription exercised by individual states impeded

---

[1] G. C. Allen and Audrey G. Donnithorne, op. cit., p. 114.
[2] Ibid., p. 115.

the formulation of a unified land administration over the country as a whole.[1]

In the organisation of the third factor of production, labour, the Malayan rubber industry was completely different from that in the rice growing areas of Siam. The rubber estates relied almost wholly on imported Indian labour. This labour formed part of the general influx into Malaya during the last decade of the nineteenth century and was composed predominantly of male labourers. It should be emphasised that this new immigration coming from India, China, and the Netherlands East Indies was distinct from the settled immigrant population (mainly Chinese) of the Straits Settlements. The general conclusion which can be drawn from the early Malayan census returns is that permanent Chinese settlement was centred in and around the ports of Singapore, Penang and Malacca, in the inland towns of Kuala Lumpur, and in the tin mining towns of Kinta and Larut such as Kampur, Ipoh and Taiping. In 1911, more than half the Chinese population of the Federated States and nearly two-thirds of the Chinese female population lived in the tin mining districts of Kinta in Perak and Kuala Lumpur in Selangor.[2] This concentration of Chinese labour in tin mining was, as we shall see later, of long standing; it was not until the end of the first decade of the present century that the demand for Chinese labour on rubber plantations seriously affected traditional occupational patterns. By contrast, the Indian population grew more rapidly than the Chinese population in the period before 1914, an expansion which was in correlation with the development of rubber estates. The percentage increase between 1901 and 1911 was 195·4 in the Federated Malay States, compared with 43·7 per cent for the Chinese population[3]; but the structure of the two populations was very different. As a direct result of the opportunities existing on rubber estates for the employment of female labour, the ratio of females to males for the Indian population was, unlike the Chinese, lower in the towns than in the

---

[1] D. H. Grist, *An Outline of Malayan Agriculture* (1936), pp. 26-30.

[2] Wong Lin Ken, 'Western Enterprise and the Development of the Malayan Tin Industry to 1914', C. D. Cowan, *op. cit.*, pp. 127 *et seq.*; see especially T. E. Smith, 'Immigration and Permanent Settlement of Chinese and Indians in Malaya and the Future Growth of the Malay and the Chinese Communities', C. D. Cowan, *op. cit.*, p. 175.

[3] T. E. Smith, *op. cit.*, p. 175.

countryside.[1] Furthermore, because most of the Indian immigrants came to Malaya to work on rubber plantations (which were largely in the F.M.S.), some 60 per cent of the total Indian population lived in the Federated States, compared with a corresponding figure of 25 per cent for the Chinese. As a consequence, the number of Straits born Indians was low, something less than 30,000 in the whole of Malaya.[2]

During the ten years after 1911, there was a check on the volume of immigration into Malaya and a corresponding effect on the growth of alien population. In the first place, there was a decrease in the use of manual labour in the tin mines as a consequence of the introduction of machinery. The labour thus displaced tended to find alternative occupation in agriculture, in this case, in the newly planted rubber areas in Keddah and Johore.[3] In these areas, therefore, the Chinese took an increasing share in estate ownership and management. As their stake in land was augmented, they tended to become more settled and adopt Malaya as their natural homeland. The census report for 1921 confirmed this, 'the return to their native country is easier, quicker and less expensive for the Indians than for the Chinese', so stated the superintendent of the census, 'and political conditions in India and China may have encouraged the Indians to return and deterred the Chinese; but whatever may be the cause there can be no doubt that the idea of a settled Malayan born community is far nearer realisation in the case of the Chinese than of the Indians'.[4] Thus, resources were made available in the shape of external supplies of capital and labour and these, combined with an abundance of suitable land and congenial climatic conditions, turned Malaya into the world's most important producer of natural rubber.

It is not easy to assess in statistical terms the true impact of this product on Malaya's economy before 1914. What figures there are cannot be readily analysed in comparative terms and the obvious inaccuracy in some compilations renders conclusion impossible. After 1921, however, there is a better degree of standardisation and it is possible to make a more precise definition. The following

[1] *Ibid.*
[2] *Ibid.*, Holt MSS., R. D. Holt Diary and related papers on Chinese and Indian migrants, 1910-15.
[3] T. E. Smith, *op. cit.*, p. 175.
[4] Census Report for 1921, p. 98, quoted by T. E. Smith, *op. cit.*, p. 176.

conclusions are based on an examination of data as nearly accurate as qualification can obtain; at least the orders of magnitude are not unduly distorted.

From a survey of the official statistics, four principal points need to be mentioned. In the first place, although it is not easy to obtain a breakdown of capital holdings and ownership of rubber estates in the early years, there are precise records for the 1930's. By that date, of the total area under production in Malaya, British companies domiciled in the United Kingdom owned 1,139,000 acres in estates of over 100 acres, while the area owned locally amounted to 300,000 acres; other European capital owned 18,000 acres and American 33,000 acres. This gave a grand total of 1,490,000 acres, of which British capital represented approximately 75 per cent.[1] Against this must be set some 504,000 acres (or 26 per cent of the total area) owned by Asiatic capital. Of the holdings under 100 acres (principally native) there were 1,279,000 acres. Thus, for Malaya as a whole there were 3,273,000 acres of which about one-third was owned by British capital.[2] In aggregate Malaya's rubber producing area represented 38·8 per cent of the world total. By comparison, in the N.E.I., which accounted for 39 per cent of world acreage, native production was just over 50 per cent, Dutch capital controlled some 31 per cent and British capital about 12 per cent.[3]

In the second place, if a retrospective view is taken of the allocation of resources to south-east Asia for the purpose of rubber production, the rapidity with which this area dominated world supply is both remarkable and astonishing. In 1910, Malaya and the Netherlands East Indies exported only 9·5 per cent of total world exports; by 1920, their exports had increased to 73 per cent.[4] In the former year the bulk of the world's rubber supply had come from South America, Africa and Mexico. Thus, within the space of a decade, the supply position had been completely revolutionised, south-east Asia taking the predominant proportion. By translating these exports into shares of Malaya's total exports by value, we come to the third point of significance. In 1906, rubber exports

---

[1] G. Rae, 'Statistics of the Rubber Industry', *Journal Royal Statistical Society*, Vol. C.1, Part II, 1938, pp. 320 *et seq.*

[2] *Ibid.*, estimated from statistical evidence given by Rae.

[3] *Ibid.*

[4] *Ibid.*, calculated from data supplied by Rae.

accounted for only 3·7 per cent of total exports; by 1912, the share was 7·8 per cent, increasing to 31·8 per cent in 1920 and to 59·5 in 1925.[1] In short, the application of resources had not only shifted the balance of supply from one side of the world to the other, but the impact of the shift had altered the scope of Malaya's export trade and had, thereby, increased the flow of cash to her planters and to her native population. The benefits accruing to the indigenous Malays, though perhaps not so great as those to the Siamese rice growers, were nevertheless considerable in that they now had a cash crop which could be extremely profitable in time of boom and used as a source of income in time of depression.

The final point for consideration is that Malaya and other southeast Asian countries, by producing a commodity so greatly in demand from the manufacturing countries of the West, became inextricably linked with the cyclical pattern of the highly industrialised organisation of Western capitalism. Out of a total of 99,500 tons imported from all sources in 1910, the United States received 42,200 tons, the United Kingdom 20,500 tons and Germany 13,700 tons, these three countries accounting for just over three-quarters of total rubber imports.[2] By 1920, both demand and supply had immeasurably increased, the United States taking 249,500 tons, the United Kingdom 56,800 tons, Germany 12,600 tons and France 16,300 tons, the total share of these four countries being about 90 per cent of world imports, with the United States receiving 65 per cent.[3] The inference from this is obvious. With growing uncertainty and erratic fluctuations in world trade after 1921, coupled with the effects of world-wide depression during the early 1930's, the demand for primary products such as rubber tended to follow the same erratic pattern and finally to sink to unprecedented levels. Malayan production was not particularly sympathetic to widespread disturbance in world markets as supplies from native growers remained inelastic to price; nevertheless, exports were adversely affected with the result that stocks piled up and rubber prices dropped to rock bottom. In such conditions, only the larger estates had sufficient resources and the necessary drive to cut costs and survive. It is not within the brief of this volume to discuss the various control schemes which were instituted in an endeavour to meet and overcome problems of

[1] *Ibid.*   [2] *Ibid.*   [3] *Ibid.*

supply in relation to demand. All that need be said in conclusion is, that as far as Malaya's external trade was concerned, the impact of depression on an economy so closely-knit with Western enterprise and production was destructive in its intensity.

*

As in the case of rubber, the second staple in Malaya's export trade, namely tin, provides an excellent example of the relationship between developed and under-developed countries, the former requiring supplies of raw material and the latter becoming the source of provision. Historically, this relationship began in the early part of the nineteenth century when the chief demand for tin came from the production of tin-plate and alloys. By the 1860's, however, it was pressure from an increasing production in the tin-plate industry which stimulated the flow of capital into new tin mining in all parts of the world. In this context, the tin market was dominated by the British tin-plate industry until 1912, when it gave way to its American counterpart, developed by skilled British immigrants within the shelter of the McKinley tariff.

Britain's demand for tin beyond the limits of Cornish production stemmed from the abolition of the tin duties in 1853 as part of the general Gladstonian policy of liberalising trading relationships. The bulk of the newly imported tin came from the Straits Settlements mainly because of its excellent quality and comparatively low price. Apart from a short period between 1875 and 1884, when Straits tin had to meet competition from an Australian tin rush, the Malayan source of supply was the predominant one serving the European and British markets. In fact, the demand for tin from industrial countries produced a shift in the balance of distribution. Until about 1850, India and China absorbed a larger proportion of Malayan tin than Europe or the United States.[1] Thereafter the greater part of the supply flowed towards Europe, especially to London which, up to the outbreak of war in 1914, was the principal market and distribution centre for Straits tin.

Unlike the production of rubber, however, there was a limited move by British and European countries to make capital available for tin mining in Malaya. As a result, the early development of tin production in response to a growing world demand was left almost

[1] Wong Lin Ken, *op. cit.*, p. 130.

entirely to Chinese enterprise, labour and capital. There were
many reasons for this. In the first place, as a consequence of the
dissolution of the Malacca Sultanate, the political structure dis-
integrated; Malay society became effete and corrupt, there was no
controlling authority and armed bands terrorised the countryside.
Taxable revenues were diverted into the maintenance of 'warring'
overlordships and, consequently, there was little incentive to
produce more than the bare essentials for existence. The Malays
were primarily agriculturalists and were not interested in the more
highly labour-intensive occupation of tin mining. Whenever the
Malay chiefs wished to augment their revenues through the
exploitation of tin resources, they had, perforce, to import labour
and capital from the Straits Settlements. In the last resort, it was
only the Chinese who were willing to risk both their lives and their
capital in such hazardous enterprise. Thus it was that, by the
1870's, the Chinese held a dominant position in the tin industry.
The organisation of the Chinese labour supply was in the hands of
secret societies composed of two main groups who, in turn, waged
intensive warfare in an endeavour to control the labour market.[1]
The strife became so bitter and severe that the tin mining industry
itself was threatened with collapse, a state of affairs which was an
important cause of the extension of British control over Perak,
Selangor and Sungai Ujong in 1874. With the restoration of law
and order, resources flowed in and, by 1883, Malaya had become
the largest tin producing country in the world, the other tin
producing countries being Australia, Britain and the Netherlands
East Indies, in order of importance.[2]

It is, perhaps, of interest to conjecture why the extension of
British rule in Malaya did not bring with it a corresponding flow of
investment in tin production. In this lies the answer to the second
reason for the dominance of Chinese enterprise. It goes without
saying that political stability was a *sine qua non* for Western
investors before they would risk their capital; but when stable
conditions were effected after the extension of British rule, the
attractiveness of Malayan tin fields as a source for British capital
was not evident. British funds tended to flow into the new mines
then being opened up in Australia, so much so that Cornish miners

[1] *Ibid.*, p. 138, quoting Annual Reports from Selangor and Perak, 1884.
[2] *The International Tin Research and Development Council Statistical
Year Book*, 1937, *passim* for relevant figures.

were fearful lest the red-shirted diggers of the Antipodes should offer a far greater threat to their own security than the Chinese labourers in Perak. In fact, the first significant movement of European capital came not from Britain but from France; this was followed in 1882 by the foundation of the Hong Kong and Shanghai Tin Mining Co. Ltd., largely supported by Western merchants in Shanghai, with the object of mining tin in Perak.[1] This undertaking was joined in the following year by two Australian companies. Thus, the early initiative in capital formation was disparate and in no way tied to the London money market.

Meanwhile, however, the newly constituted British authority in Selangor had begun to offer concessions of land and, as an inducement to overseas investors, had reduced the duties on tin production. Some 3,800 acres had been granted by 1884, the majority of the holders being resident in Singapore. Among the latter was Jardine Matheson and Co., which advanced funds for mining enterprise in Selangor. The extent of the involvement increased and, in 1882, Jardines became possessed of the Rawang Tin Mining Co. that was managed by the Singapore agency house of Scott and Co., which in turn was linked with the principal European agency house, Messrs Hill and Rathbone, in the protected states.[2] This linkage of financial and other interests might well have formed the nucleus of Western tin mining enterprise in Perak and Selangor. Unfortunately, however, most of the companies floated at this time soon came to grief, the two chief causes of disaster being bad management and failure to control supplies of Chinese labour. Western companies were saddled with high fixed costs arising from heavy capital investment and large managerial staffs' salaries. They could not, therefore, compete with the low cost labour-intensive methods of the Chinese, who employed their resources in comparatively small units and paid their labourers in kind under the terms of a prevailing truck system. One further and perhaps curious fact helping to strengthen Chinese tin mining enterprise arose from the extension of British administration itself. As Dr Wong Lin Ken has shown, traffic in opium and rights in gambling were farmed out to Chinese capitalists and this provided them with alternative sources of revenue at times when tin prices

[1] Wong Lin Ken, *op. cit.*, p. 137.
[2] *Ibid.*, see also *Straits Times*, 3 April 1889.

were low.[1] Furthermore, there was little initiative directed towards the suppression of the secret societies controlling the supply of labour to the Chinese mines and preventing such labour from working for Western companies. The innumerable difficulties besetting the employment of Western capital in the early development of the Malayan tin industry were, therefore, derived from a wide range of causes. As a result, Chinese capital and labour dominated production within the limits of oriental tradition and custom. In fact, the few surviving Western companies, in the 1890's, operating on the west coast 'were working to a greater or lesser extent upon the Chinese tribute system whereby the Chinese labourers worked the land for their own profit subject to the payment of a certain percentage of the output to the companies'.[2] This wholly unsatisfactory state of affairs could not be long maintained in the face of a rapidly expanding world demand for tin. With the application of new technological ideas, with the introduction of hydraulic mining and with better systems of management, Western capital was induced to find employment in Malaya. Then, and only then, was the Chinese monopoly in tin mining broken by a new spirit of competitive enterprise and Western companies were able to obtain positions of economic importance in the peninsula.

*

The extension of hydraulic mining, first introduced in Perak by F. D. Osborne, manager of Leh Chin Mining Co., had two immediate effects. By the late 1890's, the new method had so effectively lightened the manual tasks involved in tin production that Indian and Malayan labour could be used in place of Chinese. The second effect was that hydraulic mining (which was superseded by the bucket dredge after 1912) involved the application of large blocks of capital within the framework of joint stock company organisation. Chinese capital was not available either in the requisite magnitude or in precise form or organisation to meet the challenge of Western technological development. As a result Chinese influence was weakened and a new balance of ownership began to appear. The whole process of Western technology in tin mining has, however, to be set against two further factors. The first was

[1] Wong Lin Ken, op. cit., p. 139.
[2] Ibid.

the changing structure of the capital market for such enterprise and the second was the expanding demand for tin and its corresponding influence on the price of the product.

Following the short-lived Pahang boom in the late 1880's, the interest of investors in Malayan tin production had dwindled to an almost complete indifference. This situation was changed by the revival of tin prices and, between 1896 and 1914, companies came into being to mine tin in Siam, Bolivia, Spain and Australia, but the main British promotional activity was directed to Cornwall, Nigeria and Malaya.[1] Since 1900, there had been a rapidly increasing flow of investment into Malaya culminating in a boom in 1907, when the shares of tin mining companies reached record heights. Such investment was ultimately controlled by two organisations, the Gopeng Consolidated Tin Co. Ltd. and the Redruth Mining Exchange; the former was a successful Malayan company, the latter had been created to accommodate broker and dealer in mining shares. By means of a series of interlocking directorships, states Dr Wong Lin Ken, these two constituents 'not only controlled a very large number of hydraulic and other mining companies in Malaya but also numerous mines in Cornwall'.[2] This was a mutually convenient association because, since the beginning of the century, the relatively high cost production in Cornwall had found increasing difficulty in competing with lower cost tin from other parts of the world. Cornish capital and mining skill had, therefore, to seek employment elsewhere as local mines closed down. Malaya was a natural outlet for Cornish mining interests. The net result of this organisational pattern was that British control of Malayan tin production increased from 10 to 15 per cent in 1906 to 26 per cent in 1914.[3]

The final question to be posed is why this successful extension of Western enterprise occurred. A fact of major importance in this process was that the Chinese had worked all the available tin fields and it was not until the end of the nineteenth century that the mining community accepted the fact that there was no likelihood of new fields being discovered. This meant that existing sites had to be reworked with a capital-intensive rather than a labour-intensive form of organisation. As we have already stated, the

---

[1] *Reports of International Tin Council*, respective tables, 1890-1914.
[2] Wong Lin Ken, *op. cit.*, p. 145.
[3] *Ibid.*; *Reports of International Tin Council*, 1890-1914.

Chinese were not conversant with, nor desirous of entering into, Western forms of company finance; consequently, their position as controllers of capital declined in relative terms. Coupled with this was their further disadvantage of not having the engineering skill or the managerial experience to cope with the new situation. Finally, as a direct result of government action, the Chinese monopoly of the labour supply, and their control over land, was broken. The secret societies and the revenue farms were suppressed and Chinese labour became free to offer its services to more lucrative forms of employment in other sections of the economy.

Parallel with this change, Western mining interests gained a much greater influence in Malayan affairs with the establishment of a Federal Council for the Malay States in 1909. Besides giving Western interests a voice in the policy controlling the mining industry, the government strengthened the power of Western enterprise through changes in land policy. The Perak government (and later, the governments of other states) resumed control of all unused land formerly granted to Chinese or Malays for develop-ment, and reallocated it as concessions to Western mining com-panies who had 'sufficient capital to work with labour saving appliances'.[1] In short, the Chinese had lost their once complete control over the factors of production and their decline in effective-ness enabled Western capital to enter the mining industry under conditions of greater freedom. In so doing, they transformed production by the application of new techniques and greatly increased output so that tin came only second to rubber in importance in Malaya's overseas trade.

*

We must now attempt a final assessment of the importance of tin in Malaya's total economic structure. Between 1851 and 1860, Malaya's average annual production of tin amounted to approxi-mately 34 per cent of the world total.[2] This share remained constant until the 1870's when it fell to less than 20 per cent, reflecting the impact of Australian tin on the world market. By

---

[1] Annual Reports F.M.S. 1910, p. 7; 1913, p. 21; also C. G. W. Lock, *Mining in Malaya for Gold and Tin* (1907), pp. 173 *et seq.*
[2] International Tin Study Group, *Statistical Year Book*, 1954, pp. 15-16; *Statistical Supplement*, 1955, p. 10; also selected *Reports of International Tin Council.*

K

1890, however, Malaya's share had risen to 37 per cent, and by 1900, to well over half of the world total.[1] In the ten years before the First World War, the share fluctuated within the narrow limits of 41 to 45 per cent, decreasing to 35 per cent after that war had ended. Of this total production from Malaya, Chinese ownership was responsible for 78 per cent in 1910; thereafter, for the reasons already given, the percentage share of Chinese-mined tin fell consistently so that, by the 1930's, it amounted to less than 30 per cent.[2]

If one turns to an examination of the relationship between Malaya's export of tin and total world consumption, the position was rather less stable. Between 1900 and 1906, world absorption ranged between 100,000 tons and 105,000 tons; there was a fall in the year of depression, 1908, to the 1900 level but, between 1910 and 1913, the general improvement in economic activity caused a corresponding demand for tin and absorption rose from 117,000 tons to 127,000 tons.[3] The coming of war disorganised the tin market and it was not until 1920 (leaving aside the freak year of 1917) that the pre-war trend was resumed. The percentage share of Malaya's supply was not greatly different from the figures already cited for its share of total world production as, in the years up to 1920, production was roughly equivalent to export. The significance of tin exports from Malaya can be better assessed in relation to its total exports. In 1906, exports of tin by value amounted to 30 per cent of Malaya's total export trade; this percentage had not changed by 1912, but by 1920 the share had fallen to about 14 per cent.[4] In this latter year, exports of tin and rubber amounted to nearly one-half of Malaya's total exports by value, a proportion which increased to well over 70 per cent by the 1930's. These two products were, therefore, the sustainers of the economy with much the same degree of importance as rice for that of Siam. In Malaya's case, however, the dependence on two products was a source of weakness; as industrial products they were tied to the fluctuating activity of Western industrial production. When severe

[1] International Tin Study Group, *Statistical Year Book*, 1954, pp. 15-16; *Statistical Supplement*, 1955, p. 10; also selected *Reports of International Tin Council*.
[2] Wong Lin Ken, *op. cit.*, p. 151; also L. L. Fermor, *Report upon the Mining Industry of Malaya* (1939), p. 64.
[3] I.T.C. Reports, selected tables for exports, 1900-1914.
[4] *Straits Settlements, Imports and Exports 1906, 1912 and 1920.*

depression led to a sharp fall in demand, as in the early 1930's, Malaya's export trade was cut by nearly 70 per cent. As in the case of rubber, it became necessary for tin production to be put under regulation by international agreement with the object of ironing out the ill effects of cyclical patterns in the supply of, and the demand for, this product.

One reads much about the impact of Western enterprise on the economic development of south-east Asia. The above examination of three major products sustaining the economies of Siam and Malaya highlights the versatility of Chinese rather than of Western entrepreneurship in the period before 1914. Because of the autarchic nature of the Siamese state, the government maintained production in the hands of its own population; but the industrial and service sides of the economy and about half the shipping using the ports were in Chinese hands. In Malaya the Chinese had a virtual monopoly over the factors of production of tin and some considerable interests through Singapore merchant houses in the supply of rubber. It was only when pressure of increasing demand necessitated the employment of more capital-intensive forms of productive organisation, within the safeguard of increasing government control, that Western influence assumed a dominant role. Such a change, however, has to be set within the framework of a new context, a context in which Far Eastern countries were ceasing to be the appendage of Western industrial society and becoming components of a new Pacific economy. In this process the technological developments which transformed the steamship into a more efficient ocean carrier played their part. The inauguration of new shipping routes across the Pacific, linking China and Japan with west coast ports in the United States and Canada, and linking Singapore and Yokohama with Brisbane, Perth, Melbourne and Sydney in Australia, gave a new perspective to an expanding world trade. The Pacific shores of three continents were infused with the expansive commercial dynamism of a new age and in this, as we shall see in the following chapter, Japan, rather than China, became the source of new energy and enterprise.

CHAPTER VII

Japan and the Outside World, 1860-1914

THE development and growth of the Japanese economy, after the Meiji restoration in 1868, has been likened to a wild bird flying from an opened cage. However one may describe it, there is little doubt that the phenomenon of Japan's persistent efforts to attain the status of a modern industrial nation is of great interest to the economic historian, partly because it provides him with a model for analysis and partly because it exhibits patterns of growth amenable to theoretical interpretation. Much has already been written on the history and economic development of Japan during the past century. For our purpose, however, we propose to isolate certain factors stimulating growth with special reference to the effect upon, and the part played by, overseas trade in the period before 1914. Within the limit of this chronology, it must be emphasised that we are investigating merely the first part of a long-term process, and that the trends examined are but preliminary to a continuous and much more dynamic development taking place today.

In purely historical terms, the first difficulty which the new régime had to solve was that concerned with the suppression of a land-owning feudal autonomy. This was effected in two ways: first, by the taking over of fiefs and the paying of compensation to the old Samurai land-holding families; and secondly, by direct military action in 1877, when civil war broke out as a direct result of the discontent with the new order engendered in a remnant of the feudal aristocracy. This action was preparatory to the establishment of a large-scale industrial organisation within the sponsorship of a new system of central and local government administration. It is true that, in the last years of the Tokugawa Shogunate both local and central governments had helped in the creation of industries modelled on those of Western nations; but the Meiji government continued to pursue this objective with the express purpose of freeing Japan from industrial domination by the West. The state naturally had to take the lead in this process. Nevertheless, while many industrial enterprises were established by the state, it did not retain the ownership or administration of them once they were going concerns. There is still much controversy about the relative importance of the various factors determining Japan's emergence as an industrial nation. While it is neither relevant in this present context nor possible to enter into the detail of such controversy, certain salient features must be emphasised as background information to this narrative.

The first and most obvious point to make is that the efforts of Western powers to force Japan to open its ports to shipping and commerce with the rest of the world were just as much an important determinant of the pattern of Japan's development after 1870 as they were of China's after 1840. According to Marius Jansen, 'the outstanding intellectual and political experience in the formative years of the Restoration activists was the discovery that their society was incapable of successful resistance to the western threat'.[1] Even before the overthrow of the Tokugawa Shogunate, changes had been taking place in the structure of Japanese society, making expansion possible once the new régime had been established. The coalescing of political groups with widely differing aims and social status was, in brief, a determinant of a new outlook; for it was generally assumed that the only way to withstand the pressure of Western commercial and industrial domination was to adopt as many Western ideas and techniques 'as seemed essential to the creation of a society and an economy which would be, at one and the same time, acceptable in the international community'.[2] The sense of urgency which these ideas instilled necessitated the acceptance of economic policies which, in Seymour Broadbridge's view, emphasised the importance of a dual industrial structure.[3]

---

[1] Marius B. Jansen, *Sakamoto Ryoma and the Meiji Restoration* (1961), p. 347.
[2] Seymour Broadbridge, *Industrial Dualism in Japan* (1966), p. 9.
[3] *Ibid.*

One central point of controversy has been that concerned with the dating of Japan's turning point from an agricultural into an industrial economy. Some Japanese economists, including Professor K. Ohkawa, have put such a turning point after the end of the Second World War. This view is also supported by Ryoshin Minami who, in a sophisticated statistical analysis, attempted to discover the date at which Japan ceased to have available unlimited supplies of labour.[1] He argued that a necessary condition for an unlimited supply of labour in the subsistence sector of the economy was for the marginal productivity of labour to be smaller than the subsistence wage rate. A sustained increase in the former would indicate that a turning point had been reached. On this assumption Minami's statistical evidence placed the turning point some time in the late 1950's.[2] If one takes the long-term view of trends in the Japanese economy over the past one hundred years, there may be some grounds (in a Schumpeterian sense) for an acceptance of this finding; but Minami included both agriculture and small handcraft industry as constituents of the subsistence sector—a fact which, one must conclude, gave a false weighting to his figures for the marginal productivity of labour. As we shall see, handcraft industry formed a basic element in Japan's dual industrial system and the expansion of this particular sector in conjunction with other dynamic phenomena may help in explaining and in confirming a much earlier date for Japan's industrial turning point, a date which, according to J. C. H. Fie and G. Ranis, occurred before the end of the First World War.[3]

*

In a consideration of Japan's industrial structure (with special reference to industrial dualism) one can, perhaps, accept Seymour Broadbridge's five criteria as important in their influence upon development. First, there was the direct effect of government policy leading to the rise of the *Zaibatsu*; secondly, there was the stimulation of capital resources through the rise of the capital and money markets; thirdly, there was a dependence on imported

---

[1] Ryoshin Minami, 'The Turning Point in the Japanese Economy', *Quarterly Journal of Economics*, Vol. LXXXII, Feb. 1968, No. 1, pp. 380-402.

[2] *Ibid.*, pp. 393 *et seq.*

[3] J. C. H. Fie and G. Ranis, *Development of the Labor Surplus Economy: Theory and Policy* (1964), p. 263.

technology and techniques; fourthly, one has to take account of the consumption and saving habits of the Japanese population; finally, consideration must be given to the structure of the labour market and to the pattern of agricultural development. All these factors were effective in their impact upon the definition of Japan's total industrial growth and, through this growth, ultimately on the pattern of Japan's overseas trade.

One has to begin with the bare fact that, in 1870, Japan had virtually no heavy industry. For more than a decade thereafter, the country was without a mercantile marine and its external trade was largely in the hands of British, American and French merchants and shipping companies. The Japanese possessed no shipbuilding industry capable of supporting an independent shipping service, no iron and steel industry to supply yards and no machine industry to establish plants. The government had, perforce, to act as initiator and promotor of industrial effort; but the directive was limited in scope and always designed in favour of enterprise stemming from private sources. Thus, the intervention of the state in the direction of economic affairs did not extend to the control of new enterprises once they had become established. The chief aim of the government was to encourage private entrepreneurship in the achievement of objectives and, to this end, the great *Zaibatsu* were offered every facility. Special banks were created to supply capital and the gold standard was adopted with the help of the large indemnity from China after Japan's victory in the Sino-Japanese War. Laws were made to stimulate the shipping and shipbuilding industries as it was decided to found the state-owned Yawata Iron Works. By 1914, Japan, though still far from obtaining economic independence in strategic industries, had made substantial progress. In 1913, domestic production of merchant ships equalled imports and the Yawata Iron Works was supplying about one-quarter of the shipbuilding industry's requirements.[1] This output, though perhaps not impressive by Western standards, has to be set against the fact that, in 1900, some 99 per cent of Japan's steel requirements had to be imported. Such effort was generally successful in producing harmonious relationships between the various sections of

[1] Seymour Broadbridge, *op. cit.*, p. 10, quoting Echigo Kazunori, *Nihon zosen kogyo-ron* (An Essay on the Japanese Shipbuilding Industry) (1956), pp. 32-3.

the community competing for the factors of production and, as a consequence, the resources of the nation were developed with discipline and restraint. Thus far, the new leadership in Japan had set the objectives and had drawn the guide lines; the result was in no sense comparable with the modern interpretation of a planned economy. Nevertheless, the process of building up a modern state presented problems which only a centralised system of administration could solve and this fact, in turn, led to an extension of bureaucracy.

In these various ways the impact of the state had a two-fold effect, upon output and investment. In his analysis of the period 1887 to 1940, Professor Rosovsky estimated that, throughout the entire fifty-three years, the government was the largest and most important investor in the economy, its share of capital formation never averaging less than 40 per cent and it was only very rarely as low as that.[1] In addition, government sales of plant (chiefly influenced by the need to obtain funds), government subsidies and contracts all helped in concentrating the development of transport and heavy industry in the hands of a small group of families. Professor Tsuchiya has pointed out that, while it would be a mistake to identify the history of political merchants having close links with factions within the government with the history of particular *Zaibatsu*, there is little doubt that there were close ties between them.[2] In fact, most of the *Zaibatsu* were founded by men who had close connections with the *Hanbatsu* or clansmen of the early Meiji period. They profited greatly from government contracts and from the government enterprises which were sold off in the 1880's. As a further stimulus to development, the *Zaibatsu* accumulated resources as a direct result of military and naval programmes, emanating from the demands arising from the Sino-Japanese War. The significant growth of heavy industry, however, did not take place until the period 1890 to 1910. Whatever the rate of progress may have been and whatever the stimuli to such progress, there can be little doubt about that of the role of the state in various branches of industrial activity. In quantitative terms, Rosovsky's analysis of government investment and military

[1] H. Rosovsky, *Capital Formation in Japan 1868-1940* (1961), p. 23.
[2] Takao Tsuchiya, *Nihon keizai-shi* (An Economic History of Japan) (1963), pp. 142 *et seq.*; also Nobuo Noda, 'Some Comments on the History of Zaibatsu', *Japan Business History Review*, Vol. 5, Oct. 1970, No. 1, pp. 94-113.

JAPAN AND THE OUTSIDE WORLD 141

demands offers convincing evidence of the influence of the state on the pattern of growth and change in Japan's economic development.

Parallel with the upsurge of industrial production was the need for resources. Here again, the government acted as initiator by mobilising capital for industrial needs. Surpluses from agriculture and taxes on consumers were directed into the new sectors. Joint stock banks became the source of funds for industrial development and special banks were created (such as the Hypothec and the Industrial Bank of Japan) to stimulate economic growth. As a result, the *Zaibatsu* were given additional strength since, as well as controlling the major commercial banks, they were able to exercise great influence in the specialised financial institutions. As a corollary, the state was enabled to exercise a control over the institutions through which capital was supplied, in addition to its function as an initiator in promoting the sources of finance. As early as 1869, exchange companies had been set up within the overall control of the Trade Bureau, to perform some of the functions of joint stock banks. Through their collaboration with the new trading companies it was hoped that stimulation would be given to both domestic and foreign trade. Thus, from the start, there was an alliance between government and business interests in the promotion of a banking system designed to support national aims and achieve national objectives. Within this framework, the government not only made laws providing for a commercial banking system, but implemented the structure through the creation of the Bank of Japan, the Yokohama Specie Bank and the Hypothec Bank of Japan. By 1902, there were also in operation some forty-six prefectural industrial and agricultural banks as well as the Post Office Savings Bank and the Industrial Bank of Japan. Such special institutions were instrumental in helping to narrow the gap between the supply of and the demand for capital; they dealt in negotiable securities and sustained real values by increasing confidence in them and by facilitating their circulation, thereby increasing the supply of capital. In particular, the role of the Hypothec Bank was important, in that it acted as a ready source of finance both to agriculture and to industry by assuming the status of a central bank for the prefectural banks. In 1911, its debenture issues formed 53 per cent of all bank debentures.[1]

---

[1] *Banking in Modern Japan* (1967), Research Division, Fuji Bank Ltd., p. 47; also Seymour Broadbridge, *op. cit.*, p. 15.

By the end of the first decade of the twentieth century, the concentration of financial resources, through the conjunction of the government, the banks and a few great industrial concerns, had virtually created an industrial revolution comparable with that which had occurred in Britain in the latter half of the eighteenth century. The foundations of the shipbuilding, heavy engineering, iron and steel, electrical power, electrical equipment and modern textile industries had been laid. A railway system was in course of construction and naval and military forces had been used to extend Japan's territorial boundaries with the object of securing control over supplies of raw materials. Above all, this activity was dependent upon imported technology, a fact which had a direct bearing on the scope and pattern of Japan's overseas trade. With reference to Japan's balance of payments position, it is reasonably clear that; in the first thirteen years after the Restoration, the lack of tariff autonomy and the widening of the domestic market had strongly divergent effects. Industries with comparative advantages were stimulated, while others were hard hit. Raw silk and tea expanded at the expense of those which had been given the previous protection of feudal autonomy. From 1868 to 1881 there was an aggregate adverse trade balance of 78 million yen. The assets in the form of gold and silver which had accumulated from the feudal period had, therefore, to be used to finance trade and other deficits. Though such means were capable of sustaining development until 1880, the intensification of inflation after 1877 and the exhaustion of the stock of gold and silver, caused by a persistent import surplus, led to the need for a strong deflationary policy.

Under crisis conditions, the finance minister, Matsukata, instituted drastic measures designed to redress the adverse trends in the economy. Taxes were raised, government properties were sold off, national bank note issues were halted and redeemed and the budget was balanced. The resulting fall in prices bore directly upon the real incomes of landlords and peasant proprietors as well as upon the financial structures of the less efficiently managed industrial concerns. Consequently, there was a considerable concentration of enterprise and the way was cleared for the *Zaibatsu* to assume a more active role in the economy. In the realm of foreign trade, this deflationary policy had an immediate effect. Imports fell from 36·6 million yen in 1880 to 29·4 million yen in 1885, while exports rose from 28·4 million yen to 37·1 million yen in the corresponding years. As Miyohei Shinohara has shown, the surpluses thus created gave a firm foundation for future Japanese industrial and commercial expansion though, in subsequent years, particularly after 1896, the recurring trade deficits were largely offset by the reparations received from China.[1] In short, political, economic and military actions led Japan towards its chosen goal; in this achievement one must also give due emphasis to the Japanese people themselves, their willingness to make sacrifices and their determination to make Japan a powerful modern nation. One means to this end lay in the creation of a flourishing overseas trade. We now propose, therefore, to examine the changing structure of this trade against the background of the more important influences directing its progress during the years before 1914.

*

The diversion of economic activity from the production of consumer goods to that of capital goods was, as we have seen, an essential objective in Japan's endeavour to create an industrial state. The translation of policy into effectual reality was achieved through the use of a variety of expedients. Funds raised by taxation were diverted by the government into the creation of new industries, or were used for the subsidisation of existing enterprises. In addition, the state used its credit to raise loans at home and abroad, loans which were used to finance heavy industry. As further inducements were required, cheap credit facilities were initiated to encourage investment. Thus, by subsidies, protective duties (once the unequal treaty provisions had lapsed) and by forming a taxation system so that it bore lightly on the profit-earner, necessary stimuli were administered. The whole policy was given greater freedom following Japan's successful military and naval victories in the Sino-Japanese and Russo-Japanese Wars. The consequent rise in political prestige enabled the country to acquire fiscal autonomy after the first war and power to borrow abroad at cheap rates after the second. Against such a background, it is not surprising that the decade from 1904 to 1914 should have witnessed a remarkable expansion of Japan's economic power.

---

[1] Miyohei Shinohara, 'Economic Development and Foreign Trade in Pre-war Japan', C. D. Cowan, *The Economic Development of China and Japan* (1964), p. 229.

Nevertheless, the securing of economic objectives was not solely the aim of the Japanese government during these years. It was also vitally concerned with the attainment of political security. For this reason Japan fought against China and Russia; for this same reason it had become interested, after 1895, in the development of resources in Formosa and, after 1905, in colonial expansion in Korea. These were necessary steps in the pursuance of a policy designed to give control over supplies of raw materials which were lacking, raw materials that were considered vital to political security. Though the development of rice in Korea and sugar in Formosa was begun as a mark of colonial stewardship, the productive capacity of these areas was directed in later years to the supplementing of local supplies which were becoming inadequate to meet the needs of a population expanding at the rate of approximately 10 million each succeeding decade. Economic penetration into Asia was undertaken for the same political motive. The production of iron and coal in Manchuria and in the Yangtse Valley was part of a conscious endeavour to render Japan, which lacked coking fuel, independent of foreign metallurgical industry—a policy which was also fortified by the establishment of the government's iron and steel works at Yawata.

These political objectives were realised only at considerable cost to the nation as a whole. Capital was diverted into enterprises which, in normal circumstances, would not have attracted investment and for which, in many cases, there was little economic justification. The development of the Formosan sugar industry, for example, absorbed much capital in an undertaking which could never have grown to substantial proportions without official subsidies and preferential treatment in the home market. Such schemes placed strains upon state finances; the additional and heavy taxation, which had been imposed at the time of the Russo-Japanese War, was maintained and large loans were raised at home and abroad to finance ventures which were as much political as economic in origin. As a result, Japan's national debt (excluding railway and iron foundry debts) rose from 445 million yen in 1903 to well over 2,000 million yen by 1912, nearly three-quarters of the latter amount consisting of foreign debt.[1] Though this situation was disquieting, there is little doubt that, by such means, the

[1] G. C. Allen, *Japan the Hungry Guest* (1938), p. 118; H. G. Moulton, *Japan*, p. 588.

industrial capacity of the nation had been raised to a level which it could not have attained in the space of time under a *laissez-faire* régime. The real danger lay in the fact that rapid development had been encouraged by government assistance, and instability occurred, or was bound to occur, should the state be unable to continue its bounties. The relevant point is that Japan's capacity for doing this was weakened through the pursuit of non-economic activities.

There were, however, countervailing benefits deriving from the structure and scope of foreign trade. This theme is of particular interest within the context of this volume and it is, therefore, proposed to devote the remainder of this chapter to an examination of the various factors making up and determining the levels of such trade. As volumes expanded, the more significant aspects were the need for the importation of technical equipment and know-how, the effort to achieve import substitution in order to offset the effect of massive adverse trade balances, the importance of handcraft products and the proportionate share of such trades taken by foreign countries. All these factors, once considered, might supply the answer to the question concerning the nature and the extent of Western influence in Japan's commercial re-volution.

*

Two important factors in Japan's external trade relationships were the initial complication of a chaotic currency system and the influence of unequal treaties imposed by Western governments. We shall deal later with the attempt to establish a stable medium of exchange and incidentally with the impact of Treaty rights and obligations. It is sufficient to state here that the Treaties of 1858 deprived Japan of tariff autonomy and that the Treaties of 1866 fixed most duties unilaterally at the low rate of 5 per cent *ad valorem*.[1] These rates persisted virtually until 1911 when there was a general tariff revision following the recovery of autonomy in 1899. An important consequence of these low duties was that Japan was forced to participate in an international division of labour devoid of any shelter from protective legislation. The Japanese had, therefore, to specialise in productive activity which gave them the best comparative advantage.

In the period immediately preceding the Restoration, Yokohama

[1] Miyohei Shinohara, *op. cit.*, p. 225.

handled about 80 per cent of the total trade of Japan and, after 1860, this trade grew rapidly at about 15 per cent per annum. This expansion was achieved despite the Shogunate's policy of discouraging exports, a policy which was based on the belief that exports would decrease the total quantity of commodities available for home consumption and thus cause inflation. Exports consisted of such semi-manufactured products as silk and tea which, taken together, accounted for approximately 80 per cent of the total export trade.[1] Silk, tea and rice comprised nearly two-thirds of Japan's export trade in the 1880's but by the mid-90's raw silk had increased its share while that of tea and rice had declined. Nevertheless, these three items in Japan's export list amounted to some three-fifths of the total. By 1900 there was a change in the structure of the trade, the effect of industrialisation making itself felt: cotton yarn and piece-goods and silk fabrics then accounted for about 22 per cent of the total with a consequent diminution in the share of the older type of exports.[2] On the import side there was an initial demand for machinery, iron and steel products and raw materials. At a later stage, however, the biggest increase occurred in raw materials, especially in the supply of raw cotton to feed Japan's expanding cotton textile industry. Much the same trend is observed in the supply of woollen manufactures. In 1867 imports of woollen textiles accounted for 22 per cent of total imports but there was, thereafter, a decreasing dependence upon foreign manufactured supplies as Japan itself took up the production of woollen fabrics.

The background to the changes in the structure of Japan's trade as a whole was formed by the fact that the Meiji government had to depend for most of its revenue on the issue of inconvertible paper money and the land tax, with no protective duties to shelter its infant industries. Its industrial programme had, therefore, to be sponsored against a flood of imported manufactured goods, mostly cotton and woollen textiles, with the result that sizeable import deficits persisted. There was, in such circumstances, an impetus towards import substitution though not all government enterprise was started with this end in view. It is evident, however,

---

[1] Masao Baba and Masahiro Tatemoto, 'Foreign Trade and Economic Growth in Japan, 1858-1937', L. Klein and K. Ohkawa, *Economic Growth, The Japanese Experience since the Meiji Era*, p. 166.

[2] Miyohei Shinohara, *op. cit.*, pp. 222 *et seq.*

that the government's investments and loans in cotton spinning, silk reeling and other consumer goods industries were made with the objective of curtailing a heavy dependence on imported manufactured goods. There was also the parallel benefit in the prevention of a gold and silver drain by replacing imports with home manufactured goods, and by stimulating the export of traditional and semi-manufactured products. For the largest imported item, cotton textiles, import substitution was rapidly advanced by establishing cotton factories under the supervision of British firms and by selling government imported spinning machinery to ten private enterprises over a period of ten years.[1] In addition, government loans on favourable terms were made to importers of spinning machinery between 1878 and 1884. In the case of woollen textiles, import substitution was promoted by the establishment in 1876 of a mill using German technology for the purpose of providing army and navy uniforms. This was the beginning of industrial production in this product, though expansion was not so successful as in the case of cotton textiles. Machinery for making glass and cement was also imported to produce these commodities at home and resulted in the cutting down of imports.

On the other side of the coin there were equally persistent efforts designed to stimulate exports, particularly of traditional and semi-manufactured products. Two model silk-reeling factories, based on French technology, were built in 1871 and 1874; these factories were largely used as training schools for the purpose of instructing Japanese labour in the mechanics of a Western factory system as well as for raising productivity in an industry which for centuries had been subject to hand processes. It is difficult to assess the effectiveness of this venture as these assets were disposed of after 1883 at very low prices compared with their original cost. As a state enterprise it was not a financial success but, in common with many other such enterprises, government assistance had laid the foundations for the acquirement of new skills and technical efficiency. As Lockwood wrote, 'the State shouldered the early risks, reconnoitred the path of technical advance and patronised many private ventures which followed on its heels'.[2] The Osaka Spinning Co. was started after 1883 without

[1] *Ibid.*, p. 232.
[2] W. W. Lockwood, *Economic Development of Japan, Growth and Structural Change, 1868-1938* (1955), p. 507.

any government aid, and the following decade saw a rapid expansion in the establishment of private spinning companies. In 1885, the domestic production of cotton cloth exceeded its import and, by 1910, exports exceeded imports. In the case of cotton yarn, the first real achievement was in 1890 when domestic production exceeded imports; the second was in 1897 when exports exceeded imports.[1]

At this point it is, perhaps, legitimate to inquire into the part played by the export of traditional and semi-manufactured goods in the process of Japan's economic growth. The short answer is that they were of considerable importance and quickly found a rapidly growing market. They succeeded in helping to finance the import of manufactured consumer goods until Japan's own industrial production had developed. They also helped in financing imports of capital goods which were used in the process of industrialisation. In other words, traditional semi-manufactured exports contributed greatly to the promotion of infant industries and were, therefore, of strategic importance in this phase of growth. An alternative answer, based on an analysis of trends in Japan's overseas trade, emphasises the economy's inherent weakness as well as potential strength. To obtain a wider understanding of the function of overseas trade in Japan's expanding economy and before conclusions can be drawn from the official trade statistics, certain fundamental facts have to be established. In the first place, it must be made clear that there is a considerable problem in arriving at a workable valuation of imports as given in official trade statistics. Before 1887, imports were valued by the prices in the exporting countries and converted into yen. Silver dollars or yen were, however, used in international transactions and, in this sense, it can be claimed that Japan was on a bi-metallic standard. After 1873, when Germany and other Western countries changed to the gold standard, silver currencies including the yen continued to depreciate against gold currencies. In the second place, therefore, official statistics need to be corrected in terms of gold yen from gold standard countries in order that discrepancies caused by the depreciation of the silver yen may be taken into account. For the purpose of our argument, we have used the corrected figures, accepted by Lawrence Klein and Kazsuhi

[1] Masao Baba and Masahiro Tatemoto, *op. cit.*, p. 172.

Ohkawa, from the statistical tables in the book which they edited on Japan's economic growth.[1]

If we first examine changes in the volume of Japan's overseas trade, the conclusion must be that there was continuous and rapid development throughout the whole period from 1870 to 1914. The indices (1913=100) show that export volumes doubled between 1873 and 1882 and doubled again in the next decade. Between 1893 and 1900, there was a slackening in momentum caused partly by adverse trends in world trade until 1896 and by the growing effectiveness of Japan's policy of import substitution. After 1902, despite a fairly close correlation with trends in world trade until 1909, there was a resumption of expansion and a virtual redoubling of export volumes in the decade 1903 to 1913.[2] The indices for import volumes show a rather different pattern of growth and time sequence. There was a slower rise until 1886 followed by a rapid rise to 1980, four years in which import volumes doubled. Between 1890 and 1895, there was a levelling off comparable with that in the export trade. By 1902 volumes had doubled and, in the following decade to 1913 (in line with exports), had doubled once again.[3]

Translating these volumes into corrected values the picture assumes a rather different aspect. Using corrected figures for imports before 1887 so that the depreciation in silver may be offset, there does not appear to have been such a large export surplus as is shown in official statistics. In the period between 1882 and 1896, however, there were favourable trade balances in each year apart from 1887 (when there was a very small adverse balance), 1890 (which was a panic year), 1894 (which saw the start of the Sino-Japanese War) and 1896.[4] These favourable balances were due partly to currency stabilisation, to import substitution and to the stimulation of exports of traditional products. By fitting the import and export functions to the data from 1879 to 1896 it is asserted that, 'although the estimated price elasticity of exports has a wrong sign, the estimated world trade elasticity of demand for exports is very high at 2·9'.[5] This was greater than the income elasticity of demand for imports. If this is a correct assessment, it

[1] *Ibid.*, p. 167, Table 6-2.
[2] *Ibid.*, p. 176, Table 6-6, Volume index of Exports.
[3] *Ibid.*
[4] *Ibid.*, p. 167, Table 6-2.
[5] *Ibid.*, p. 174.

L

means that the export demand for Japanese traditional semi-manufactured products was very elastic and accordingly contributed to export expansion. As we have seen, exports grew hand in hand with imports and had a balancing effect. From this it is reasonable to conclude that exports did not have a dominating influence on economic growth in Japan, though their rate of expansion was an important contributory cause. In such a context, one cannot ignore the effect of reparations received from China following the Sino-Japanese War. The equivalent of some 365 million yen was received between 1895 and 1898 (compared with the war expenditure of 200 million yen), and was a considerable injection into the Japanese economy at that time. In fact, it was comparable with import deficits during the period from 1894 to 1903, i.e. 354 million yen.[1] Such resources provided a well-timed stimulus for the seven-year government programme of expansion in both the state and private sectors of the economy. This programme included re-equipment for the army and navy, the building of railways, the foundation of universities, the establishment of banks and the inception of the Yawata Steel Mills. Of all the benefits derived from reparations, however, perhaps the greatest was that they enabled Japan to change over to the gold standard in 1897, the year in which Japan's exports of cotton yarn exceeded the import of the same commodity. For these and other reasons the year 1897 might well be regarded as a turning point in the country's economic development. Thereafter, in terms of growth, the percentage contribution of exports to the growth in G.N.P. was more significant. If one takes the ratio of the increase in exports (at 1913 prices) to the increases in real G.N.P. (in 1913 price), there was a sharp change in the role played by exports in the process of economic growth. A comparison of three successive periods will be sufficient for our purpose. Comparing the quinquennium 1876-80 with that from 1894-98 the contribution was 8 per cent; from 1895-99 to 1911-15 it was 29 per cent and from 1921-25 to 1934-38 it was 39 per cent.[2]

We must now turn to a more general examination of the effects of Japan's overseas trade. Having isolated some of the sources of strength, it is necessary to stress points of weakness. By 1914, Japanese annual overseas payments had not only become burden-

[1] Miyohei Shinohara, op. cit., p. 229.
[2] Masao Baba and Masahiro Tatemoto, op. cit., p. 177, Table 6-7.

some but highly inelastic. The somewhat intractable nature of these difficulties was caused partly by the necessity to pay interest on large foreign loans, partly by the continuous drain for naval and military expenditure at home and abroad, and more especially by the imports of equipment needed for industrial development. By contrast, the export trade, though increasing in volume, was liable to extreme fluctuations. It was, as we have seen, highly specialised, raw silk, silk fabrics and cotton goods accounting for some 55 per cent of the total by 1913.[1] To add to the uncertainties besetting this trade, the outlets were confined to two main markets, China and the United States, cotton goods being chiefly exported to the former and raw silk and silk fabrics to the latter. Some 64 per cent of all Japan's exports went to these two countries before the First World War.[2] The vulnerability of so narrowly based a trade is obvious, especially when it is realised that exports of raw silk were highly sensitive to fluctuating fortunes in the United States' economy. In relative terms, therefore, while Japan's annual payments were fixed, its trade receipts were liable to extreme fluctuation. This single fact was responsible for periodic conditions of strain, a state of affairs not easily resolved as Japan's central bank was rarely in a position to attract short term funds. To some extent Japan's acceptance of the gold standard led to a mitigation of these difficulties as large foreign balances began to be accumulated and some of these were owned by the Bank of Japan. Such funds were counted as part of the gold reserve against its note issue; but the strength of this reserve fund was, in turn, dependent upon the balance of payments position. In the four or five years before 1914, this reserve, mainly because of Japan's worsening trade balance, became a dwindling asset. The outbreak of war in 1914 saved the country from serious financial embarrassment for, as a result of conflict in which its chief Western competitors were engaged, it emerged as a creditor rather than as a debtor nation in the world economy.

*

We come finally to the effectiveness of foreign merchants and shipping companies in the promotion of Japanese trade; that is to

[1] G. C. Allen, *op. cit.*, p. 119, quoting *Financial and Economic Annual of Japan*, and *The Statistical Year Book of the Empire of Japan*.
[2] *Ibid.*, p. 120.

say, to the commercial aspects of development. It would be misleading if the above sections of this chapter gave the impression that Japan's determination to shape its own economic future was sponsored almost entirely by the efforts and will of native resourcefulness under the guidance of government intervention. There was a wide area, particularly during the last thirty years of the nineteenth century, in which foreign merchants could, and did, play a vital part in the process of modernisation. Despite assertions to the contrary, the imprint of their commercial system and code of behaviour was not only clearly stamped upon the economy as a whole but, in many respects, persisted long after their active participation had ceased to exist.

Although Japan had a flourishing internal trade at the end of the Tokugawa régime, such trade being elaborately organised in the hands of long-established business houses, there was virtually no experience of the finer techniques involved in the promotion of overseas trade. As a result, there was little acquaintance with the needs of foreign markets and the potential benefits to be derived from contact with new sources of supply. It was natural, therefore, that from the outset, foreign firms should have secured a predominant position in the financing and the direction of particular trades. It might have been expected that this predominance would have been short-lived for techniques and information could easily be acquired; in fact, it lasted until the end of the nineteenth century. The explanation of this derives from the simple fact that, in matters commercial, technical competence is not enough; there must, in addition, be the power to win and hold the confidence of suppliers and customers, a function in which Western merchants excelled whereas their Japanese counterparts had to undergo a long apprenticeship in its attainment. In theory, the essential element was that of goodwill; in practice, the inhibition was centred upon the price and uniform quality of the product and credit-worthiness of the Japanese merchant himself. As late as 1897, a British consular report stated categorically that 'until the Japanese obtain the knowledge and foresight in business transactions which can only be acquired by experience, and succeed in inspiring the commercial world with confidence, their credit is not sufficiently high for direct dealings with foreign countries'.[1] The

[1] Quoted Allen and Donnithorne, *China and Japan, op. cit.*, p. 198: *British Consular Reports*, Miscellaneous series, 440, 1897.

obvious implication was that foreign merchants were not only more efficient than their Japanese rivals, but that their supreme knowledge of the channels of trade and their skill in providing resources for the promotion of trade would remain unassailable. So much for the sublime conceit of the Western mind. From the very year in which the above report was written, the hold of the foreign merchant on Japan's markets began to relax and the power of the Japanese merchant to increase. We propose, therefore, to examine the causes of this change-over not merely in the context of Japan's economic sovereignty, but in the resultant effect upon Western merchants and shipowners alike.

The merchants who settled in Yokohama (and later Kobe), consequent upon the opening of the first ports to foreign trade, were mainly those who already had connections in China and other Far Eastern countries. One of the first British companies to establish a foothold at Yokohama was Jardine Matheson. They sent William Keswick to Japan in 1858 and, as a result of his efforts in the development of commercial contacts, their ships were soon sailing between Yokohama, Kobe and Chinese ports. This was followed by the incursion of John Swire and Sons who, in the 1860's, began to ship cotton, woollen and worsted goods to Japan on behalf of various constituents, including Richard Shackleton Butterfield.[1] Shortly after the foundation of the firm of Butterfield and Swire, a branch house was opened in Yokohama (and eventually at Kobe), bringing with it the agency for Holts' Blue Funnel Line ships. By 1866, there were more than forty foreign merchant houses trading at Yokohama; this number increased as other ports developed their potential as trading centres.

There were, nevertheless, many initial difficulties inhibiting the foundation of sound commercial practice. Chief among these was the fact that there was little understanding of the nature and scope of the market or of the goods likely to have a reciprocal demand. Before 1869, there were export surpluses in the commodity trades, but after the Restoration as a result of the government's purchases of ships and munitions, a more precise definition was given to Japan's needs as well as to its capacity to supply Western markets. There was also considerable confusion arising from the chaotic state of the various media of exchange, a fact which helps to explain the peculiarity of Japan's trading balances

[1] Sheila Marriner and F. E. Hyde, *The Senior*, *op. cit.*, p. 17.

and, incidentally, why foreign merchants obtained so firm a grip on the organisation of external trading contracts. Basing their approach on traditional methods employed in the financing of Pacific trade, the first merchants brought to Japan, not goods, but shiploads of Mexican silver dollars. This merely accentuated the problem of exchange values for, under the Treaty of 1859, the Mexican dollar was to be exchanged weight for weight with Japanese silver coins. The Tokugawa government exercised a monopoly over mining and had derived advantage from the over-valuation of silver in terms of gold. The gold-silver ratio had been fixed at about 1 : 5, compared with a ratio of about 1 : 16 in the outside world. The possibilities of so wide a discrepancy were not overlooked by foreign merchants. They imported Mexican dollars and exchanged them weight for weight with Japanese token silver coinage; they then re-exchanged the latter for gold coins at a ratio of 5 : 1, shipped the gold to Shanghai and there bought silver at 16 : 1.[1] It may well be true that the initial attraction of foreign merchants to Japan was stimulated as much by the prospect of profit from exchange transactions as by that of gain from trade in commodities. Be that as it may, the effect of the over-valuation of silver meant that tea, silk and copper-ware could also be purchased by the foreigner at artificially low prices. These conditions could not be allowed to persist and, after 1860, the ratio of gold to silver became the equivalent of that in the outside world. Nevertheless, before such parity was achieved, the Japanese economy had suffered a loss which it could ill afford; on the other hand, there was an undoubted gain because such chaotic conditions led to a more rapid expansion of commercial contacts with the West than could have been established in a different set of circumstances.

It is reliably estimated that in 1864 the number of foreign residents in Yokohama numbered 300 while in Nagasaki there were about 200.[2] Of this total, some 250 were British. A majority

---

[1] G. C. Allen and Audrey G. Donnithorne, *op. cit.*, pp. 199-200, also D. H. Leavens, *The Gold-Silver Ratio in the Early Foreign Relations of the Far East* (1928); U.S. Dept. of Commerce, *The Currency System of Japan* (1930), pp. 5-6.

[2] G. C. Allen and Audrey G. Donnithorne, *op. cit.*, Appendix F, p. 270, quoting the *Statesman's Year Book* (1870), p. 676; and M. Paske-Smith, *Western Barbarians in Japan and Formosa in Tokugawa Days 1603-1868*, p. 218.

of these foreign residents were merchants, but the classification of function and employment is difficult to make because official statistics refer only to those who were employed in the service of the government. In 1872, for example, the central government employed 214 foreigners, of whom 119 were British, 50 were French and 16 were American.[1] Most of these found occupations in railways, lighthouses, communications, shipbuilding and educational services. In addition, foreign nationals were employed by the prefectures and in various government arsenals. By 1880, some 237 foreigners are recorded as being in the government or prefectural service. Throughout the whole decade from 1871 to 1880, approximately half the foreign residents were British, the remainder being French, American and German, in that order of importance. In 1879, the total number of Western residents in Japan was 2,475 of whom 1,106 were British, 479 were Americans, 300 were Germans, 230 were French and 209 were Russians.[2] In the absence of precise information, it must be assumed that many of these were merchants or shipping agents. By 1913, the total number had more than doubled but, thereafter, the figure remained comparatively stable, thereby indicating that Japanese firms were taking over the functions hitherto performed by foreigners.

There are, however, certain important changes within the structure of the picture given above which need to be mentioned. As we have seen, foreign merchants were not only concerned with the purely commercial aspects of Japan's chief exports of tea and silk but also with the preparatory processes of tea cultivation, silk egg production and silk reeling.[3] This extension of control gave them an initial advantage in directing the flow of exports to particular markets. It has been estimated that, in 1887, nearly nine-tenths of Japan's foreign trade was in the hands of foreign merchants. Up to that date, it was only in the trade with China that Japanese merchants had any real function. During the next decade, however, the relative strength of Japan's own commercial structure began to increase. This was caused by the increasing activity of trading companies such as Mitsui Bussan Kaisha (founded in 1876) and by government encouragement to private merchant houses to enter the arena. As a result, in 1894, the Japanese firm of Horikoshi began to export silk fabrics to the

[1] *Ibid.*   [2] *Ibid.*, p. 271.   [3] See above, pp. 43, 46, 48.

United States, a venture which, by its success, encouraged other firms to take part in the trade. The consequence of such persistent efforts was that Japanese merchants extended their direct control over trade from 20 per cent of the total in 1890 to 40 per cent by 1900. This relative increase, however, does not necessarily imply a diminution in the volume of trade handled by foreigners, as total imports and exports doubled during the decade. Nevertheless, it was the Japanese merchant rather than the foreigner who now controlled the marginal increase. Furthermore, as the effects of industrialisation began to be felt, the native merchant enlarged his control over the export of manufactured and semi-manufactured products and the import of raw materials. The net result was a shift in the influence of foreign merchants. Whereas Britain had taken the lead in the development of Japan's trade up to the mid-1880's (most of the imports were British in origin), the shift in sources of supply from countries selling manufactured goods to those selling raw materials resulted in a diminution of Britain's share in the Japanese market. There was a corresponding expansion of the American market for raw silk and the Chinese market for cotton goods. The trend into the new century witnessed the growing strength of American and German participation in Japan's trade, with Japanese merchants handling a fair proportion of the trade with the Chinese coastal ports. In relative terms, however, these changing emphases were not significant when compared with the rapid extension of Japan's own commercial enterprise. Such was the scale of transformation that, by the 1920's, foreign activity in the import trade (apart from certain specialised branches such as machinery and engineering products, which required maintenance and the supply of spare parts) had become of minor importance. The import of raw materials generally fell into the hands of a few large-scale Japanese trading organisations such as Mitsui Bussan Kaisha, Mitsubishi Shoji and Okura. The major export commodities had also fallen into Japanese hands, cotton piece-goods for example being controlled by a few large firms who, in turn, imported the major share of the raw cotton needed for their manufacture. Finally, one must take account of a continuous rise in Japan's trade with its colonies, Korea and Formosa. The main channels through which this particular trade passed were Japanese. By the end of the First World War, the only significant part of the commodity trade left in foreign hands was that of tea to the United States, and silk piece-goods and miscellaneous manufactured products to Western countries. As Allen and Donnithorne have stated, 'in these classes of goods and in those markets, their western connections, their knowledge of western tastes and the goodwill which they enjoyed with purchasers overseas, still gave them an advantage over their Japanese competitors'.[1]

*

Much the same pattern of developing control can be observed in the expansion of Japan's mercantile marine as in its commercial organisation, though the timing of the change-over of control was slightly different. The tonnage of foreign shipping entering Japanese ports rose from 440,000 in 1873 to approximately 12 million in 1913. In examining changes in the relative shares of the carrying trade, one finds that, up to 1885, foreign vessels carried over 90 per cent of Japan's overseas trade and represented about 83 per cent of the steamship tonnage entering and clearing Japanese ports[2]; by 1900, the respective shares were 70 per cent and 65 per cent.[3] In spite of the rapid expansion of Japan's own shipping services after 1895, foreign ships were still carrying about half of its trade in 1913, though very shortly afterwards, as the result of dislocation caused by the First World War, the balance was tipped in Japan's favour and foreign shipping lost its predominance. From this time onwards, Japanese shipping companies secured an increasing volume of the carrying trade and by the early 1930's more than 70 per cent was being shipped by national lines.

At first, Japan's shipping services were developed over short distance Pacific routes such as those between Yokohama and coastal ports in China, Korea and the islands of Formosa and the Philippines. The longer oceanic routes to Europe, the west coast ports of Canada and the United States (and later, to Australia) were all well served by foreign shipping lines and subject to the pressure of intense competition. In the building of national maritime supremacy, therefore, Japan began by concentrating on those routes where foreign competition was less intense and where Japan itself had reasonably well-organised commercial contacts.

[1] G. C. Allen and Audrey G. Donnithorne, *op. cit.*, p. 204.
[2] Holt MSS., Swire correspondence, Swire to Philip Holt, 2 Mar. 1885.
[3] Swire MSS., Estimates of Shipping Tonnage in Far Eastern waters, June 1900.

As the strength of its shipping companies increased and as agency houses were established, the services were extended across the Pacific. The final phase came when Japanese ships ventured beyond the North Pacific to the Indian, South Pacific and Atlantic Oceans thus, by implication, giving the Japanese mercantile marine an international status and a competitive equality with the shipping lines of other maritime powers.

Of the European shipping interests which first carried cargoes to Japan, the P. and O. and the French Messagéries (both subsidised for the carriage of mails) were the most important; the latter company had begun services to Japan in 1866 and was followed in 1867 by the P. and O. with an extension of that company's route from Shanghai. In this way, Yokohama was linked, through the medium of a British line, with India—a fact which acquired much greater significance at a later date when Japan's own shipping companies began to extend their trans-oceanic influence. The two European companies were joined by Alfred Holt's Blue Funnel Line in the 1870's, though direct and regular sailings of the Holt vessels were not started until the mid-1880's.[1] Blue Funnel ships quickly gained an ascendancy in the carriage of Japanese cargoes, both outwards and homewards, capturing some 70 per cent of the total carrying trade between Britain and Japan.[2] As the net receipts from their voyages indicate, this leading position was maintained (at least up to 1914) in face of growing competition from other lines, especially that from Japan's most powerful company, Nippon Yusen Kaisha, and to a lesser extent from the secondary line, Osaka Shosen Kaisha.[3]

The first lively interest shown by Japan in shipping matters occurred in 1875 when Mitsubishi and other allied concerns began to operate ships on the route between Shanghai and Japanese ports. This venture came into conflict with ships of the Pacific Mail Steam Ship Co., which, in the previous year, had started a bi-monthly service between Shanghai and San Francisco. The main staple of trade was raw cotton from China—a product in increasing demand from Japan's growing textile industry. The provision of shipping services for the carriage of this product from China attracted the powerful attention of Japanese merchants

---

[1] F. E. Hyde, *Blue Funnel*, *op. cit.*, p. 27.
[2] Holt MSS., Swire correspondence, Swire to A. Holt, 30 Oct. 1889.
[3] F. E. Hyde, *Blue Funnel*, *op. cit.*, pp. 126-32.

and cotton manufacturers; so much so that, in 1885, an alliance of government-sponsored shipping concerns (under the controlling influence of Mitsubishi) was formed to create Nippon Yusen Kaisha. This company eventually became Japan's leading shipping interest. At its inception, the company had 58 ships with a gross steamship tonnage of 65,000—a figure inviting favourable comparison with the fleets of the P. and O. and Holts' Ocean Steam Ship Co. The government guaranteed dividends of 8 per cent on the company's capital for a period of fifteen years and, in return, exercised supervision over its trading routes.[1] By contrast with Holts, however, Nippon Yusen Kaisha was paid an annual subsidy of 880,000 yen. At first the company had to rely on foreign captains, engineers and pursers to run their ships and it was not until the end of the First World War that the line was staffed entirely by Japanese personnel. This shipping line's foundation was contemporaneous with the creation of a second company, Osaka Shosen Kaisha, a company formed by the amalgamation of a number of small firms engaged in the coastal trades. Osaka Shosen eventually became Japan's second largest shipping firm and, with Nippon Yusen, carried cargoes on all the major sea routes of the world.

The nature and scope of Japan's maritime power can only be understood in relation to its economic and industrial development if the strategic importance of the geographical situation is given weight; for, apart from the promotion of a mercantile marine by government action, there were non-political and non-economic reasons affecting the competitive strength of Japan's shipping services. The chief factor was undoubtedly Japan's advantageous geographical position: first, in relation to the shorter shipping routes to the Chinese mainland and the Pacific Islands; secondly, in relation to its position as a junction for long distance trans-Pacific routes vital as lines of supply to its industrial growth. In this latter context, the shipping services between Japan and the west coast ports of Canada and the United States were of great importance, especially through their links with the trans-continental railway systems. To the west were the teeming markets of India and south Asia, while to the south lay the coastal ports and

[1] Nippon Yusen Kaisha, *Golden Jubilee, History* (1935), p. 11. See also G. C. Allen, *A Short Economic History of Modern Japan* (1946), pp. 85 *et seq.*

towns of the vast and underdeveloped continent of Australia. It was mainly on the over-capitalised steamship route *via* Shanghai, Hong Kong, Singapore and Suez to Europe that Japan's new shipping companies could expect to meet the overwhelming strength of other maritime powers. The full story of how Japan broke into these various trades forms an interesting chapter in maritime history. For the purpose of this narrative, however, we can only refer to the salient points of interest which marked the rise of an oriental mercantile marine competitive in all respects with Western rivals.

As already stated, Nippon Yusen Kaisha began by consolidating its contacts and influence in the short-distance trades with ports on the China coast, particularly in the carriage of cotton from Shanghai and sugar from Hong Kong. A fair proportion of the sugar cargoes were shipped from Swire's Taikoo Sugar Refinery which, by 1888, sent some 37 per cent of its production to Japan. By 1894, Taikoo was supplying 46 per cent of the total demand in Yokohama and Kobe[1] but this share of the market could not be maintained. Import duties were imposed in 1898 and, as a result, Hong Kong sugars were replaced by production from protected Japanese sources of supply. Similar changes in the balance of control over commodity trades were but a reflection of a policy with wider implications which, as we have seen, dominated the import trades when Japan began to demand raw materials on an increasing scale. As a logical extension of interests in line with national requirements, Nippon Yusen Kaisha started a direct service to Manila in 1890 and in 1893 to Bombay. In this latter port the company met and overcame the competition of Western lines and captured the major part of the trade in raw cotton to Japan.[2] Three years later, Japanese shipping was given direct encouragement by the passing of the Navigation Subsidy Act. This enabled the two main shipping companies to order larger ships capable of competing on all the main cargo-liner routes of the world. Nevertheless, although the Japanese companies might desire to test their growing strength over longer distances, the competitive forces arrayed against them were formidable and, on occasion, inhibited successful operation of their ships. The struggle

[1] Sheila Marriner and F. E. Hyde, *The Senior, op. cit.*, p. 103.
[2] Swire MSS., John Swire Memoranda, 1890-1896, Statement on Japanese Mercantile Marine.

to enter the Bombay cotton trade had been conducted against the background of a fierce rate-cutting war with the P. and O., which lasted for three years; but the culmination was a victory for persistent effort. In 1896, Nippon Yusen Kaisha was admitted to the Bombay-Japan Conference. In fact, the year 1896 was *annus mirabilis* for it witnessed the beginning of three long-distance services to North America, Australia and Europe. We shall deal with the trans-Pacific trade in the following chapter, but it is pertinent to the present theme to deal briefly with the service to Europe—a service which linked London and Antwerp with Japan *via* the Suez Canal.

The strength of this link grew outward from previous collaboration in both commercial and financial identification of interests. It is true that Nippon Yusen Kaisha made use of local European merchant houses, but there were in existence long-standing connections which helped in the overcoming of initial difficulties. The line was served by the Japanese house of Buhierosan Tannaker which had been established in London as early as 1879[1]; but it was with the firm of Samuel and Co., which had supplied many of the war-time needs for Japan's conflict with China, that the majority of the business was transacted. In fact, Marcus Samuel had become the London banker of the Japanese government and had been instrumental in floating a sterling loan in 1899.[2] With this kind of backing, therefore, Nippon Yusen Kaisha had every reason to believe that a successful shipping trade could be developed with Europe, provided always that its ships could be run with efficiency and kept competitive in operation. The nature of the entry of Japanese ships into European ports, however, induced retaliation. The new lines' subsidised mail service from Japan was a direct threat to the long-established position of the Messageries Maritimes and the P. and O. As a countervailing measure, the P. and O. inaugurated, after 1896, an intermediate service between London and Japan and, in the boom following the Russo-Japanese War, other competing services were started: by Brocklebanks from Liverpool, by the Messageries jointly with Chargeurs Réunis, by the Prince Line from the U.S.A. and by the North German Lloyd from Australia. As a result, shipping tonnage to and from Japan *via* the Suez Canal increased

[1] D. A. Farnie, *op. cit.*, p. 361.
[2] *Ibid.*, p. 453.

from 1,168,000 in 1904 to 2,290,000 in 1905; this despite the fact that Nippon Yusen Kaisha, whose services had been interrupted by the war, did not resume sailings through the Canal until 1906.[1]

How then did Japan's principal shipping company meet and overcome opposition on the European route and what advantages accrued from the extension of trade to Western ports? To a large extent, the choice of route was designated by the Japanese government as one of national importance. It followed, therefore, that Nippon Yusen Kaisha was being used as an instrument of national policy and that, as a consequence, normal commercial considerations did not apply in the conduct of its business. Dividends were guaranteed and subsidies helped to cover losses. According to John Swire, who had personal relationships with some of the company's directors, Nippon Yusen Kaisha could never have shown a real profit on its voyages to Europe without massive state assistance.[2] Even so, the Japanese government's purse was not bottomless and efforts were made, whenever possible, to maintain receipts at economic levels. For this reason, the company sought admission to, and became a member of, the China Conference in the late 1890's.[3] As we shall see later, it also entered into pooling arrangements and freight agreements on most of the other routes which it served. Thus, wasteful competition and rate-cutting wars were avoided and revenue was maintained. There were also positive achievements to record. As we have seen, a dominating control had been achieved in the Chinese and Bombay cotton markets and there was a parallel achievement in the supply of raw silk to Europe. By 1909, the volume of Japanese raw silk shipments exceeded those from China and competed powerfully in the French and other European markets. This was an integral part of a build-up of Japanese maritime strength. Japan had become a focal point for new steamship services across the Pacific and had captured the major share of many trades with China, India, the U.S.A. and Australia by 1914. The outbreak of war presented the country with new opportunity; in 1916, the ships of Osaka Shosen Kaisha were reaching out *via* the Cape to the service of markets in South America and, in the following year, those of Nippon Yusen Kaisha were returning homeward with valuable cargoes of Argentinian

[1] D. A. Farnie, *op. cit.*, p. 498.
[2] Swire MSS., Swire to R. D. Holt, 27 Oct. 1897.
[3] Minutes China Conference from Holt MSS., folio 6, 1895-1900.

hides and wheat, Brazilian coffee, sugar and fruit. In short, Japan had secured to itself a dominating control of shipping services in all the major markets of the world, where it could find outlets for its own manufactured products and exchange them for vitally-needed supplies of raw materials.

In retrospect, it is possible to argue that, in its successful competition with foreign shipping lines, the Japanese mercantile marine was assisted not only by official subsidies, but also by the fact that it was an integral part of the powerful business houses whose interests were also engaged in trade, industry and finance. It is doubtful, however, whether the thrust of a nationalistic economic policy or the incentive from an integrated organisation within the economy were primary contributors to the rise of Japan's mercantile power. Japan possessed many natural advantages essential to the development of shipping services and native enterprise was successful in cultivating them. Within the context of Japan's industrial and economic growth, shipping and trade were essential elements, but growth was not entirely dependent on such services being in Japanese hands. The fact that national control was established brought a new emphasis to the Pacific economy as a whole. It is likely that foreign shipping enterprise gained far more from the rapid extension of Japan's overseas trade than it lost through the emergence of a powerful Japanese mercantile marine. In the matters of shipping and trade there had been a shift in the balance of power; new stimuli had been provided in the promotion of world trade as a whole, and the definition of the Far East had ceased to be confined to the areas within specified ports on the fringe of a great ocean. It had now become the pulse of a Pacific economy and, through that economy, a powerful influence in a new and multilateral pattern of world trade.

CHAPTER VIII

Changes in the Pattern of Trade and the Extension of Shipping Services across the Pacific

THE opening of new trades across the Pacific through the provision of steamship services was stimulated by an initial extension of both tramp and cargo-liner routes and by the southward thrust of Japanese mercantile enterprise to Australia. The shores of the three continents fringing this ocean had been linked with Western markets by sailing ship companies whose graceful clippers added romance to the hard economic facts of their struggle to maintain their trades. Eventually, they were driven from the deep seas by the power of steam, the western ports of South America being brought within the control of such famous shipping concerns as the Pacific Steam Navigation Co., and the Pacific coast ports of North America by the ships of the China Mutual, Harrisons' Charente Steamship Co., the Pacific Mail Steamship Co. and many others. To the south, Australia was served by the P. and O. and British India companies which, for a time, divided Britain's passenger and mail traffic between them. They were later joined by Lund's Blue Anchor Line, the Orient Steam Ship Co., Shaw Savill and Holts' direct Blue Funnel service from Glasgow. For our purpose, however, we are more concerned with the provision of trans-Pacific steamship routes by which the trades of such ports as Singapore, Hong Kong and Yokohama were given greater diversity. Furthermore, although recognising that many such trans-Pacific steamship services were successfully undertaken, we propose to confine this present survey to four routes, namely Holts' service in conjunction with Bethell and Trinder to Fremantle, the services of the China Mutual, the Pacific Mail and Nippon Yusen Kaisha between

Yokohama and San Francisco, Swire's China Navigation Co.'s services from Hong Kong to Sydney and Melbourne and, finally, the institution of a direct line between Japan and Australia. In much of this new enterprise one can perceive the active and initiatory participation of John Samuel Swire, for it was his persistent belief that the trade, and indeed the whole economy of the Far East, should not be wholly dependent on Western markets, but that they should be given as much scope as possible in establishing links with ports in other parts of the world.[1]

The merits of the new steamship route to the Far East *via* the Suez Canal and the general economic implications of this waterway have already been discussed.[2] It is, perhaps, because of its obvious importance as a vital and strategic route that such great emphasis has been given to the link which it provided between Europe and the Pacific. Nevertheless, from the date of its opening, there was much discussion about the merits of an alternative route from China and Japan to Europe. This alternative route had been made possible by the completion of the trans-continental railroads across the United States, linking west coast ports with those of the eastern seabord. At a later date, a third route was opened across Canada and was made available when the Canadian Pacific Railway was opened. These new lines of communication offered a powerful inducement to China merchants not only to ship their goods eastwards but to travel homewards by a more temperate and faster route than that *via* the Red Sea. As a result of this and other reasons the P. and O., whose ships took 60 days to get home *via* Suez as against 35 days for the eastern route, lost about 20 per cent of its Far Eastern traffic during the 1870's.[3] By 1871, silk was being despatched eastbound from Yokohama to Liverpool in 47 days.[4] This route also became highly competitive in the carriage of green tea and captured a large share of the export trade from China (and later Japan) to the American and European market. Thus, as this new lateral line of communication became established, there was a diminution in the relative importance of the Suez Canal. There was, however, little justification for the hope, then being

---

[1] Swire MSS., Memoranda on Far Eastern trade, Oct.-Dec. 1880.
[2] See above, Chapters 1 and 2.
[3] Boyd Cable, *op. cit.*, Chapter XXIII for a general statement of the position; D. A. Farnie, *op. cit.*, p. 190; Swire MSS., Swire to A. Holt, 1 Jan. 1874.
[4] D. A. Farnie, *op. cit.*, p. 190.

M

freely expressed by American merchants, that the trans-continental routes would eventually divert from the Canal the bulk of the trade from Asia.[1] In the final analysis, as D. A. Farnie has shown, the Canal remained far cheaper than the railway (apart from a few trades) because it was an all-water route and thereby avoided transhipment costs. It facilitated traffic to the extent that cargo could be carried from China to New York by sea at one-fifth of the combined sea and rail charges imposed on the route across the United States or Canada.[2]

Despite this general conclusion, however, there were potentially large profits to be earned from the employment of ships on this northern Pacific sea link. Its inception had encouraged a proposal in 1870 for a steamship and railway service between England and Australia in 40 days and had stimulated the beginning of a paddle steamship service from San Francisco to Sydney. In the trades to and from the China coast and Japan, the Pacific Mail held a virtual monopoly of the steamship trade to San Francisco during the late 1860's. As a result of an increase in the volume of trade, this company started a bi-monthly service in 1874; by the 1890's, nearly 200,000 tons of goods were carried annually on this route, a fact which did not escape the notice of other shipowners.[3] Shipping companies long-established in Pacific trades, as well as new companies, were attracted by the profitability of this route and embarked upon a competitive struggle by putting their ships into the trade. John Swire had, from an early date, been attracted to the starting of a steamship trade between China or Japan and the west coast ports of America. His interest was such that, in 1870, he obtained a detailed account from Yokohama of the sailings, vessels and freight rates of the Pacific Mail Steam Ship Co.'s service during the three previous years.[4] Through their agency for the White Star Line, Butterfield and Swire could offer passages to New York from Japan *via* Liverpool, using Ismay's crack liners for the trans-Atlantic crossing. Swire saw every possibility for the inauguration of an east-bound service *via* San Francisco and, in 1874, he wrote to Rufus Hatch, a director of the Pacific Mail, tendering for the

[1] D. A. Farnie, *op. cit.*, p. 191.
[2] *Ibid.*
[3] Holt MSS., Minutes China Mutual, 1890-1895; also F. E. Hyde, *Blue Funnel, op. cit.*, pp. 115 *et seq.*
[4] Swire MSS., Butterfield and Swire to John Swire, 15 Mar. 1870.

line's China and Japan agency.[1] The tender was not accepted, but it is clear that one of the major considerations in Swire's mind for maintaining his Yokohama and New York branches was the possibility of entering this trade. In 1898, Bowrings started a service between San Diego and China and Japan in conjunction with the Atchison, Topeka and Santa Fé Railroad. Using chartered steamships, it was hoped that, in return for tea and silk, an export trade in cotton, wheat and manufactured products might be developed with the Far East.[2] Butterfield and Swire were appointed agents; but unfortunately, the demand was not sufficient to sustain business. Cargoes were light and receipts failed to cover costs. Added to this, the driving force of John Swire's guidance had been removed by his death in 1898. The service was discontinued in 1902.

The protagonists on the north Pacific after 1900 were Holts' Blue Funnel Line and Japan's Nippon Yusen Kaisha. According to estimates made by Richard Holt in 1913, these two companies carried 65 per cent of total cargoes in 1899 and, in the following decade, this percentage increased to 75.[3] Of these amounts Holts' ships carried about 60 per cent of teas and silks shipped from China, while Nippon Yusen controlled three-quarters of the trade to and from Japan. There was, therefore, a reasonably well-ordered division of the carrying trade, freight rates being regulated by common consent rather than by formal agreement, except in those years when cargoes were light. Holts' participation in this trade stemmed from their acquisition of a controlling interest in the China Mutual in 1902. A fairly regular service had been started by the latter company between China, Japan and ports on the west coast of Canada and the United States. When the China Mutual came under joint management with Holts this service was gradually expanded and became an important element in earning capacity. 'The outward cargoes from Europe are general', stated the managers' report for 1903, 'and are such as have hitherto been carried in sailing ships. Homeward, wheat and tinned salmon are shipped to Europe and other classes of cargo to Japan, China and the Philippines. The steamers will usually return home *via* the

[1] Swire MSS., Swire to R. Hatch, 10 July 1874.
[2] Swire MSS., Agency memoranda, July 1898.
[3] Holt MSS., R. D. Holt papers, June 1913. Correspondence and memoranda on Pacific trades.

East and the Suez Canal, but occasionally a full cargo offers for Europe *via* Cape Horn. An arrangement has been made experimentally with certain American railroads which largely control the trade.'[1] The initial hope that this venture would prove to be lucrative was more than justified. In the first three years of operation, the net voyage receipts from the north Pacific trade accounted for 20 per cent of Holts' net voyage receipts as a whole; in subsequent years it amounted to 25 per cent and, by 1913-14, the share had risen to about 27 per cent.[2]

There was, therefore, every justification for the large expenditure of capital for new ships built specially for this route. By contrast, the ships of Nippon Yusen Kaisha were mainly old and second-hand, many of them having been purchased from Holts when this latter company rebuilt its fleet in the 1890's.[3] The new Holt ships, being of the latest design, were highly competitive, working costs being marginal. With full holds, therefore, net receipts were maintained at a maximum. The Japanese ships barely returned a profit and were only kept on the services by virtue of subsidisation, the sea route having been designated as one of national importance by the Japanese government. Apart from the carriage of cargo, Holts succeeded in capturing a large proportion of passenger traffic. Thus, by 1911, the managers reported that large new steamships had been put on the north Pacific 'with improved provision for Chinese passengers who form a large and growing element in the trade in both directions across the Pacific'.[4] In this way, advantage had accrued from an alternative route to Suez, and steamships, by extending sea lanes, had brought China and Japan within the concept of a more comprehensive Pacific economy.

*

In the trades southwards from Singapore to Australia, communications before 1885 were dominated by sailing ship companies. This was so long after the steamship had opened up ports along the China coast to Western trading enterprise. The links between Australian ports and those in the Far East were sustained by the

[1] F. E. Hyde, *Blue Funnel, op. cit.*, p. 154; Holt MSS., Minutes O.S.S. Co., Feb. 1903.
[2] Holt MSS., Minutes O.S.S. Co., Voyage receipts, 1902-1914.
[3] *Ibid.*, 1892-1898.
[4] Holt MSS., Minutes O.S.S. Co. for 1911.

clipper, such famous ships as *Cutty Sark*, *Lightning* and *Thermo-pylae* being engaged in fierce competitive rivalry. In 1890, however, the attention of the Holt managers was drawn to the possibility of starting a steamship service between Singapore and western Australia. For some years previously, the firm of Bethell and Trinder had operated their steamship *Australind* on this route with apparent financial success.[1] With an eye to the prospective profitability of this trade, Holts declared that transhipment of cargoes from western Australian ports 'would help to fill the Company's main line steamers from Singapore'.[2] Their interest had been assured by the active advice from John Swire for he had long been toying with the idea of sending ships to Australia, either directly from the China coast or from Singapore. His earlier business associations with that continent had imbued him with a persistent desire to tap the potential demand for steamship services southwards across the Pacific. The Holts had, in fact, anticipated this desire by sending an occasional ship from Singapore to western Australian ports in the late 1880's, and this service was given a more regular character through the establishment of joint trading arrangements with the firm of Bethell and Trinder. Swire thereupon entered into negotiations with Bethell and Trinder on Holts' behalf, with a view to the creation of a joint service with Holts' ship *Saladin*, which had been specially built for this type of trade.[3] It was agreed that Dalgety and Co. should act as the agents in Australia, taking 5 per cent on cargo and passengers procured at Fremantle and 2½ per cent on inward freights.[4] Earnings were pooled and a discriminatory freight rate was charged by both companies in order to induce Australian merchants to use the Singapore route to London for their cargoes of wool. As Swire pointed out, this arrangement would favour Holts, as the Ocean Steam Ship Co. would act as the sole carriers for Bethell and Trinder's cargoes from Singapore to England in return for the latter company acting as brokers for Holts' ship *Saladin*.[5] When Bethell and Trinder raised objections that such a pooling agreement might adversely affect their earnings on short cargoes, Swire

[1] F. E. Hyde, *Blue Funnel*, *op. cit.*, p. 93.
[2] *Ibid.*, pp. 96-7.
[3] *Ibid.*, p. 96.
[4] *Ibid.*, Holt MSS., Swire correspondence, Swire to Dalgety and Co., 2 July 1889.
[5] F. E. Hyde, *Blue Funnel*, *op. cit.*, p. 97.

replied characteristically, 'if you agree to the O.S.S. Co. being sole carriers of through cargoes per *Australind* homewards, we will give you the option at the end of the first twelve months either of keeping your own upward earnings or of pooling on gross registered tonnage downwards. We must pool if you are to be London brokers for *Saladin* and, if you are not her brokers, competition will, of necessity, bring down freights to a low level.'[1] The pool was put into operation and, at the end of a year, it was obvious that freight rates were higher (some 25 per cent according to Swire) than they would otherwise have been in a freely competitive market.[2]

The outward cargoes in this new trade were principally miscellaneous, capable of sustaining the needs of up-country stores. In return, the principal commodity was wool. After 1895, however, as a consequence of new gold discoveries, the scope changed, outward shipments consisting of mining machinery and consumer goods in return for both bulk and high value cargoes. At first, the volume of trade was small and Holts' profits on voyages were in the region of £5,000 per annum.[3] Nevertheless, a second ship *Sultan*, under joint ownership, was put into service in the expectation that trade would increase. As settlers poured into the area volumes did, in fact, increase and annual net voyage receipts rose to a level of £9,000 (1896-1900).[4] Future prospects seemed bright and, as an earnest of their continuing faith, two new ships were added to the fleet between 1896 and 1899, the Holts buying out Bethell and Trinder's share in *Sultan*. By this purchase, joint ownership was ended and henceforth each company owned two ships.[5] As trade grew, larger and faster ships were ordered and, as a final act to destroy the lingering competition from sailing ships, steam-lighters were used to speed the loading process. All these factors contributed towards the efficient working of this small fleet and profits rose as costs fell and earnings increased. By 1914, Holts' average annual net earnings (1911-14) had risen to £17,000.[6] In other

---

[1] Holt MSS., Swire to Charles Bethell, 23 Nov. 1889.
[2] Holt MSS., Swire to Philip Holt, 23 Dec. 1890.
[3] Holt MSS., Minutes O.S.S. Co., Voyage receipts from Western Australian trade, 1890-1895.
[4] *Ibid.*, 1896-1900.
[5] F. E. Hyde, *Blue Funnel, op. cit.*, p. 98.
[6] Holt MSS., Minutes O.S.S. Co. for years 1911-14, Voyage receipts from Australian trade.

words, the venturing of capital into such an enterprise had been justified and John Swire's foresight had, once again, been vindicated.

Having made a success of the west Australian trade, Holts were strengthened in their belief that lucrative opportunities would attend the inauguration of a direct service to the principal Australian ports. The trade figures provided justification for such a service, average annual exports from Britain to Australia having increased from £19,482,000 to £21,798,000 for the successive periods 1891-95 and 1896-1900; while imports from Australia had increased from £23,801,000 to £24,624,000 for the corresponding periods.[1] In view of this general expansion, and with the growth of Australian business with the north of England and Scotland, the embarking of capital in such a venture could not ultimately fail to secure large returns. Apart from the carriage of wool, which was a staple of the trade, there were also seasonal cargoes of fruit—for which the ships had to be fitted with refrigerated holds. The history of this development has been written elsewhere,[2] but there are certain facts relevant to our present theme which need to be emphasised. By starting a direct service with Adelaide, Melbourne, Sydney and Brisbane, Holts were brought into contact with new agents, viz.: Gilchrist, Watt and Sanderson of Sydney, G. R. Wills of Adelaide and Sanderson and Murray of Melbourne. Gilchrists had long been interested in bringing to Australia cargoes of sugar from Java, Manila and Mauritius as well as tea from India and China. In the direct trade with Britain they took shares in, and became agents for, the Orient Steam Ship Co. in the 1870's. They were also (together with the other two houses) agents for William Lund's Blue Anchor Line. The experience and expertise of these Australian houses gave Holts a dominating position and indirectly brought them transhipment cargoes for many cross-Pacific trades. In this way, the tenuous links between Australia, the Philippines, Japan and, ultimately, of the United States, were fostered.

*

We must now return to the activities of John Swire's China Navigation Co. As we have already seen, this company had

[1] *Trade and Navigation Returns of U.K. 1890-1900.*
[2] F. E. Hyde, *Blue Funnel, op. cit.*, pp. 110-14.

gradually extended its services along the China coast and, by the 1890's, it was trading outwards to Manila, Java and other south-east Asian ports. In the 1880's, however, a major decision had been taken to engage in a direct trade between China and Australia with four large passenger ships constructed for the purpose.[1] Though a powerful inducement had been to secure a hold on the carriage of emigrants from China, the cargo side of the business had not been overlooked. The main commodities carried southward were tea, sugar and rice, while return cargoes consisted of coal and, later, of flour, gold, wool, lead and gold bullion. The organisation of this China Navigation Co.'s service in Australia was undertaken by Swire's agents, Lorimer, Marwood and Rome, a firm with a detailed knowledge and experience of shipping business. It was, therefore, natural that Swire should enter upon an Australian service, provided that the time was propitious. That it was delayed so long was due to the fact that sailing ships held the monopoly and it was uncertain whether steamships could compete successfully. By 1875, it was becoming obvious that, although clippers still retained their hold on the tea trade, steamships were beginning to compete seriously in the carriage of general cargoes.[2] Swire thereupon instructed his agents to make a careful survey of the changing conditions while, at the same time, Butterfield and Swire were inquiring into the potential passenger traffic between China and Australia. The result of these investigations was not encouraging and Swire had to wait until 1881 before conditions were favourable. Exploratory voyages were made to Australia in 1882 and a regular liner service using three ships was in operation by 1883.[3] In the agreement with Jardines concerning the division of the Yangtse trade, a clause was inserted restricting the south Pacific voyages to China Navigation Co. ships. The general route included Foochow, Hong Kong, Manila and the Australian ports, with occasional visits to Japan to load rice.[4]

The only other serious competitor on this service at this time was the Eastern and Australian Steamship Co. This liner service was run by McTaggart, Tidman and Co. of London, using Gibb, Livingstone as agents at Hong Kong and Gibbs, Bright and Co. as

[1] Sheila Marriner and F. E. Hyde, *op. cit.*, pp. 92 *et seq.*
[2] *Ibid.*
[3] *Ibid.*, p. 92.
[4] *Ibid.*, Appendix I.

agents in Australia. In October 1883, Tidmans suggested that Butterfield and Swire might take over the Hong Kong agency, but the negotiations broke down and eventually the business passed to Russells.[1] Having failed to create an interlocking agency, Swire and Tidman entered into a pooling agreement dividing the China-Australian cargo trade between the Eastern and Australian Steamship Co. and the China Navigation Co. The pool, however, did not include passenger traffic nor the carriage of coal from Australia, the latter trade in particular being subjected to fierce competition from casuals and tramps. As might have been expected, Gibb, Livingstone, whose interests in the trade had been ignored, raised strong objections to the arrangement; so much so that John Swire, who was anxious to work his ships with as little friction as possible, was forced to admit that Gibb, Livingstone had been badly treated by Tidmans and, consequently, an agreement based on an injustice could not be maintained.[2] Tidmans, however, refused to negotiate with Gibb, Livingstone and the latter company retaliated by offering bitter competition both with Tidmans and with the China Navigation Co. Livingstone, who had a large and thriving connection with Chinese merchants, got the better of the contest with the result that the receipts to the China Navigation Co. were cut by nearly 25 per cent.[3] Despite John Swire's efforts at mediation, no settlement had been reached when the agreement expired. By 1888, the prospects of profitable development in this trade were not bright; there was cut-throat competition between the shipping companies and, as a complicating factor in the conduct of trade as a whole, it appeared likely that the Australian government would soon impose restrictions on immigration and the importation of particular cargoes such as sugar. Such inhibitions would threaten not only the returns from the passenger traffic but also those from ancillary services. In particular, the provisioning of ships outwards from Hong Kong would suffer as Chinese emigrants needed large supplies of stores to maintain their diet. The situation was so depressing that John Swire's natural optimism was replaced by regret that his ships had entered such a hazardous business.[4] The

---

[1] Swire MSS., Swire to J. Lorimer, 19 Sept. 1884.
[2] Swire MSS., Swire to J. H. Scott and E. Mackintosh, 27 March 1885.
[3] Swire MSS., Swire to T. A. Gibb and Co., 27 Mar. 1885; also Holt MSS., Swire correspondence, 1 April 1885.
[4] Swire MSS., Swire to E. Mackintosh, 11 May 1888.

four large passenger ships of the China Navigation Co., however, continued to operate despite adverse conditions. There was further apprehension in 1891, on the death of Mr McTaggart, when it appeared likely that the ships of the Eastern and Australian Co. might be sold to another competitor; but the immediate financial difficulties of this company were overcome and there was a re-organisation of assets in 1894. In the following year, a pooling agreement with the China Navigation Co. was signed for the carriage of rice from Kobe to Australia. For a short time thereafter, the conflict between the two companies was relieved by a rise in demand for cargoes and shipping services, and this led to each line securing a growing volume of business. By 1900, however, conditions had changed once again, largely as a result of the incursion of German and Japanese ships into the trade, a fact which posed the threat of serious competition from external sources.

As we have seen, Japan's shipping company, Nippon Yusen Kaisha, was an instrument of government policy, subsidies being given in return for control over and designation of shipping routes. The Australian market assumed a potential importance for Japan after 1890, particularly in the supply of wool and ores. There were odd fluctuations in the balance of trade but, by 1900, Japan generally had an adverse pattern of settlement. Through the starting of a direct line between Japan and Australia, Nippon Yusen Kaisha was able to offer a cheap and efficient service for the carriage of both passengers and cargo and, within four years, it was reported that this company 'was sweeping the board both down and up'.[1] In 1896, Nippon Yusen Kaisha accepted an invitation from the China Navigation Co. and the Eastern and Australian Co. to work an agreement for the maintenance of freight rates and, in 1900, North German Lloyd, which had increased its services to the area, was admitted to this Conference. Even so, the Japanese and German ships were working at lower costs per ton mile (by virtue of subsidisation) than those of the two British companies. They were able to make a reasonable profit on voyages whereas Swires' ships barely covered costs.[2] The effectiveness of competition and the declining profitability of service on this route induced Swires to look elsewhere for cargoes and, as a consequence, they diverted

---

[1] Swire MSS., John Swire and Sons to Butterfield and Swire, 27 July 1899.
[2] Sheila Marriner and F. E. Hyde, *The Senior, op. cit.*, p. 94.

some of their ships to a new (and ultimately a large) trade, namely the supply of frozen meat from Australia to the Philippines. This diversion of resources had two important effects: it strengthened Nippon Yusen Kaisha's hold on the direct trade and helped to establish a feeder service between the islands for Holts' main line services to China and Japan. As a result, the holds of Blue Funnel ships were increasingly filled with additional cargoes of sugar, oilseeds and sisal from a new source and without any initial outlay of capital by way of innovation. In 1900, G. S. Yuill and Co., together with Smith, Wood and Co., built a store in Manila to serve the frozen meat trade. John Swire and Sons took a one-third share in the venture and fitted out two ships with refrigerated holds.[1] The trade increased rapidly, profits were maintained at a relatively high rate and Swires' ships were kept fully laden in a trade with few competitors. In short, the threat from Japanese ships to Swires' earning capacity had been averted and, at the same time, the trans-Pacific link with Australia had been maintained. To a large extent this new and expansive trade helped in off-setting losses incurred by the decline in the sugar and tea trades; though in the case of the latter commodity, losses were less severe and the trade as a whole survived longer than that in sugar. 'Our main object in shipping tea to the Colonies', wrote Swire, 'is to control cargo for the China Navigation Co.'[2] Herein lay the reason for Swires' Pacific enterprise and a clue to their search for new ventures under conditions of an expanding world trade.

*

These shipping ventures in the Pacific assume greater importance if they are set against the changing pattern of Far Eastern trade as a whole. From the point of view of Britain's relationship with China, the loss of the tea trade to India and the decline in the supply of cotton yarn and textiles has to be set within the general context of a more serious decline in all branches of the export trade. As a corollary, shipping companies were impelled to divert resources into new trades and invest capital in new types of construction. It was only by such means that a relatively high marginal efficiency of capital could be achieved in conditions of relative decline in trade.

The old triangular pattern of settlement between Britain, India

---

[1] *Ibid.*, p. 95.   [2] *Ibid.*, p. 48.

and China, which had operated during the first half of the nine-teenth century, was modified considerably after 1885. Britain's import of China tea fell from 137 million lb. in 1873 to 16 million lb. in 1913; whereas China's imports from Britain and Japan rose steeply after 1902.[1] China was forced to seek new outlets for its tea and silk and these outlets, as we have already seen, were secured in Europe and Russia. To add to the complications of a changing pattern of trade, Britain's main staples of export to China, cotton yarn and cloth, underwent severe and adverse fluctuation. Trade in coarse cotton drills and sheetings was lost to American exporters and that in yarn to Indian and Japanese spinners. To some extent, these losses were offset by a rise in capital goods of all kinds after 1880 and even exports of printed cottons expanded between 1881 and 1883; but the rise was short-lived and a decline set in once again in the following years. Plain cottons, however, were not so severely affected and sales to China were maintained throughout the 1880's.[2] On the other hand, the monopoly which Britain had enjoyed since 1870 in the supply of yarn to China was destroyed by Indian and Japanese competition. In 1885, Britain had supplied 20 million lb. of yarn to China; twenty years later India was sending ten times that amount and, by 1913, Britain's exports were a mere 2 million lb.[3] Competition from America in the Chinese market was equally severe but, fortunately for Britain, the growing strength of the Japanese textile industry in the production of low cost cotton cloth competed far more with American textiles than with those from Britain. It is, perhaps, not an overstatement of fact that the fortunes of the British cotton industry were largely determined by developments in the Far East. Though Britain continued to be the largest single exporter in all the principal markets of the world, the British failure to expand trade with China was a retarding factor in the years after 1900. This was so despite the fact that, by 1913, Britain was responsible for nearly 60 per cent of world trade in cottons.

Overseas demand for all descriptions of British iron and steel products and machinery increased up to 1907, to be followed by an

[1] S. B. Saul, 'Britain and World Trade, 1870-1914', *Economic History Review*, Vol. VII, No. 1, Aug. 1954, p. 50.
[2] S. B. Saul, *Studies in British Overseas Trade, 1870-1914* (1960), p. 105.
[3] P. Ray, *India's Foreign Trade since 1870* (1934), pp. 199 *et seq.*; also S. B. Saul, *op. cit.*, p. 189.

almost universal collapse in the next year. Orders for railway
equipment had been good, particularly from Japan; in fact, in the
markets of both China and Japan exports of machinery were
maintained, while those from America remained well below the
levels of exports from Britain and Germany. By 1913, exports of
electrical machinery from British firms to China were four times
greater than those from America.[1] Thus, despite fluctuations and a
decline in some of the main staples, there were gains in newer types
of products and these were generally capable of sustaining the
shipment of an increasing volume of primary products from the
Far East to Europe.

These changes in the composition of trade were reflected both in
the design of ships and in flows of investment into the rebuilding of
fleets. This was certainly the case of the highly organised Blue
Funnel Line and, to a lesser extent, in other cargo-liner companies
such as the Shires, Castles and Glens. The conclusions about the
future pattern of trade with the Far East induced Holts to invest
approximately £1·5 million in the re-equipment and rebuilding of
their fleet during the 1890's and early 1900's. Whereas, formerly,
the cargoes to China used to consist almost exclusively of Manchester and Yorkshire goods, they had now become more diverse
in character and included scrap iron, chemicals, machinery for
Japanese cotton mills, plant for woollen, paper, rice and sugar mills,
marine boilers, patent manures, iron houses and limited quantities
of railway equipment.[2] In particular, the shipments of machinery
to Japan were reported in 1896 as being 'very large' and special
attention had to be given in the construction of new ships 'to the
cargo gear and the facilities for lifting and storing large and heavy
pieces such as boilers, weighing in some instances over 30 tons'.[3]
This new type of cargo was very different from the more familiar
cargo of bales and cases and thus required new methods and a new
policy to deal with it. In retrospect, the Holts increased their
carrying capacity somewhat beyond the requirements of the trade,
and there were many years between 1901 and 1910 when ships
were returning homewards with empty space.[4] In such circumstances, it was mainly by virtue of the efficiency with which they

[1] S. B. Saul, *Studies in British Overseas Trade, 1870-1914* (1960), p. 36.
[2] F. E. Hyde, *Blue Funnel, op. cit.*, p. 76.
[3] Holt MSS., Minutes O.S.S. Co., 1890-1900, *passim*.
[4] *Ibid.*, Minutes 1901-1910, *passim*.

handled their ships, and the maintenance of freight rates within Conference agreements, that they were enabled to survive the difficulties arising from over-investment.

Other Far Eastern shipping companies were similarly affected by the change in the pattern of trade and, in general, two main consequences flowed from such change. Like Holts, they had to look to ports other than those in China in order to fill up holds with alternative cargoes of sugar, rice, sago, timber and wool. Superimposed upon this stimulus to seek additional cargo was the factor of increasing costs as voyages, perforce, had to be extended. By 1899, there had been a rise in the price of south Wales coal. To offset this rise in cost, most shipping companies were forced to increase their dependence on the supply of Eastern coal, particularly from India and Australia. For Holts, this change in the source of supply was not so great a disadvantage as for their competitors. By arrangement with Swires' trans-Pacific service, they could obtain Australian coal either in Hong Kong or at Yokohama.[1] Furthermore, in their quest for new cargoes they began loading homewards from the Philippines where, it will be remembered, China Navigation Co. ships were developing a thriving trade in Australian frozen meat. Apart from odd transhipment cargoes, however, this market supplied valuable cargoes of sugar and hemp, the latter commodity being subject to a pooling agreement among the regular steamship lines.[2] In 1905, however, the whole situation was again complicated by an 80 per cent increase in the price of Far Eastern supplies of coal, and contracts in Japan had to be cancelled in favour of alternative sources of supply from India and Australia.

Despite year-to-year fluctuations in particular trades, most British shipping companies were able to take advantage of what was generally described as 'rapid development all over the Far East and the Pacific'.[3] In this context, Holts reported in 1907 that the company was getting a fair share of 'the material that is going out'. Some of these outward shipments such as rails and rough cargo did not pay a high level of freight, but the managers of Holts thought it best to cater for the whole trade, 'giving no opportunity for rivals to get a footing'.[4] The loss of traditional staples and the consequent

[1] Holt MSS., Minutes O.S.S. Co., 1898-1910.
[2] Ibid.; see also F. E. Hyde, Blue Funnel, op. cit., p. 128.
[3] Ibid., Minutes for 1906 and 1907.
[4] Ibid., Minutes for 1907, 1908.

need to diversify went on apace until 1914. In 1907, rival companies entered the Saigon rice trade, competing with French lines in the carriage of that commodity homewards to Europe. In the following year, new cargoes of frozen produce were shipped from Hankow and bean cake for cattle in north China, together with sugar-cane from Java for that same purpose. In these various ways, therefore, the problems arising from a shift from light measurement cargo to heavy deadweight cargo were overcome.

The second consequence stemming from these changing emphases in Far Eastern and Pacific trade was concerned with the relative position of London and Liverpool as loading ports for that trade. Liverpool had always been the main loading port for Lancashire cotton yarns and cloth as well as for Yorkshire woollens. In fact, much of Holts' strength in the China trade had been based on their close association with northern textile exporters. John Swire and Sons had acted as their agent for the unloading of their ships in London, but the major part of the loading of cargoes outwards to the Far East had been done at Birkenhead. Now, however, with the change to deadweight cargoes, the Holt source of supply became increasingly centred in the Midlands. As there was very little difference in the cost of sending shipments either from Birmingham to Birkenhead or from Birmingham to London, such cargoes were likely to go either way. As a result, London began to assume a relatively greater importance than Liverpool as an outward loading port to the Far East. This importance was accentuated after 1890 when Liverpool, by reason of monopoly charges by both dock and railway authorities, became a relatively high cost port.[1] In addition, as we have already seen, it had to withstand growing competition from Manchester and a growing diversion of trade to that new port once the Manchester Ship Canal had been opened. By 1913, it was estimated that some 25 per cent of Birkenhead's loading capacity to the Far East had been captured by London brokers working on behalf of Liverpool-based shipping companies serving Pacific routes,[2] a fact which affected the Mersey's position as a port, but which had little relevance to the profitability of the various shipping companies' trades to the Far East.

[1] F. E. Hyde, *Blue Funnel*, *op. cit.*, p. 77; also F. E. Hyde, *Liverpool and the Mersey* (1971), *passim*.
[2] Holt MSS., R. D. Holt to L. Holt, 12 May 1913.

As already stated, the extension of trades in the Pacific led to the investment of large blocks of capital in new ships especially designed for carrying a wide variety of products. In the main, cargo-liner companies attempted to achieve this end without making calls upon their shareholders, though in the case of the P. and O. there were specific clauses in the continuing mail contracts which regulated capital expansion, and debentures had to be issued to cover short-term financial arrangements. Companies such as Holts' Ocean Steam and Swires' China Navigation Co. were largely self-financing, though there were periods before 1914 when the exigencies of adverse fluctuations in trade led to some tightening of resources. By contrast, the emergence of the Japanese mercantile marine was not so specifically affected, mainly because their ships had been purchased from British firms secondhand at low prices. As a result, depreciation charges were almost non-existent though working costs were relatively high. In the final analysis, subsidisation proved a most effective weapon in maintaining their services at competitive rates.

Much of Holts' ability to provide new ships for the north Pacific and Australian trades out of their own resources sprang from their cautious policy in maintaining large reserve funds. As we have seen, nearly £1·5 million was spent on rebuilding the fleet during the 1890's and early 1900's and, for this purpose, the reserve investments were a constant source of supply, though on this particular occasion the size of the rebuilding programme was such that Holts had recourse to short-term bank finance. Such a policy was dependent upon good trading conditions because the replenishment of funds could only be made from voyage profits. Accordingly, though profits increased considerably after 1894, surpluses were added to the reserves, much to the annoyance of stockholders who expected higher dividends. By 1900, the managers were able to report that, 'if shipping continues prosperous there is every reason to hope that, before very long, the cost of the great increase to the fleet now in hand, will be paid off out of reserves and voyage profits'.[1]

Of all the uses to which Holts' reserve investments were put in the years before 1914, however, the most important was in the purchase of the China Mutual in 1902. This necessitated the selling

[1] Holt MSS., Minutes O.S.S. Co. for 1900.

of £200,000 worth of securities and resulted, not only in adding further strength to the fleet as a whole, but in increasing the power of the company, particularly in the north Pacific trade. If a comparison is made with Japan's Nippon Yusen Kaisha, it becomes obvious that while Holts' heavy capital costs gave them certain competitive advantages in possessing a modern fleet which could be worked at low costs, Nippon Yusen Kaisha had a low capital cost fleet and relatively high working costs. This was so because most of the latter company's ships had been bought secondhand, Holts alone having sold eleven of their old ships to the Japanese between 1894 and 1898 for an approximate total of £86,000.[1] While these ships were soundly built and capable of continuing service, they had become wholly non-commercial as profit-earners within Holts' financial framework. To the Japanese, however, they were viable both as ocean carriers and as profit earners. Richard Holt estimated that, under Japanese management, their purchase price had been paid off within two and a half years, and that subsidies had helped in maintaining their competitive strength in all the Pacific trades.[2] By further contrast with the P. and O. there were distinctive differences worthy of emphasis. It will be remembered that the P. and O. was subsidised for the carriage of mails, a subsidy which enabled it to maintain a dividend of not less than 6 per cent. With growing competition on the Far Eastern route however, the total amount granted under successive mail contracts fell steadily and capital for the building of the fleet had to be drawn from a variety of sources. By 1887, the P. and O. fleet consisted of fifty ships totalling 200,000 tons. Up to that date, nearly £3 million had been put aside for new ships and £2·5 million had been spent on them in the period 1878 to 1887. In six years from 1875, debts amounting to £800,000 borrowed on debentures had been paid off.[3] The total assets of the company in ships, land, wharves, workshops and machinery in all parts of the world were valued at just under £4 million. By 1912, the paid-up capital was £2,340,000 in preferential stock and £1,160,000 in deferred stock. To maintain the fleet efficiently and to finance capital requirements, there had been a judicious use of reserves coupled with a policy of short-term borrowing. In short, there was

---

[1] *Ibid.*, Minutes for 1894-1898.
[2] *Ibid.*, R. D. Holt memoranda, 30 Dec. 1900.
[3] Boyd Cable, *op. cit.*, p. 183.

a fairly continuous flow of resources, but capital charges were much in excess of those paid by Holts and very considerably in excess of those paid by the Japanese.

As the China Navigation Co. extended its services across the Pacific, the fleet had to be expanded so that, by 1900, it consisted of fifty ships. The initial capital of £360,000 was increased in 1883, on the amalgamation with the Coast Boats Ownery, to £500,000. Apart from this, most of the expansion was financed without adding to the nominal capital, though approximately £2 million had to be spent on the building of new ships between 1873 and 1900.¹ In addition, nearly £500,000 was expended on the purchase of land, wharves, go-downs and other properties. Butterfield and Swire, as managers, had to find ways of meeting heavy commitments and, as a consequence, considerable strain was imposed from time to time on the resources of the Swire organisation as a whole. In general, John Swire endeavoured to finance the China Navigation Co. without making calls upon the shareholders. As an earnest of this determination he was prepared, on occasion, to make advances from John Swire and Sons in London until profits could cover disbursements. At other times, he arranged loans from personal friends, for example, some £57,000 in 1875 from Philip and Alfred Holt.² Debentures were issued in 1883 to finance the amalgamation with the Coast Boats Ownery and three years later there was a further issue of £160,000 for short-term finance.³ The need for working capital increased in direct proportion with the range and scope of the company's interests. By June 1891, John Swire and Sons had advanced no less than £235,000 to cover cash balances and to meet the cost of new ships.⁴ 'At this time, only £13,000 of debentures were outstanding, so it was decided that a further £140,000 should be issued at 4 per cent, half to mature in December 1892 and the rest in December 1893'.⁵ In addition, a loan of £145,000 was arranged with the Commercial Bank of Scotland so that, by these various means, the debt to John Swire and Sons was reduced to £20,000 by February 1892. These were only short-term expedients, however. Swires could not afford to tie up too much capital in an extension of trans-Pacific shipping services; their other interests, such as the Taikoo Sugar

---

¹ Sheila Marriner and F. E. Hyde, *The Senior, op. cit.*, p. 95.
² *Ibid.*   ³ *Ibid.*, p. 96.
⁴ *Ibid.*   ⁵ *Ibid.*

Refinery, were absorbing large amounts of capital. The accounts show that, by June 1893, the indebtedness to John Swire and Sons stood at £50,000 with £86,000 of debentures still outstanding.[1] In the following year, arrangements were made with the Commercial Bank of Scotland for new debentures amounting to £100,000. Thereafter, for the remainder of the 1890's, the problem of providing short-term finance was solved by the improvement in trade which resulted in large profits and, from these profits, reserves were built up, to the extent that the China Navigation Co. was able to meet most of its demands for working capital. Only £52,000 of debentures were outstanding by the end of 1896, the debt to John Swire and Sons having been repaid; by 1899, all debentures had been liquidated and only a small debt of £5,000 was outstanding to Swires.[2]

This record of financial achievement bears favourable comparison with that in many other well-organised shipping companies at that time. Loans were raised to cover temporary difficulties, while the building of ships and investment in port facilities were ultimately financed from reserves. In the case of the China Navigation Co. those reserves were built up consistently, the depreciation reserve standing at £260,000 in 1882 (the insurance fund at £10,000), and rising in 1896 to £1,086,645 when the reserve depreciation, boiler, and insurance accounts stood at that amount.[3] Three years later, these same items totalled nearly £1½ million. By the 1890's, therefore, the China Navigation Co. was in a strong financial position. Swires' trading strength had been assured by the establishment of pooling agreements, especially those for the Hong Kong-Manila trade and for the rice trade between Japan and Australia. Within the framework of such agreements, the earnings of the China Navigation Co. shot up despite the dislocation caused by the Sino-Japanese War. After 1900, as Swire had forecast before he died, there was an intensification of competition from outside lines, particularly from Germany and Japan. Referring to the China Navigation Co.'s business J. H. Scott wrote in 1899, 'Germans and others are showing such keenness to gain a footing on all routes, it is more in our interest to carry all the cargoes at rates reduced by squeeze claims than to allow such a vast

[1] *Ibid.*, also Swire MSS., Swire to J. H. Scott, 2 June 1893.
[2] *Ibid.*, Swire MSS., Balance Sheets for 1896 and 1899.
[3] Swire MSS., Balance Sheets for 1896 and 1899.

proportion to be diverted from us'.[1] The rising tide of competition, however, could not be stemmed by pandering to the needs of shippers. The membership of the various Conferences had to be widened to include the shipping of all nations.

There were years of adversity for most companies trading to the Pacific between 1906 and 1910, the basic causes being accentuated by crop failures in China leading to short cargoes and low earnings. There was also disorganisation in Manchuria following the Russo-Japanese War and this, in turn, disrupted the north-south grain trade. These conditions were further exacerbated by the sharpening of competition on shipping routes and, as a result, the China Navigation Co. failed in four successive years to earn sufficient to cover depreciation charges on the fleet and, for the first time, no dividend was paid for three successive years.[2] Thus, from the point of view of the shareholders they were called upon to exercise restraint in years of prosperity mainly for the purpose of securing financial stability; and, in times of adversity, they received a nil return on their investment. To this extent, it might be said that they were helping to underwrite developments of shipping services in the Far East and the Pacific and, through shipping, the direction of trade in the areas served.

As far as shipping was concerned, the changes in the pattern of trade and the growing diversity of services across the Pacific had a stimulating effect on the technological development of the steamship. Practically all the shipping companies engaged in the trade were impelled to invest heavily in new and more suitably designed ships. Larger hold space had to be made available and more efficient engines installed. If, as a result, some excess capacity was created, particularly in years of seasonal adversity, costs were reduced by a sufficient margin to ensure reasonable profitability. Holts' new ships (4,000 tons G.R.), for example, could carry cargo at 0·0258d per ton mile, this being the average cost for the fleet as a whole on a specific year's working in the 1890's; whereas their older compound tandem ships (2,100 tons G.R.) had been worked in 1880 at 0·0514d per ton mile. After 1900, the corresponding figure for a 7,000 ton ship was 0·0142d per ton mile, representing a reduction of 73 per cent on the figure for 1880.[3]

[1] Sheila Marriner and F. E. Hyde, *The Senior, op. cit.*, p. 90.
[2] *Ibid.*, p. 198.
[3] F. E. Hyde, *Blue Funnel, op. cit.*, pp. 115-16.

If trade alone is considered, there were three important factors affecting change in the pattern and structure: the decline of the tea trade homewards; the decline of cotton yarn and cloth as outward staples; the rise of Japan as a competitor in all sections of the trade. Against such a background, the efforts which were made to diversify and enter new trades throughout the Pacific assume importance. These activities not only helped in safeguarding returns on an increasing capital in shipping, but were also effective in linking Far Eastern ports with those of industrial and developing economies in the Pacific as a whole. In this way, the domination of Western demand was lessened and Far Eastern countries had a wider choice of market for the disposal of exports. This was particularly true of the traditional agricultural products, though much less so in the case of new products such as rubber and mining products such as tin. These latter continued to be geared to demand from Western industrial markets, Japan alone being excepted. Having established this change of emphasis, however, we must proceed to pose a further question as to the importance of Far Eastern trade as a whole in the wider compass of an expanding world trade, in particular how these changes affected the pattern of international settlement.

CHAPTER IX

Far Eastern Trade and International Settlement

THE emergence of Far Eastern and Pacific trade within the compass of world trade can, perhaps, best be illustrated in terms of the general pattern of settlement in both trading and other accounts, the additional items apart from trade balances being bullion movements, interest charges on international loans and certain other invisible items. In such an exercise, the relative importance of India to Britain as a focal point in inter-imperial trade must bear obvious comparison with Holland and Dutch Indonesian possessions. Side by side with this division, however, one has to take into account the change in the patterns of trade, particularly those resulting from the effective emergence of Japan and the shift in China's commodity trades with the outside world. The role of Europe and the United States was no less important but perhaps less central to our theme.

In the eighteenth century, the lack of balance in the trade between Britain and China had to be resolved by the continuous export of specie to China. In the first decades of the nineteenth century, however, as a result of increasing trade with India, the flow of precious metal was curtailed. India began exporting opium and, to a lesser extent, quantities of cotton to China, receiving in return raw silk, sugar and nutmeg. The balance turned strongly in India's favour. Thus it happened that Britain's purchases of China tea were paid for by Indian exports of opium and cotton, the triangle being completed by British exports of manufactured goods to India, by the freights earned by British ships taking part in Eastern trade and by the dues payable by Indians to the East

India Co. This pattern did not change substantially until the 1870's. After 1875, however, changes of a more complex character began to take place. China's total foreign trade (i.e. both imports and exports) rose from 125,108,000 Haikwan taels in 1868 to 973,468,000 in 1913, representing a 7·5-fold increase in terms of silver. The most rapid increase occurred after 1900 when railways were in process of penetrating the interior and when Manchuria had been thrown open to foreign commerce. In fact, the rate of growth of China's total trade for the thirteen years after 1900 was twice that of the preceding thirty-two years.[1] If allowance is made for the depreciation in the value of silver, the actual increase was approximately three and a half times over the period as a whole. If, on the other hand, we examine volumes of trade (see Appendix I), imports increased about four times and exports about three times. Against this background one can make an assessment of China's trade balances, though all figures before 1887 have to be adjusted, in order first to take account of smuggling through Hong Kong and Macao, and secondly to bring the market values of imports and exports (as expressed by Chinese Maritime Customs) into line with f.o.b. and c.i.f. prices. When such adjustments are made, it would appear that China had a favourable trade balance between 1864 and 1887, exports exceeding imports by an aggregate of 262,745,000 Haikwan taels; from 1888 to 1900, however, there was an adverse trade balance, imports exceeding exports by an aggregate of 531,389,000 Haikwan taels.[2] This adverse balance was further augmented from 1900 to 1913 by as much as 1,604,577,000 Haikwan taels.

If the above figures are given further adjustment by relating them to bullion movements and homeward remittances from Chinese emigrants working abroad, it is clear that, up to about 1900, China's foreign trade was primarily in the nature of merchandise exchange. Thereafter, its international trade became much more closely linked with international capital movements. As Yu-Kwei Cheng has shown, in addition to China's heavy adverse trade balance after 1900, the country imported 14,691,267 Haikwan taels worth of gold and silver more than it exported. Some part of this amount was offset by Chinese homeward

[1] Yu-Kwei Cheng, *Foreign Trade and Industrial Development of China* (1956), p. 12.
[2] *Ibid.*, p. 13.

remittances but most of it was invested in China, a major part of which was in the form of loans to the Chinese government.

These changes in the structure and pattern of China's trade can only find relevance if they are related to other changes currently taking place in the Pacific area as a whole, to the growth of trade between Japan and China as described in Chapter VII, to the change in India's trading relationship with both China and Japan and finally to the shift in the pattern of Britain's trade with Malaya, China and Japan after 1890. In general, traditional patterns of trade were sundered by changes in demand. In the first place, there were pressing demands for an increase in the production of foodstuffs to feed rapidly expanding populations in Far Eastern countries. From 1890 onwards, accruing surpluses were drawn into a complex system of cross-trades. Flows from the rice-producing areas of Burma, Siam and Indo-China, from the sugar plantations of Java, from the tea and coffee plantations of Indonesia and Japan were channelled through Singapore, Batavia and Hong Kong in a vast *entrepot* trade. In the second place, there was a growing two-way demand between Britain, Europe, the United States and the Far East for sugar, coffee, tea, tobacco, silk, and later tin and rubber, in return for capital goods to build up industrial potential in China and Japan and textiles to clothe the teeming populations of the Orient. This particular pattern was modified after 1890, partly by the growing importance of India and Japan as manufacturing and trading nations and partly by changes in the sources of supply for particular commodities.

Thus, China turned to Japan and India for supplies of cotton textiles and Japan to India for cotton yarns. Again, in order to offset the serious decline in the British market's demand for Chinese tea, China had to develop new export markets in Russia, Europe, the United States and Japan to which it could send increasing quantities of new products. In this way, it was possible for China to find resources for the imports of railway equipment and engineering products in demand from Britain. In much the same way Japan began to extend its influence in immediate Pacific markets for the supply of foodstuffs and to expand its export markets as a means of satisfying the persistent requirements for machinery of all kinds, railway equipment and capital goods for industrial expansion. On the other hand, Malaya, and to a lesser extent Indonesia, became a heavy exporter of tin and rubber to Western countries, thereby building up trade surpluses which, in turn, were used less for the import of Western products and rather more for those from India and Japan. In short, traditional demands within traditional markets gave way to new demands ensuing from the pressures of a changing economic environment. As a result, a much wider basis was created for the settlement of trading and other accounts.

*

It is only possible to make a broad and general assessment of the direction of Far Eastern trade. As far as trade with China is concerned, origins of imports and exports are obscured by the position of Hong Kong as an *entrepot*; in much the same way trade with Malaya and the East Indian islands is complicated by the growth of Singapore as a focal point of trade. In spite of the difficulties inherent in trade returns however, it is possible, very largely owing to the work of men such as H. B. Morse,[1] to establish a general outline of the changes taking place in the source and distribution of trade with the assurance that orders of magnitude are not unduly distorted.

Up to about 1900, it is clear that Britain and its imperial territories (excluding Hong Hong) dominated the foreign trade of China, especially the import trade. Admittedly, the domination was a declining one for, as China's trade grew, Britain's share decreased. In 1868, for example, the British share of total trade was 70 per cent; between 1888 and 1896, direct trade accounted for about 25 per cent of the total. If the figures for trade between Hong Kong and China are separately analysed for the year 1868, the share of Britain and its dependencies in Chinese imports *via* Hong Kong amounted to 90 per cent, while the corresponding percentage for exports was 78. These proportions of Hong Kong's trade with China were diminished in later years as that port became more international in scope; in other words, as Hong Kong became a distribution centre for goods originating in Japan, the United States and south-east Asia, the proportion of these imports rose in conjunction with a corresponding increase in exports to these sources. Consequently, Britain's share fell. Nevertheless, when Morse made his analysis of China's trade in 1906, including Hong

[1] H. B. Morse, *The International Relations of the Chinese Empire*, Vol. II, pp. 398-9, 402-3.

Kong in his calculations as an international port within the commercial area of China, British Empire countries were shown as contributing about one-half of China's total imports and absorbing about one-fifth of its exports.[1] On the same basis of calculation, Japan's trade with China showed a consistent increase, the Japanese share growing from 4·3 per cent in 1888 to 8·4 per cent in 1896; by 1906 the percentage was 14·2 and by 1914 it had reached almost 20 per cent.[2] The United States and Russia also increased their trade with China in both relative and absolute values, the former's share of China's exports remaining relatively stable at between 8 to 10 per cent throughout the whole period, while its share in China's imports grew from 1·1 per cent in 1868 to 10·4 per cent in 1906.[3] Russia steadily enlarged its trade with China (apart from a short period of stagnation 1904-05 following the Russo-Japanese War), its share of total trade reaching 6·8 per cent in 1913. France and Germany each had somewhat less than a 5 per cent share, although there was a contrast between them, China having a negative balance with Germany while France took about 10 per cent of China's exports in the form of silk, returning only 1 per cent as a contribution to China's imports in the years 1906 to 1913. Accordingly, China built up a favourable trade balance with France and this amounted to some 20 to 30 million Haikwan taels annually.

By comparison with China, the disposition of Japan's trade has to be viewed against the background of overseas payments which, by 1914, had not only become burdensome but also highly inelastic. As we have already stated, the intractable nature of this particular difficulty was caused by the necessity to pay interest charges on large foreign loans. Nevertheless, there was great resilience on trade account, Japan's exports being highly specialised but increasing at a rapid rate. In the 1880's, silk, tea and rice constituted approximately 66 per cent of the total trade but, by 1895, raw silk had increased its share while that of tea and rice had declined. The effects of industrialisation considerably altered the pattern of exports after 1900, cotton yarn and piece-goods and silk fabrics acquiring a greater share as the older and more

---

[1] *Returns of Trade and Trade Reports*, issued by Inspectorate General of Chinese Maritime Customs, 1906, Part I, pp. 46-7.
[2] Yu-Kwei Cheng, *op. cit.*, p. 18.
[3] *Ibid.*

traditional type of export declined in relative importance. On the import side, there were also substantial changes, the initial demand for machinery, iron and steel, and raw materials giving way, partly by reason of a direct policy of import substitution, to a demand for raw cotton and cotton yarn. We have already examined the indices of Japanese trade, but it is relevant at this point to remind ourselves that Japan's export volumes doubled between 1873 and 1882 and doubled again between 1883 and 1892, though there was a slackening in the rate of growth until 1896; after 1900, however, expansion was resumed and volumes were again doubled in the decade 1903 to 1913. Imports followed a similar trend though with a rather different time span.

In the years between 1882 and 1896, Japan was able to acquire favourable trade balances for each year apart from 1887, when there was a small deficit, 1890 and 1894 when trade was interrupted by the outbreak of the Sino-Japanese war. Underlying this apparently satisfactory position, however, was an undoubted weakness caused by the narrow base of Japan's exports and the limited markets for these exports. The highly specialist nature of raw silk, silk fabrics and cotton goods, which together accounted for some 55 per cent of total exports by 1913, was vulnerable and fraught with uncertainty. In addition, as we have seen, the outlets for these products were confined to two main markets, China and the United States, cotton goods being chiefly exported to the former and silk and silk fabrics to the latter; some 64 per cent of all Japan's exports went to these two countries before 1914. Any dislocation in the American economy was, therefore, bound to have a disproportionate and adverse effect on Japan's trade. Japan thus found itself in a position where its annual payments were fixed and trade receipts subject to fluctuation from the ebb and flow of a major Western market. As far as Britain's trading relationships with Japan were concerned, more than 75 per cent of imports were of British origin up to the mid-1880's. Thereafter, Japan's import trade became more diffused and countries such as Germany cut into Britain's share. In short, the source and distribution of Japan's trade, though more narrowly based than that of China, underwent considerable change during the fifty years before 1914. The result was an appreciable change in the pattern of international settlement and, consequently, a new emphasis in the spectrum of world trade.

The changing relationship between Britain and the Far East

was defined by new magnitudes in the pattern of overseas settlements. In the early 1880's, when there was a relatively small
volume of overseas investment, Britain had trade and bullion
deficits with Europe and the United States amounting to £105·4
million. When adjustments are made for invisible items in the
balance sheet, the deficit was still as high as £60 to £70 million.[1]
This amount was increased by a further £14 million on trading
account with the rest of the world. Against this, however, has to
be set a credit balance of some £25 million from India, thus
leaving about £60 million to be covered by invisible earnings from
the rest of the world. By 1910-11 the deficit on all accounts with
Europe and the United States was in the region of £95 million.
In addition, there was a deficit of £50 million with the rest of the
world being made up to the extent of £48 million from imperial
countries and £2 million from Argentina. Against this, Britain
had credit balances of £118 million, thus leaving a gap of £27
million which was apparently covered by a large number of small
invisible items from a wide range of countries such as Siam,
Indonesia and Indo-China.

The above statement is a very broad one and obviously needs
much qualification as to detail. For our purpose, however, we can
make adequate use of it to emphasise the relative importance of the
Far East to Britain in this present context. In 1910 Britain had
credit balances of £26 million with China and Japan while, in the
following year, China had annual trade and bullion deficits of
£10 million with India and £3 million with Japan, a substantial
part of these deficits being caused by a rising importation of
Indian and Japanese cotton-piece goods. As a partial counter to
these deficits, however, China had built up favourable balances
of £3·5 million with Russia and £6·5 million with Continental
Europe. In this way, according to S. B. Saul, 'a local pattern of
multilateral trade was dissolved by the process of growth of the
world economy generally and became part of a world-wide network'.[2] The essential reason for this was that, over the years, both
India and Japan had established large and complex patterns of
settlement with the rest of the world.

If we now examine the changes in trading and other balances

[1] S. B. Saul, *Studies in British Overseas Trade, 1870-1914* (1960),
pp. 56-7.
[2] S. B. Saul, *op. cit.*, p. 45.

for the rest of the world, the relative importance of an emergent Far East becomes apparent. Up to about 1885, the United States, apart from Europe, had a positive balance only with Australia, of a little less than £1 million, with deficits (in 1881) of £3·5 million to both India and China and about £3 million to Japan. By comparison, its deficit with Europe was only a little over £0·5 million. With the very rapid rise in the industrial capacity of the United States after 1885, there was a corresponding rise in demand from the American market for Eastern and south-east Asian products. There was, however, no reciprocal proportionate demand for United States manufactured goods, mainly because of low income levels in all the eastern primary producing countries. Such markets were being increasingly served by the highly competitive and lower cost products from India, Europe and Japan. Thus, the United States continued to have adverse balances with the Far East. On the other hand, though Britain had heavy debit balances with Europe and the United States in the years around 1900 (and by 1910 with Canada in particular), Britain increased its earnings from India, China and Japan on trade account, together with high income from Australia after 1908, caused mainly by interest payments on loans and repatriation operations.[1] Offsetting this generally favourable situation, Britain had a deficit with the Straits Settlements (including trade with Malaya) of some £11 million. This deficit was not easily reduced, particularly in trading account, as Britain's staple export to the Straits Settlements, namely textiles, was progressively threatened by competition from Indian manufacturers.[2] Apart from this, however, the main settlements with Europe and America were, in the years before 1914, through the Far East, Australia helping to close the multilateral pattern linking Britain and Europe. Again, as S. B. Saul has pointed out, the key to Britain's balance of international payments lay in India, this latter country financing some two-fifths of Britain's total deficits before 1914.[3]

*

The part played by the changing structure and direction of Far Eastern trade, as elements in the pattern of international

[1] *Ibid.*, p. 60.
[3] *Ibid.*, see Appendix to Chapter III, p. 237.
[2] S. B. Saul, *Economic History Review, op. cit.*, p. 64.

settlements, invites comparison between the two colonial powers, Britain and Holland. We have already traced the historical background to the extension of Dutch influence in the East Indies. As far as shipping and trade were concerned, the outstanding point to notice is that Dutch control was greatly reduced in both sectors during the period 1870 to 1914. Indonesian exports rose from 175 million florins in 1880 to 671 million in 1913, representing in real terms a possible three-fold increase. In 1870, about 76 per cent of total exports from Indonesia went to Holland, of which 60 per cent was carried in ships of either Dutch or of Dutch-Indonesian origin. By 1912-13, the average share of total exports to Holland had fallen to 26 per cent, and of this amount only 28 per cent was carried in Dutch ships.[1] According to J. A. M. Caldwell, Holland's economic control in Indonesia had declined from a position of virtual monopoly to a point where its share in its colonies' trade was lower than that of any other comparable imperial power.[2] Furthermore, as a large part of such exports to Holland was re-exported, retained imports were considerably reduced, a reduction which, in some years, amounted to less than 10 per cent of total Indonesian exports to Holland.

By contrast, Britain's share of its imperial trade was considerably larger than that taken by Holland. The proportion of colonial produce in Britain's total import trade remained fairly constant between 1870 and 1900. Thereafter, until 1914, the share of food imports rose while that of raw materials fell. By 1913, some 25 per cent of Britain's imports came from imperial sources and, if re-exports are taken into account, about 20 per cent was retained.[3] If individual commodities are considered, the emphasis is considerably altered. These sources provided about half the wheat, rice, tea, cheese, cocoa, wool, jute, tin and rubber imported. Like Holland, however, Britain profited greatly from the re-export of colonial produce, total receipts in 1913 being valued at £56 million.[4] This balance provided Britain with resources for multilateral settlement and so gave direct relief against undue fluctuation of trade in other markets.

[1] J. A. M. Caldwell, *op. cit.*, p. 96.
[2] *Ibid.*
[3] S. B. Saul, *Studies in British Overseas Trade, 1870-1914* (1960), p. 223.
[4] *Ibid.*, p. 225.

The main point of this discussion, however, is the importance of India as a bulwark in the financing of Britain's overseas trade. Although Britain's share of trade with China and Japan decreased, British balances on trade and other accounts were turned from debit to credit. Holland's share of its trade with Indonesia, however, declined absolutely and the Dutch had no comparable source, such as that which the British had in India, to act as fulcrum in its international balance of payments. In fact, it was through India that Britain acquired the flexibility necessary for a great trading and capital-exporting country. As Britain's adverse balances were built up with Canada, the United States and the Argentine in the years before 1914, the increasing surpluses with China, Japan and India assumed much greater significance. The surpluses with China and Japan helped towards offsetting deficits with the Straits Settlements and Malaya, while the large credit balances with India amounting to some £60 million went far towards covering other deficits, both imperial and foreign.[1] Thus, as long as Britain continued to export large quantities of goods to India, it could indirectly overcome foreign tariff barriers through India's own export trade. From the point of view of international payments for example, India was able to contribute to Britain's dollar settlements by exporting primary commodities to the United States.

The wider implications of these changing factors in the pattern of international settlement can be seen in the new relationship caused by the emergence of Far Eastern countries into the expanding network of world trade. As we have seen, Britain had, by 1914, rising balances with India, China and Japan on trade account and a deficit with the Straits Settlements. On the other hand, India had an excess of exports to the rest of the Empire of £15·8 million and one of £48·6 million to foreign countries, £30 million of which came from trade with Europe, £10·3 million from China and Hong Kong and £6·8 million from Japan.[2] Thus, the old closed triangular pattern of settlement between Britain, India and China had, by 1914, become much wider in scope and character. Whereas previously Britain had deficits with the Far East, there were now sizeable surpluses. The growth in Pacific

---

[1] S. B. Saul, *Economic History Review, op. cit.*, p. 65.
[2] *Ibid.*, p. 64.

trade as a whole had altered the balance, and both India and Australia were involved in filling the gaps in Britain's trading account caused by deficits elsewhere. In this sense, the new and lively changes in the structure of Far Eastern trade played a vital and important part in world trade as a whole.

CHAPTER X

The Function of Capital in Far Eastern Trade

WITHIN the terms of reference governing the contents of this volume, our text should be primarily concerned with enterprise resulting from the activities of the individual rather than that sponsored by governments or by institutions. Behind all the statistics of relative growth and decline in particular Far Eastern trades stand men who were prepared to risk their capital and work with untiring enthusiasm in the pursuit of an idea. That idea, it is true, was usually fostered by acquisitive desire which, in basic terms, could be translated into a profitable return on capital employed; but it would be wrong to suggest that this was their sole motive. Many shipping companies and merchant houses contributed generously to the foundation of schools, universities and other recreational and educational institutions in the Far East, while others created opportunities for the dissemination of Western technology through the provision of tea factories, silk and rice mills, sugar refineries and dockyards. In aggregate terms of expenditure, these efforts did not amount to any significant sum when compared with the gross receipts from shipping and trade; but they indicate a sense of responsibility towards the areas served and a desire to promote the well-being of certain, albeit small, sections of the indigenous population.

It is quite impossible to make a valid comparison of the various types of enterprise which contributed to the growth of Far Eastern trade. There were men with ideas such as Ridley, Bennett and Hooker who were not only conscious of the potential profitability of starting a new primary source of production in the planting of rubber trees, but were also objective in their assessment of the future economic benefits which would accrue to south-east Asia as a whole. Equally important were the ideas of men like Bogaardt and Nienhuys in their promotion of trade with the East Indian islands, and those of Van den Ahrend and Jacob Cremer in the development of the Deli tobacco trade. On yet another plane, the promotional activity of such monarchs as King Mongkut of Siam in opening up his country to Western trade, of Prince Henry of the Netherlands and of Japanese and Chinese business men must be given due emphasis. In sponsoring technical innovation there was a long list of men with exceptional capability, whose strength of purpose in a particular field eventually led to an increase in productivity and to growth in trade. In commercial matters however, it was the merchant and the shipowner who wielded the greatest influence over the production and direction of supplies in answer to the changing pattern of demand. Through the adaptation of their resources to the requirement of trade, through their willingness to risk capital in the starting of new trades and through their sensitive and responsive attitude to market conditions, their wide range of enterprise was made manifest. From among so numerous a body, one can only attempt a very limited assessment based on a small range of companies and, for this reason, we have chosen to examine British rather than other foreign enterprise, drawing our conclusions from three organisations (which in themselves comprehended a fairly diverse range of companies), whose joint influence on Far Eastern trade was probably greater than any other combination of interests. The three organisations chosen are those of Rathbones, Holts and Swires, Rathbones representing the more traditional type of trading existing before 1875, Holts that of the new steamship company, and Swires the new and highly developed structure serving a variety of needs in a rapidly expanding market.

The essence of commercial enterprise lies in the ability of the merchant or shipowner to provide credit and capital for the whole range of his operations, in seeking out new avenues for the profitable employment of resources and in applying experience and knowledge to a prospective use of such resources. Fundamentally, Rathbones, Holts and Swires relied on their own capital, and the credit which could be generated from such capital, as the springboard for future activity. In Rathbones' case, this was in sharp

THE FUNCTION OF CAPITAL 199

contrast with a good deal of contemporary practice; for most houses engaged in the early China trade operated almost entirely on credit made available to them by other firms. Thus, as Dr Marriner has shown in her study of the Rathbone organisation, the problems which the partners had to solve arose largely from the difficulties inherent in the utilisation of their own capital rather than from external sources of finance.[1] In much the same way Holts placed great faith in the efficacy of large resources, and this, as we have seen, induced a policy of conservatism, reduced their competitive strength in the 1880's and brought them almost to the verge of ruin.[2] It was only in the 1890's, when they were rebuilding their fleet, that they called upon external sources to help them fulfil their commitments. The Swire organisation also made use of bank finance and the issue of debentures to embark upon programmes of construction for the China Navigation Co. The real point is, however, that whenever indebtedness was incurred the strength of financial management and organisation ensured quick repayment.

In the period before 1850, Rathbones were primarily concerned in building up their resources to keep pace with their own and with their correspondents' activities, a phase, be it remembered, when they were engaged in both the American and the China trades. After 1850, however, their major preoccupation was to discover ways of sustaining credit operations and of maintaining their accumulating capital in profitable employment. As a result, the impact of their financial policy had repercussions over a wide field of trading commitments. They used their capital directly in the China trade or indirectly as a reserve fund from which they could create credit for the financing of their own activity and that of their many correspondents abroad.[3] In general, their capital was used as a reserve to support credit operations necessary for their trading ventures. Their foreign exchange transactions were largely promoted through the sale of bills of exchange drawn on them by correspondents under letters of credit. This was a system which was fairly common and long-established in commercial practice. It was, nevertheless, a procedure open to risk, especially at times when other China houses were engaged in speculative transactions

[1] Sheila Marriner, *Rathbones of Liverpool, op. cit.*, pp. 121 *et seq.*
[2] Holt MSS., Swire correspondence, 1881-90; also Minutes O.S.S. Co., Accounts and Voyage Profits, 1880-1890.
[3] Sheila Marriner, *op. cit.*, p. 206.

and operating almost entirely on London credits, without adequate reserves of their own. In such circumstances, Rathbones took special care in safeguarding their reputation by relating the issue of letters of credit to outstanding liabilities at any given time. Only by such a method could they conserve funds for their own produce dealings and have adequate resources to meet maturing bills.[1] Thus, by dint of careful planning and by scrupulous attention to the likely demands upon them, they were generally able to keep their reserves fully employed. At the same time, by suiting the requirements of the market to their available resources, they were able to avoid undue risk, especially in those produce operations which were liable to sudden and intense speculation. In fact, bills could only be drawn under Rathbones' credits up to a certain percentage of the invoice value of the goods purchased, the proportion varying with the prospects of the market.[2] By such prudent management Rathbones were able to build up a large and relatively successful credit acceptance business, at a time when very large internationally based financial houses such as Barings and Rothschilds were concentrating this type of business in their own hands.

In the case of bills drawn against the purchase of tea or silk shipped direct to Rathbones for sale, the receipts from such sales were usually to hand in time to cover the bills at the date of maturity. If, by chance, sales were delayed, correspondents were requested as a matter of course to send funds; but, regardless of practice, it was always a matter of principle with Rathbones to see that cash was available as a surety against the possibility of default. In 1857 and 1873, for example, their capital was used effectively in sustaining the financial standing of their own and other trading houses. The China trade, in particular, required measures of generosity to correspondents. As bill transactions became more difficult and, as a result of improvement in transport facilities, produce operations became strictly seasonal, Rathbones were induced to widen the scope of their interests in order to keep their capital employed throughout the whole year. It goes without saying that they endeavoured to confine any new enterprise to safe and non-speculative trades even though these provided a relatively small profit margin. The China tea trade was one in which risks were coupled with a slow turn-over of capital; silk, on the other

[1] Sheila Marriner, *op. cit.*, p. 207.
[2] *Ibid.*, p. 208.

hand, was subject to a somewhat narrower range of fluctuation in prices, this latter trade being regarded by Rathbones as 'one of great safety and capability'.[1] If their business was conducted within limits of safety, however, the scope of their enterprise was not so restricted; their strength sprang from their financial stability and this, in turn, was buttressed by the multifarious extension of interest and activity. Nevertheless, in all operations, they applied the strict ruling that their capital should earn a minimum of 5 per cent and, as Dr Marriner discovered, they always made a debit charge of this amount on their capital involved before declaring a profit.[2]

Apart from its use in financing produce trades, Rathbones gave their capital two other principal functions: in the first place, they made frequent loans to correspondents (particularly in time of crisis) and thus, by securing loyalty, directly promoted their own business interests[3]; in the second place, they undertook agency work for foreign banking and insurance companies. This involved them in claims on behalf of customers of the companies, the insurance firms depositing with them first-class security covering the amounts they were likely to have to disburse, though Rathbones had to maintain cash balances to meet current claims.[4] These various ways of using capital, however, did not always solve their problems, particularly those concerned with surplus cash in hand. At times, when produce operations were diminished or when seasonal flows of cash preceded the maturing of bills by several months, the accumulation of cash was likely to cause acute embarrassment. By 1868, William Lidderdale, their London partner, was writing regretfully that he could 'not suggest any new ways of relieving R.B. and Co. of money'.[5] The whole lack of balance in this situation was caused primarily by peculiarity in the China trade in that cargoes arrived and were sold some six months before settlement was due. There was, nevertheless, one single advantage accruing from periodic seasonal fluctuations of this kind. Large cash balances provided a source of strength for Rathbones in times of crisis; but, apart from this, the holding of liquid assets

[1] Rathbone MSS., W. S. Brown to S. G. Rathbone, 31 Oct. 1854.
[2] Sheila Marriner, *op. cit.*, p. 211, quoting Rathbone MSS., Rathbone Bros. and Co. to F. B. Birley, April 1851.
[3] Sheila Marriner, *op. cit.*, p. 213.
[4] *Ibid.*, p. 215.
[5] Rathbone MSS., Lidderdale to T. K. Twist, 28 Oct. 1868.

constituted a cause for anxiety—anxiety which could only be alleviated by a sound investment policy for the channelling of balances into long and short-term securities.

Rathbones' investment policy was, perhaps, indicative of new emphasis, especially as it applied to the function of a merchant house trading with China. Their investment policy was governed by two principles: the avoidance of speculation and the maintenance of securities in a readily accessible form to provide cash. This in no way differed from current practice among the more reputable China houses but, contrary to contemporary custom, they did not become providers of capital to large external institutions. Many houses, for example, had begun as traders and, having engaged in acceptance business, finally ended as finance houses. The major part of Rathbones' capital on loan went to their own trusted correspondents.[1] While it is true that they did not collect funds from the general public in order to advance loans or security operations, they did attempt, in 1866, to obtain advances from the Bank of England against Consols as security.[2] In general, though they were primarily interested in merchanting operations, it is clear that their ultimate success depended on how profitably they handled their wider financial interests. Any profits accruing from produce transactions could quite easily have been cancelled by losses arising from an unwise investment policy. In the direction of the firm's investments, the wise counsel and judgment of William Lidderdale, their London partner who in 1870 became a director of the Bank of England, were of significance and, in the practical issue of safeguarding their assets, of great importance.

Though Rathbones may be considered as traditional in their management of the China trade, the scope and organisation of their total business broke new ground. The fact that a merchant house needed capital to back up its credit and financial operations had led in the past to a wide and disparate use of resources. Rathbones proved, however, that though capital could not be confined entirely to merchanting functions, it could be utilised in a variety of associated ways to attract more trade. The China trade, by virtue of its fluctuating character, was one in which it had always been difficult to keep capital fully employed. Rathbones showed how this

[1] Sheila Marriner, *op. cit.*, p. 220.
[2] *Ibid.*, p. 221. Rathbone MSS., Lidderdale to S. G. Rathbone, 22 May 1873.

innate difficulty could be overcome. Their practice of providing cover for contingencies, using funds as a generator of credit and employing short-term cash reserves as a source of investment, undoubtedly led to the development of specialist financial services in the promotion of trade. The valid point to notice is that this provision was in being on the China coast some time before British financial institutions had reached a mature degree of efficiency. By demonstrating successfully that part or even the whole of a firm's capital could be employed outside normal trading activity, Rathbones contributed a new element to the structure and organisation of a China merchant house. In this sense they established the link between the older type of colonial merchant and the new power of the steamship agent who, after 1870, was to provide an increasing array of services based on specialised forms of communication.

*

Though the Rathbones were shipowners as well as merchants, the Holt organisation was based on a somewhat different concept, both in management and, obviously, in the type of service offered. When Alfred and Philip Holt sent their first ship to China in 1866, they had no knowledge of conditions on the China coast nor of the type of commercial structure needed to secure cargoes. Their main concern had been to build a ship capable of making such a long-distance voyage. Having achieved this, their next problem was how to make that ship pay its way. Holts' efforts in accomplishing this end comprehend a very different measure of enterprise from that of the Rathbones, even when one allows for the distinctive and specialist nature of their service. Yet one would hesitate before suggesting that Holts' activities were less profound in their influence on the course of Far Eastern trade than those of the Rathbones. The latter were not innovators in the Holt sense; they were representative, admittedly enlightened in their attitude and policy, of an old order. Holts were, by chronology and technology, the exponents of the new. If their enterprise was different in scope and magnitude, it achieved the same result by bringing China and the Far East into closer contact with Western capital and, through this contact, it improved the productive capacity of the region and secured a wider distribution of the products of native labour. What, then, were the distinguishing features of the use of capital in steamship enterprise?

Holts' Ocean Steam Ship Co. (the Blue Funnel Line), founded
in 1865 with an initial capital of £156,000, was owned and
controlled by a small group consisting of members of the family
and close personal friends. In this, the organisation was no different
from that of the Rathbones or the Swires. By 1872, the capital had
grown to £532,500 and it was decided, in view of good trading
prospects and the satisfactory level of reserves, that no further
calls for capital need be made.[1] Apart from certain short periods
when large-scale reorganisation of the fleet had to be put in hand,
the cost of all new ships was (until 1914 at least) met out of earnings
and the reserves. The nominal capital was adjusted when the
steamship company was incorporated in 1902 and, until comparatively recently, remained at a figure of £425,337.[2] Within ten years
of the company's foundation, the reserves stood at £294,000,
largely invested in railway stock and United States government
bonds. The income from these investments (£17,000 in 1875) was
used to offset deficits in various accounts, and the reserves themselves were a constant source for the replenishment of tonnage, as
well as fulfilling their original function of maintaining financial
stability. Without such backing Holts might well have gone out of
business in the 1880's, when losses at sea, poor trading years and
competition from the China Mutual all but crippled their re-
cuperative power. In general, the level of the reserves was maintained by paying a moderate rate of dividend and by channelling all
available surpluses into the various reserve accounts. In no year
after 1881 did reserves fall below £350,000, except in 1902 when
the purchase of the China Mutual shares necessitated a reduction
to £269,000.[3] If, however, one adds in the company's holding of its
own stock, its interests in the East India Ocean Steam Ship Co.
and the Dutch Blue Funnel Line (N.S.M.O.), the absolute amount
in reserve investments never fell below £500,000 in the whole
period 1886-1902.

In the absence of complete documentation, it is difficult to
apply techniques of measurement when attempting to assess the
growth of a firm. In Holts' case, however, it is possible to compare
employed capital (i.e. total assets less liabilities) for the two periods

[1] F. E. Hyde, *Blue Funnel*, *op. cit.*, p. 144.
[2] Holt MSS., Minutes O.S.S. Co., 1903; F. E. Hyde, *Blue Funnel*,
op. cit., p. 144.
[3] Holt MSS., Minutes O.S.S. Co., Accounts 1881-1902.

1903-04 and 1913-14. In the former years, their employed capital in round figures was £1,800,000, while in the latter period it was just short of £4 million.[1] When necessary adjustments are made, it is a reasonable conclusion that Holts' assets doubled in the ten years before 1914. An alternative view would suggest that this growth in ten years was equivalent to that which had taken place in the preceding forty. This rate of growth (particularly the varying pace of growth) is reasonably consistent with rates of growth for Pacific trade as a whole. This is one further indicator that, by virtue of capital expansion derived in this case from voyage profits, Holts' share in a growing Pacific trade was being maintained. In proof of this statement one has only to look at the growth of receipts from their purely Far Eastern interests (i.e. the Singapore coal account, the Australian steamers, the Island steamers, the Shanghai and Hankow wharves) to measure the correlation; earnings from these sources were £31,600 in 1903-04 and rose to just under £200,000 in 1914.[2] In other words, the outflow of capital from what was originally a purely shipping activity by itself generated many other subsidiary interests of a commercial nature; as genesis and growth of Holts' resources ran parallel with Far Eastern economic development as a whole, the returns were, therefore, in correspondence with general trends.

This somewhat conservative policy of financial strength through capital accumulation caused John Swire considerable apprehension, and led to forthright criticism of the Holt brothers in the management of their resources. 'Divide your reserve fund,' he urged, 'and add to your fleet by issuing new shares at a premium equivalent to the value of the old stock.'[3] In Swire's judgment, the only way in which Holts could sustain their position on Far Eastern trading routes was by building new ships capable of competing on favourable terms with their competitors. On the Holt side there was, perhaps, a wider view of the efficacy of large reserves. They enabled the company to enter upon large-scale activity with complete freedom from dependence on external sources of capital. If Swire thought of their reserves in terms of potential tonnage, Alfred and Philip Holt looked to them as a source for the extension of their trading interests in the Far East. Thus, during the 1890's,

[1] F. E. Hyde, *Blue Funnel, op. cit.,* p. 156.
[2] *Ibid.*
[3] Holt MSS., Swire correspondence, Swire to A. Holt, 7 Dec. 1880.

they not only reorganised and rebuilt their fleet, but at the same time consolidated their trade with Malaya, Siam and Sumatra, developed trade with western Australia, entered the Java trade through the foundation of their Dutch company, provided wharfage and lighterage facilities at Pootung, Hankow and Kowloon and, by purchasing the China Mutual, gained access to new routes across the northern Pacific to Canada and the United States. In such promotional use of their capital, John Swire could scarcely have forborne to give approval and praise.

As Holts' enterprise expanded, success in the use of resources depended on growing efficiency in management. If such success can be measured in terms of economy in the design and use of ocean carriers, in mounting profits, in reduced costs and greater capital resources, then their management was, indeed, efficient. Nevertheless, they were forcibly made aware of the hard economic fact that, once a firm has attained a certain size, momentum in the efficiency of organisation can only be sustained if capital is readily available. In Holts' case, their determination to keep control of capital within their hands not only enabled them to pursue a reasonably consistent course in the spreading of risks, but also to seize every favourable opportunity for the expansion of activity. In this respect, their policies were in tune with prevailing changes in economic conditions in the Pacific. As far as Britain was concerned, the change in the sources of raw material supply had come with suddenness and, from 1880 onwards, the level of real wages was largely determined by the terms on which it could obtain imports, those terms, in turn, depending on the investment of capital in developing countries.

Thus, in every aspect of Holts' shipping business with the Pacific, capital, somewhat painfully accumulated from earnings, had been used in a variety of ways to expand the company's control of a growing market. In this, their view of the promotional function of capital was not basically different from that of the Rathbones. The new element in the concept of capital usage sprang from the inherent direction of a steamship company's resources, because the efficient management of such resources involved a wider perspective of the role of a firm in its relationship with the growth and development of overseas trade. Holts' reliance on the strength of large reserves may have given them a sound financial structure, but it resulted in a conservative use of resources. Up to 1892, the extension of their influence in the Far East had been circumscribed by an over-cautious policy. Though capital had been used to widen the scope of services, it had not been applied to maintaining the efficiency of the fleet and, as a consequence, Holts' competitive strength had declined. After 1895, however, younger partners such as Richard Holt gave a new direction to Holt enterprise. The principles which John Swire had urged upon them since 1880 were rigorously applied and capital was given a more dynamic role in the promotion of trade. According to John Swire, financial stringency was much less a hazard than the danger of using obsolete ships in highly competitive trades. If capital were employed in making ships efficient, returns would be maximised and *ipso facto* larger cash flows for future development could be made available. So ran the argument; and it is, perhaps, no coincidence that under such stimulus Holts' fortunes began to rise. It remains to be seen whether Swire's own interests, intermingled as they were with the fluctuating prosperity of the Holts, could find newer and more profitable uses for capital in the maintenance of his own Far Eastern enterprise.

*

An attempt has been made elsewhere to assess the nature and profitability of the Swire organisation and associated enterprises.[1] The deficiencies in the records of the two Far Eastern constituents, Butterfield and Swire and the China Navigation Co., do not allow a precise calculation to be made; but the ledger accounts of the parent company, John Swire and Sons, which incorporated balances from the two Eastern companies, are sufficient to give a picture adequate for our purpose. The summary of the annual profit and loss accounts probably give an accurate, though general, idea of the earnings of John Swire and Sons (London), though they do not contain the detail essential for precise analysis. The profit and loss accounts in the private ledger held in the London house are fully supplemented, as far as London business is concerned, by a complete set of general ledgers, journals and cash books for the period 1868 to 1879. The lack of detailed information for the organisation as a whole makes it difficult for us to attempt anything more than a general assessment of the profitability and use of aggregate capital resources.

[1] Sheila Marriner and F. E. Hyde, *The Senior, op. cit.*

The first point worthy of emphasis is that fairly heavy losses were sustained in produce operations for specific years in the 1870's and that there was a rapid decline in this type of business after 1884.[1] These apparent losses may have been offset in some measure by commissions charged by Butterfield and Swire for handling the business, but there is no information in the accounts of the magnitude of such earnings. From Swire's point of view, the whole commercial atmosphere in the 1870's was bedevilled by falling prices, financial stringency, bankruptcies and failures. In general terms, the balance on trading account may be cast as follows: from 1868 to 1880, the loss on goods exported was approximately £97,000; the loss on silk imported, approximately £78,000; the loss on tea to America, £44,000; exports of tea to Britain also registered losses until 1879. At that point an exceptionally good season returned so large a profit that all previous losses were covered and a surplus of £23,000 was retained.[2] Against this formidable array of loss on produce operations during the 1870's have to be set the various credit items from Butterfield and Swire, the earnings from commissions on work undertaken by John Swire and Sons in London, and the earnings from the insurance and other accounts. These sources of income enabled the firm to weather the commercial storms of the 1870's, though the margin must have been a very narrow one. This margin was not much larger in the 1880's, but the profit and loss situation in this decade was masked by the fact that John Swire and Sons' capital was rising and interest payments on this were met internally through the interest account. It is true that, on occasion, this account was in deficit but, during the 1880's and 1890's, it was receiving an increasing volume of credit from the firm's rising investments. The reward for long years of effort came only after 1890, when profits began to show a substantial rise. With the exception of 1891 and 1892, trading losses were greatly reduced, though losses on exchange transactions were persistent if not disastrously heavy. The interest account was in credit throughout the decade, being constantly replenished by dividends on investment and loans mainly granted to the China Navigation Co. and the Taikoo Sugar Refinery, and also from rents charged by Butterfield and Swire on properties in China. Thus, increasing receipts from these particular

---

[1] Sheila Marriner and F. E. Hyde, *The Senior*, *op. cit.*, p. 187.
[2] *Ibid.*, p. 191. Swire MSS., ledger accounts.

items were sufficient to cover the growth in interest payments on the partners' capital. The comparatively large increase in Butterfield and Swire's earnings can be accounted for by the growth of commissions from the sale of Taikoo sugar and from the expansion of the trading ventures across the Pacific of the China Navigation Co.'s fleet.[1] All this was, of course, exclusive of the commissions earned from Holts' Blue Funnel agency, earnings which, in relation to the amount of business done, were comparatively small but which were, nevertheless, on a rising trend after 1890.

If, instead of looking at annual returns, we make a calculation for successive decades, a rather better picture of the profitability of Swire's enterprise may be gained. Including the amounts credited as the interest on Swire's family capital, but excluding the interest credited to Eastern partners, the comparative profits were:

1868-80, £366,024; (annual average £28,155)
1881-90, £412,552; (annual average £41,255)
1891-1900, £748,561; (annual average £74,856)[2]

In the first twenty years of the Swire organisation's promotional effort on the rivers and along the coasts of China, comparatively heavy losses on produce transactions bore directly on return to capital. This situation was exacerbated by the withdrawal of Butterfield's capital and legal complications concerning the partnership agreement. The result was that Swire found himself short of liquid resources for trading and development purposes. It was not until the 1890's that this particular difficulty was resolved. As a corollary to the decline in produce transactions there was a change in methods of finance. Acceptance business by bills of exchange fell sharply from £510,000 in 1871 to £86,894 in 1879. To offset the gap caused by this decline, there was a corresponding increase in bank finance through credits and overdrafts.

In attempting to assess the demand for capital over the whole field of operations in the Far East, one has to consider the needs not only of John Swire and Sons but also those of Butterfield and Swire, the China Navigation Co., the Taikoo Sugar Refinery and, at a later date, the Taikoo Dockyard and Tientsin Lighter Co. It is clear that the parent company, John Swire and Sons, had to bear responsibility in times of stringency for the financial stability of constituents. The problem, therefore, was to manage the business

[1] Ibid., p. 193.   [2] Quoted ibid., p. 196.

of this company so that it could act as a buffer in times of need and as a generator in times of expansion. The essence of such a policy is inherent in the concept which John Swire himself had of the use of reserves, in the function of his own and of his partner's capital and in the nature and profitability of other forms of enterprise. As far as shipping policy was concerned, John Swire, as we have already seen, regarded reserves as potential tonnage. By maintaining the efficiency of shipping services, by investing in wharves, go-downs, lighterage and other port facilities, by spreading capital over such industrial enterprises as the Taikoo Sugar Refinery and Taikoo Dockyard, the Swire organisation secured high average returns under conditions of limited risk. In directing this policy, Swire was himself acting on the good advice which he so often gave to the Holt brothers. He preferred to use resources rather than to hoard them, taking a somewhat shorter view of the efficacy of capital than did the Holts.

Perhaps the best way of estimating the financial results of Swire's enterprise is by a consideration of the increase in his own capital. At his father's death in 1847, John Swire inherited £1,000. By 1867, when he had started his direct interest in Far Eastern trade, the ledger of John Swire and Sons shows his capital as £39,192; when he died in 1898, he left approximately £220,000.[1] There is a degree of correlation between the rate of growth of Swire's private resources and that of the organisation as a whole, though within the compass of growth there are some interesting facts relevant to this context. He had, some time before his death, relinquished his share in the profits of John Swire and Sons in favour of his two sons, receiving only the interest on his capital. His estate would undoubtedly have been greatly increased had he taken the profit due to him during the prosperous years of the 1890's. The extent of Swire family resources available for financing trade was given in 1868 as £96,345, by 1875 the total was £427,840 and by 1879 the amount had risen to £503,404.[2] These aggregates were made up from the resources of John Samuel Swire, William Hudson Swire and from balances in the general accounts of Butterfield and Swire. The fact that capital growth in the early years was slow was but a reflection of depression in the China trade.

[1] Swire MSS., Ledger John Swire and Sons, 1867 *et seq.*; also Will of John Samuel Swire, 12 Aug. 1898, probate 27 Jan. 1899.
[2] Swire MSS. Additional records ledgers, for 1868, 1875 and 1879.

Net receipts from trading were, therefore, not a ready source from which capital accounts could be replenished.

Both John Swire and his brother, William, contributed directly to the resources of John Swire and Sons by allowing the greater proportion of their profits and the interest on their capital to accumulate in the firm's accounts. At the end of 1876, when William retired, his capital amounted to £136,819 and he left £100,000 of this on loan to the firm, subject to certain provisos.[1] The remainder was transferred to John Swire's partnership account which, by 1880, had grown to £210,037. Nevertheless, William's retirement had posed a problem to John concerning the advisability of taking a new partner or of merging with another firm. The urgent need was for more capital. One obvious solution lay in a new partnership, a course which, after due consideration, Swire rejected. Despite the many calls which were then being made on him, he decided to carry the whole burden of management and bear sole responsibility for the financial implications of such action.[2] For many years, financial considerations continued to dominate the firm's policy. Swire could always find much more profitable employment for capital than the total amount over which he had control, and his constant endeavour was to keep reserves in a liquid form. It thus became necessary for him to keep a strict watch on the whole range of activity in order to ensure a profitable use of resources. By the 1890's, however, through the abandonment of produce transactions and by the increasing dependence on bank loans and other financial expedients, this particular problem had become less acute. In its place arose the more insistent problem involving the delegation of managerial responsibility as the whole enterprise grew in magnitude and complexity.

By the 1890's, the situation had changed and the whole organisation had control of, and command over, substantial resources. The extent of the change can be judged from the fact that, when a new partnership agreement was signed in 1892, the partners of the Far Eastern companies, having themselves accumulated considerable capital, were given sanction to leave money on deposit with the parent company to a maximum of £100,000. By 1896, the capital

[1] Ibid.; see also Sheila Marriner and F. E. Hyde, The Senior, op. cit., p. 212.
[2] Ibid., p. 25.

of John Swire and Sons stood at £750,000 with liabilities on its own account for goods and acceptances amounting to a mere £22,000; whereas its liabilities to the Commercial Bank of Scotland and to Hambros on behalf of the China Navigation Co. and the Taikoo Sugar Refinery totalled £250,000.[1] Herein lies the clue to John Swire's view of the function of capital in the promotion of Far Eastern trade. His essential aim was to make it work in as many ventures as possible, each unit being employed to full capacity. John Swire and Sons acted as clearing house and undertook responsibility for liabilities incurred by the insatiable demands of the Far Eastern constituents. Between 1910 and 1914, for example, John Swire and Sons advanced £200,000 to the Taikoo Dockyard alone and, as we have seen from this text, the natural flow of resources to constituents in time of stringency formed strong internal links uniting Swire's interests as a whole, as well as providing a bulwark against external pressures. As a result, Swire's reputation for financial integrity became established, built up as it was on prudent management during long lean years of adversity. When more prosperous conditions began to prevail after 1890, the strength of the organisation as a whole enabled management to achieve much greater flexibility in the promotional use of its capital.

*

We have examined three distinctive attitudes adopted by British firms in their promotion of Far Eastern trades. There are obviously many variations on this theme, but the examples, chosen because of the width of interest involved, cover a not unimportant section of Far Eastern trade in the period before 1914. By virtue of this fact, one can legitimately claim that these examples were reasonably representative of current enterprise and commercial practice. In all three cases, capital was accumulated from a wide range of diverse sources though, in the main, reserves were built up by ploughing back profits and by keeping outgoings (including dividends) as low as possible. As trade grew and commitments increased resort was had to bank and other forms of institutional finance, though liabilities were always kept within reasonable limits. As a consequence, real capital grew at a rate consistent with that in the growth

[1] Sheila Marriner and F. E. Hyde, *op. cit.*, p. 33; Swire MSS., Financial statement for 1896.

of trade generally. The chief distinction is that, whereas Rathbones could not always find profitable employment for surplus cash in hand and Holts kept (at certain periods) too much capital in reserve, Swires, at least until the 1890's, could have used far more capital than the limited amount at their disposal. In this, the range of activity sponsored by managerial enterprise and governed by the opportunities for promotional investment stood out in sharp contrast. All that one need conclude from this is that, over a wide section of Western enterprise in the Far East before 1914, these distinctions were common and well recognised.

It was, however, in the close inter-relationship between these three organisations that the importance of their resources became clear. Unfortunately, the peak of Rathbones' involvement in the China trade had passed by the mid-70's, the period when both the Holts and the Swires were building up their strength and activity. Nevertheless, Holts and Rathbones were closely connected and each contributed capital to the other's ventures, particularly in those connected with the tea trade. The many forms of co-operation between Holts and Swires were more fundamental in character and, though many changes have taken place in the past hundred years, close ties still exist between them. What then, were the particular reasons for this kinship and how did it affect the course of Britain's trade with the Far East and the Pacific?

Swire's relationship with the Holt brothers was certainly not based on any inducement of financial reward. The one item in the list of Swire's earnings which never really returned a profit was that of the Blue Funnel agency. In this apparently insignificant fact lies the answer to Swire's stormy love-hate relationship with Alfred and Philip Holt and, by implication, to the wider connections in their business activities. Swire's judgment was sound and he had an uncanny knack of being proved right after the event. Consequently, when his strong will was opposed by men of equally firm determination, acrimonious debate would take place and sparks would fly. Yet, through all his serious disagreements with the Holts, he never forgot that it was Alfred Holt who had given him the opportunity to start in business on the China coast. As already stated, Swire's receipts from the Holt agency rarely covered overheads and, accordingly, the links between both groups of companies must have been engendered by something more powerful than calculations of profit and loss.

P

The Ocean Steam Ship Co. and Swire's two Eastern companies had grown out of a common identity of purpose. Their mutual interests acted as a spur to enterprise; 'to have abandoned the Holts in the critical years of the 1880's might have assuaged John Swire's business conscience, but would have been morally indefensible'.[1] Apart from ethical considerations, there were sound economic reasons why the connection should have been sustained. Holts' main line ships, steaming between Britain and Far Eastern ports, formed a life-line which gave purpose, direction and stimulation for widespread initiative. The uninhibited functioning of such an artery was of vital importance to the well-being of the Swire constituents and to that of many other houses trading on the coast. A prime concern for Holts' economic welfare was, therefore, basic to successful operation in wider and related spheres of activity. In the practical expression of this concern, John Swire's promotion of the first China Conference can be explained, as it was a device for the protection of Holt ships against ruthless competition. His interest and support for the extension of Holts' shipping services outwards from Singapore was also a reflection of this concern. It would, however, be a false assumption that, in his constant quest for capital, John Swire's attitude to the Holts impaired either his judgment or his long-term expectation of profit. The range of his interests was manifold. He mastered the intricacies of produce trades as a necessary prerequisite to the employment of resources; he possessed expertise in merchanting, in the management of ships, in insurance, finance and exchange operations; he was equally successful in his grasp of the techniques and economics of sugar refining and wool-growing. In legal matters, his knowledge was more than adequate for the successful prosecution of his business. In short, Swire epitomised much that was best and, perhaps a little that was worst, in Western enterprise during the years before 1914.

*

In the long term range of economic development over the past one hundred years, Far Eastern countries have played an increasingly dynamic role. In the fifty years between 1865 and 1914, Western influence was paramount in opening up the trade of these countries and in supplying lines of communication. Large areas of

[1] Sheila Marriner and F. E. Hyde, *op. cit.*, p. 205.

the world which for centuries had been closed to the foreigner, whose populations were subject to custom, aristocratic privilege and all the refinements of corrupt administration, were suddenly beset by the insistent power of Western capital and technology. The products of their peasant agriculture were subject to the blast of competitive market forces. It has taken more than a century for these populations to learn the arts of foreign enterprise but, having achieved the mastery over their potentially powerful economies, they have become not merely the rivals of Western civilisation but exponents of new and more highly explosive forms of society. Perhaps the last word may be left with John Swire who, in a moment of unusual philosophical contemplation, penned the following words on the fly-leaf of one of his cash books: 'We came to an inhospitable shore and found a people embalmed in custom and the wisdom of the ages. We gave succour to their needs and, in return, took our just reward. At first we never really understood their motives nor they ours. Behind the impassive face was the thought that we were barbarians entering into a civilised world. But after more than twenty-five years of association with Johnny Chinaman, the best that can be said is that we have made many friends and, as far as my knowledge goes, left behind us no enemies.'

This, at least, was a final qualitative measure of success in the pursuit and promotion of Far Eastern trade.

Appendices

APPENDIX IA
Exports of China
(Source: Chinese Customs reports)

Year	Total value (HKT 1,000)	%	Tea %	Silk, Silk Goods %	Seeds, Oil %	Beans %	Hides, Leather, Skins %
1868	61,826	100	53·8	39·7	—	1·0	—
1880	77,884	100	45·9	38·0	0·1	0·2	0·5
1890	87,144	100	30·6	33·9	0·6	0·4	1·4
1900	158,997	100	16·0	30·4	2·5	1·9	4·3
1905	227,888	100	11·2	30·1	3·4	3·0	6·6
1913	403,306	100	8·4	25·3	7·8	5·8	6·0

Year	Cotton %	Wool %	Coal %	Eggs, Egg Products %	All other items %
1868	0·9	—	—	—	4·6
1880	0·2	0·4	—	—	14·7
1890	3·4	1·6	—	—	28·1
1900	6·2	1·9	—	—	36·8
1905	5·3	3·7	—	0·9	35·8
1913	4·1	2·4	1·6	1·4	37·2

APPENDIX IB
Imports of China
(Source: Chinese Customs reports)

Year	Total value (HKT 1,000)	%	Opium %	Cotton Goods %	Cotton Yarn %	Cereals, Wheat, Flour %	Sugar %
1868	63,282	100	33·1	29·0	2·5	0·8	0·8
1880	79,293	100	39·3	24·9	4·6	0·1	0·4
1890	127,093	100	19·5	20·2	15·3	9·6	0·9
1900	211,070	100	14·8	21·5	14·3	7·0	3·0
1905	447,101	100	7·7	25·6	15·0	2·9	5·1
1913	570,163	100	7·4	19·3	12·7	5·2	6·4

Year	Tobacco %	Coal %	Kerosene %	Metals & Minerals %	Machinery %	Railway Materials, Vehicles %	All others %
1868	—	2·1	—	4·8	—	—	26·9
1880	—	1·2	—	5·5	—	—	24·0
1890	—	1·6	3·2	5·7	0·3	—	23·7
1900	0·5	3·1	6·6	4·7	0·7	—	23·8
1905	1·4	1·6	4·5	10·4	1·2	1·8	22·8
1913	2·9	1·7	4·5	5·3	1·4	0·8	32·4

APPENDIX IIA

Exports of Indonesia

(Source: Compiled from figures in CKS 165)

Year	Annual average value of exports (000 f.)	% increase	Annual average weight of exports (000 m. tons)	% increase	Average value of each metric ton of export (f.)
1865-69	93,664	—	273·3	—	0·34
1870-74	123,871	32·3	320·8	17·4	0·39
1875-79	188,131	51·9	405·9	26·5	0·46
1880-84	187,655	−0·2	511·5	26·0	0·37
1885-89	186,997	−0·4	619·8	21·2	0·30
1890-94	196,305	5·0	708·3	14·3	0·28
1895-99	219,805	12·0	1,044·2	47·4	0·21
1900-04	263,057	19·7	1,644·6	57·5	0·16
1905-09	379,916	44·4	2,640·1	60·5	0·14
1910-14	573,700	51·0	3,318·8	25·3	0·17

APPENDIX IIB

Exports of Tin from Indonesia

Year	Annual average export of tin	
	weight (000 metric tons)	value (000 f.)
1865-69	—	6,466
1870-74	—	6,948
1875-79	8·4	6,892
1880-84	9·2	8,035
1885-89	10·5	11,937
1890-94	11·6	11,022
1895-99	13·7	10,827
1900-04	18·0	23,335
1905-09	13·0	16,935
1910-14	15·2	30,081

APPENDIX III

Production (and Export)* of Tin-in-concentrates from Malaya
Annual average in (000) long tons.

Year	Long tons
1851-60	6·5
1861-70	8·5
1871-80	7·2
1881-90	19·6
1891-1900	41·7
1901-10	48·8
1911-15	49·8

Source: International Tin Council

*During these years production was virtually equivalent to export.

APPENDIX IVA

Exports and Imports of Japan 1868-96

(In thousands of yen)

Year	Export	Import (Official)	Import (Corrected)	Volume Index (1913 = 100) Export	Volume Index (1913 = 100) Import
1868	15,553	10,693	—	(4)	(4)
1869	12,909	20,784	—	(3)	(6)
1870	14,543	33,742	—	(3)	(9)
1871	17,969	21,917	—	(4)	(5)
1872	17,027	26,175	—	(4)	(6)
1873	21,635	28,107	—	5	6
1874	19,317	23,462	(24,487)	6	6
1875	18,611	29,976	(31,899)	6	7
1876	27,712	23,965	(26,544)	8	7
1877	23,349	27,421	(29,979)	8	7
1878	25,988	32,874	(37,722)	9	9
1879	28,176	32,953	(38,015)	8	10
1880	28,395	36,627	(42,246)	8	11
1881	31,059	31,191	(35,767)	9	10
1882	37,722	29,447	(33,354)	11	10
1883	36,268	28,445	(32,449)	12	10
1884	33,871	29,673	(33,617)	11	10
1885	37,147	29,357	(33,499)	11	10
1886	48,876	32,168	(37,364)	14	11
1887	52,408	44,304	(53,153)	15	15
1888	65,706	65,455	—	20	19
1889	70,061	66,104	—	20	19
1890	56,604	81,729	—	15	24
1891	79,527	62,927	—	23	19
1892	91,103	71,326	—	22	22
1893	89,713	88,257	—	21	24
1894	113,246	117,482	—	25	26
1895	136,112	129,261	—	27	29
1896	117,843	171,674	—	24	38

APPENDIX IVB
Exports and Imports of Japan 1897-1914
(In thousands of yen)

Year	Export	Import	Volume Index Export	Volume Index Import
1897	163,135	219,301	32	45
1898	165,754	277,502	30	58
1899	214,930	220,402	37	45
1900	204,430	287,262	32	48
1901	252,350	255,817	44	43
1902	258,303	271,731	45	51
1903	289,502	317,136	49	57
1904	319,261	371,361	53	60
1905	321,534	488,538	49	82
1906	423,755	418,784	57	67
1907	432,413	494,467	54	76
1908	378,246	436,257	54	66
1909	413,113	394,199	65	67
1910	458,429	464,234	77	74
1911	447,434	513,806	71	74
1912	526,982	618,992	85	88
1913	632,460	729,432	100	100
1914	591,101	595,736	101	84

Index